# White Bread

# Social Fictions Series

Series Editor
Patricia Leavy
USA

The *Social Fictions* series emerges out of the arts-based research movement. The series includes full-length fiction books that are informed by social research but written in a literary/artistic form (novels, plays, and short story collections). Believing there is much to learn through fiction, the series only includes works written entirely in the literary medium adapted. Each book includes an academic introduction that explains the research and teaching that informs the book as well as how the book can be used in college courses. The books are underscored with social science or other scholarly perspectives and intended to be relevant to the lives of college students—to tap into important issues in the unique ways that artistic or literary forms can.

Please email queries to pleavy7@aol.com

**International Editorial Advisory Board**

Carl Bagley, University of Durham, UK
Anna Banks, University of Idaho, USA
Carolyn Ellis, University of South Florida, USA
Rita Irwin, University of British Columbia, Canada
J. Gary Knowles, University of Toronto, Canada
Laurel Richardson, The Ohio State University (Emeritus), USA

# White Bread

*Weaving Cultural Past into the Present*

**Christine Sleeter**

SENSE PUBLISHERS
ROTTERDAM / BOSTON / TAIPEI

A C.I.P. record for this book is available from the Library of Congress.


ISBN 978-94-6300-065-9 (paperback)
ISBN 978-94-6300-066-6 (hardback)
ISBN 978-94-6300-067-3 (e-book)


Published by: Sense Publishers,
P.O. Box 21858,
3001 AW Rotterdam,
The Netherlands
https://www.sensepublishers.com/

Cover image by Christine Sleeter

*Printed on acid-free paper*

# ADVANCE PRAISE FOR
## *WHITE BREAD*

Using her own experience of exploring her family's immigration history, renowned educator Christine Sleeter has crafted a captivating story that weaves together interrelated themes: investigating family histories, teaching children of diverse backgrounds, and forging personal relationships across lines of race and culture. After reading this engaging novel, readers may be motivated to delve into their own family histories and, along the way, to reflect on what it means to be an American in our complex, multicultural and multilingual nation. – **Sonia Nieto, University of Massachusetts, Amherst, author of *What Keeps Teachers Going?***

This is a provocative and moving story about how coming to know oneself, including one's own family history, can lay the foundation for acting in solidarity with others. Addressing the complex topics of teaching, identity and community, *White Bread* will serve as a valuable resource for pre-service and practicing teachers, as well as for teacher educators. In fact, I can't wait to use it in my own courses that aim to advance learning about the challenges and joys of teaching in today's increasingly diverse schools. I highly recommend this book! – **Jamy Stillman, University of Southern California**

Sleeter imaginatively engages family history as a tool of critical collective reflection, recovering community cultural wealth as a matter of urgency in our classrooms and beyond. – **Tara J. Yosso, University of California Santa Barbara, author of *Critical Race Counterstories along the Chicana/Chicano Educational Pipeline***

With *White Bread*, Sleeter artfully explores the challenging topics of race, culture, history and identity critical to the success of white teachers in multicultural settings. That she manages to do this in a page-turning, multigenerational novel complete with mystery and romance makes this a must-read not just for teachers, but for everyone. – **Bree Picower, Montclair State University, author of *Practice What You Teach***

Refreshingly innovative, creatively telling, and heart-wrenchingly intelligent, *White Bread* not only captures the everyday minutiae of teaching in culturally diverse U.S. classrooms, it also documents the emotional, psychological, and spiritual transformation one undergoes when self-investing in racial justice. Through the humanistic characterization of Jessica, a white, middle class school teacher, Sleeter provides a concrete answer to how the historical nuances of white privilege influence identity, society, and, in particular, education. A must read for the almost 90% white teaching force in the United States! – **Cheryl Matias, University of Colorado Denver**

Jessica's questions, her history, and the situations she finds herself in enable the reader to reflect on the challenges many of us find in the classroom and in our lives on a daily basis. Thoughtful, engaging, compassionate and reflective, *White Bread* is one of those books that's easy to read, and go back to, again and again. – **William G. Tierney, University of Southern California, author of** *Academic Affairs: A Love Story*

In *White Bread*, Christine Sleeter has woven together a wonderful narrative of life in America, one that includes multiple layers of identity, ever-shifting and forever shaping the deeply entrenched experiences of everyone. The book seamlessly floats back and forth between a time more than a century ago that was not fully documented, and aimed to assimilate a white German past, and a contemporary time in which Mexican-Americans are facing similar concerns. The narrative and characters are delightful, real and compelling. This very thoughtful book presents an engaging vision of social justice. I very much enjoyed reading it. – **Paul R. Carr, Université du Québec en Outaouais, author of** *Revisiting the Great White North?*

*White Bread* tells a wonderful story of how a young, white, novice teacher comes to critical consciousness around issues of race as she studies her own family history and learns to connect with her Mexican American students. *White Bread* should be read by everybody, but especially teachers and teacher educators as they work to transform their practices to reach our increasingly diverse student populations. In particular I think *White Bread* has the power to help white teachers explore their own identities and better understand how legacies of racism and oppression impact communities of color. – **Wayne Au, University of Washington Bothell, author of *Pencils Down!***

# TABLE OF CONTENTS

# ACKNOWLEDGEMENTS

You would not be reading this book had I not been supported by several fantastic people. I am deeply grateful to Patricia Leavy whose vision led to the creation of the groundbreaking Social Fictions series, and who enthusiastically welcomed my manuscript into it.

To the dear friends who read earlier drafts of chapters – giving me honest feedback and suggestions, improving my use of Spanish and German, and encouraging me to keep writing the story – thank you! I am immensely grateful to Linda Turner Bynoe, Judith Flores Carmona, Deborah Hearn Gin, Sara Hiemstra, Frauke Loewensen, Bobbi Long, Mary MacCormack, Twinkle MacCormack, Josina Makau, Jean Moule, Marsha Moroh, Leslie Patiño, Diana Paul, Juanita Perea, Terri Pipes, and Katharine Richman. From your comments to me on the bike path and suggestions over lunch, to emailed chapter re-writes, to detailed suggestions throughout the manuscript, this book is much stronger because of you. Caroline Leavitt's invaluable coaching through this first novel improved the characters and the writing tremendously. Thank you, all!

Cory, an Asset Protection Specialist at Best Buy, filled me in about the process of job promotion, correcting some inaccuracies and misconceptions on my part.

I appreciate the support of my colleagues in Central Coast Writers of California, who have helped me think through the process of writing, publishing, and marketing fiction. The Number One Ladies' (and Gentlemen's) Book Group was wonderfully supportive of me through this writing process, adding *White Bread* to its reading list when the book was completed.

Finally, to my most valued writing critic, supporter, and life partner, Joe Larkin, even if you show up in only three sentences in this book, I never would have had the confidence to write it without your steadfast encouragement and love.

# PREFACE

*White Bread*. How many times have I heard White teachers describe themselves that way in response to my attempts to show them the importance of culture and ethnicity in their classrooms? I used to regard statements like "I'm just white bread" or "I'm just an American" as attempts to shrug off implications that racial and ethnic identity might matter. But I gradually realized something deeper going on: In the rapidly shifting demographics that make up our schools, our neighborhoods, and our public spaces, many of us – especially those of us who are White and unsure that there even is such a thing as collective identity for white people – aren't sure where (or if) we fit. Unable to place ourselves within a nuanced collective memory, we retreat into denying its value.

What I didn't reveal for a long time was that I, too, was not able to place myself and my family into a larger historical memory, except in the most general of terms. Of course I had studied U.S. history in school, but in abstract, impersonal terms. I knew my father was of German descent and my mother was of mixed European descent. But beyond my grandparents lay a huge lacuna. One day I jumped into the website Ancestry.com, and became quickly obsessed with tracing my family roots. As I discovered a goldmine of online resources, I created family trees and stories about ancestors, shared them with family members, then began to play with situating my family within larger narratives of U.S. history and culture.

Out of this work came Critical Family History (http://christinesleeter.org/critical-family-history/), a process for placing any family's story within a wider socio-cultural and historic panorama. Eager to find out whether this process made sense to anyone else, in the summer of 2014, I tried it out on thirty-eight racially and ethnically diverse classroom teachers in Colorado for two weeks. The depth of their learning and enthusiasm exceeded my ambitious expectations.

Writing *White Bread* turned out to be the best venue I could use to portray struggles and questions around issues of culture and identity in schooling. Jessica, a White fifth-grade teacher who endeavors with only mixed success to teach her culturally diverse students, is prompted to explore her family's past by an unexpected discovery. Simultaneously, she begins to grapple with culture and racism through suggestions offered by others around her, principally a handsome Mexican American teacher who helps her understand her students.

*White Bread* pulls readers into a tumultuous six months of Jessica's life as she confronts many issues that turn out to be interrelated. Why does she (and many other people, she comes to realize) know so little about her family's past? Where did the stories go? Why does her husband seem to want something different from life than she does, why do her wishes threaten him, and why has she simply been going along with his wishes? Why does she crave community as she feels increasingly isolated, and does she have any power to change the isolation modern life seems to hand White people today? (From her vantage point, people of color seem to experience communal bonds she lacks.) Why would Latino teachers want to make their classroom curriculum more Latino, when it seems like their students would be better off becoming American? Can she actually become a good teacher who sparks learning in her students, different from her as they are?

Ultimately, Jessica learns why her family's past was buried, how to retrieve much of it, and how to use it as a lens to work through these issues. The story line of *White Bread* alternates between past and present, introducing readers to German American communities in the Midwest during the late 1800s and early 1900s. While the stories set in the present are products of my imagination, grounded in my decades of work with teachers in multicultural contexts and my ongoing work with ethnic studies, the stories set in the past rest on very detailed archival research of my father's side of my family, described at the end of this book.

*White Bread* can be used to prompt discussion and reflection in teacher education, ethnic studies, and sociology courses. A short resource guide for instructors using this book in class can be found on my website (http://christinesleeter.org). Beginning teachers who see many of their own struggles reflected in Jessica's classroom and her conversations over lunch with fellow teacher Cath will likely gain ideas they might try. *White Bread* provides an entre into considering where White people might fit within ethnic studies. In addition, *White Bread* can be used, in conjunction with my Critical Family History blog, to engage students across the disciplines in researching their own family histories, and learning to situate their families within a larger context. Indeed, embedded in Jessica's ongoing exploration is a step-by-step process for family history research. Or, *White Bread* can simply be read for pleasure.

*Christine Sleeter*

#### CHAPTER 1

*August, 2012*

Jessica's stomach sank as she anticipated a second year teaching fifth-graders who seemed to come from Pluto while she hailed from Mercury. She scanned thirty-three new faces, about half Mexican, the rest white, most poor. Would she reach them any better this year?

"What did Michelle enjoy most about camping with her family?" she asked about the story they just read. Only the third day, she was still attaching names to faces. She glanced at a card taped in front of a bronze-skinned boy whose short black hair reminded her of a shoe brush. "Jerome?"

Jerome whirled around and whispered, "Don't *do* that!" to the boy behind him, who stifled a giggle. Then to Jessica, "Getting chased by ghosts?"

"Ooooh, ghosts of Sherwood!" Álvaro, sitting behind Jerome, pantomimed drawing back a bow.

"They told ghost stories at night, they weren't chased by ghosts. Diana, what did Michelle enjoy most about camping?" Jessica repeated, mentally marking the two boys to keep an eye on.

"That isn't how you say her name, Mrs. Westerfield," offered Mark, blond hair falling across his eyes.

Puzzled, Jessica looked at the name card again. "Sweetheart, how do say your name?"

"At home it's Dee-AH-nah, but my teachers always say Diana." She studied the page, apparently searching for the answer. "Here it is. 'The thing Michelle enjoyed most was the river's big swimming hole.'"

"Thank you, Diana." Jessica made a point to use Spanish pronunciation. "How many of you have been to a swimming hole?"

Three hands shot up. "Matt?"

Before Matt could open his mouth, Álvaro blurted out, "We go swimming at Lake San Antonio, teacher."

Jessica's mental image of the story suddenly evaporated. Gone were the snow-capped peaks, pine forests, and waterfalls from

1

her camping trip with Tim the weekend before. In their place, picnic tables rose from gravel alongside a large California reservoir rimmed by dusty, brown hills and trees too sparse to offer shade.

"I asked Matt." But she barely heard Matt's reply as she affixed a stern look to her face just as a book crashing to the floor snatched away students' scant attention to the camping story.

\* \* \* \* \*

Who were those kids and who was she to them? Jessica wondered as she drove home. Teaching turned out to be so much harder than she had imagined a year ago, certainly harder than her own teachers made it seem. She couldn't picture what might be going through most of her students' heads. She wasn't even sure how to place them in her world, or herself in theirs. Her fifth-grade colleague Esteban had pointed out that much just two days ago.

As the school year began, he had given an informal presentation to the rest of the Milford Elementary School teachers -- all white -- about cultural identity and the fact that half their students could scarcely find anyone like themselves in the curriculum. Holding up a reading book, a science book, and a social studies book, he recited in less than a minute their references to Mexican Americans, then suggested what teachers could include.

When he finished, one teacher remarked, "These kids are all Americans, or at least that's what their families want them to become. Wouldn't we do them a disservice by teaching them to be Mexican rather than American?" Jessica wondered the same thing.

"Mexican American *is* American," Esteban said. "My family, for example, was born here. We're Americans. But we aren't white Americans, we aren't Black Americans, we're Mexican Americans."
At that point Jessica, sitting in a corner, looked up from her cell phone where she was surreptitiously playing solitaire. As far as she was concerned, his classroom radiated too much of Mexico – the kids sang songs in Spanish, a big United Farm Workers flag graced the front of the room (although he *had* pointed out that it represents an *American* labor union).

So she raised her hand. "Esteban, you might be teaching what you're familiar with, but don't expect us to teach things we don't know. I'm just plain white bread American, that's what I know and that's what I teach."

He studied her, then asked, "White bread American? What's that? Who are you, Jessica?"

The room fell silent. Then grandmotherly Marge, all graying hair and tortoise-shell glasses, stood. "Well, I guess I'm white bread, too. You can teach the way you want, Esteban, but I'm not you and don't see why I should try to be." The meeting concluding, she left.

As the rest filed out, Esteban offered to loan Jessica a few books she could try out in her classroom, "just to see how the kids respond," he said. Did he know how much she struggled to excite them about learning? Then again, occupying the classroom next door, how could he not know?

A half hour ago, he had appeared at her door as she was straightening the general chaos her students left behind as though their efforts to put things away had launched a small tornado. As she pushed in chairs and picked up bits of paper like a human vacuum, she heard a light tap on the doorframe. Looking up, she saw Esteban. "Hey, I thought you might want to borrow these." He entered and set a few books on her desk.

"Thanks." She saw four children's novels and a hefty history text, all by Spanish-surnamed authors.

Following the direction of her eyes, he explained, "This one is to give you some background. The others are for the kids."

"Thanks," she repeated. "I'll take a look at them." As a flush began to warm her neck, she turned back to her classroom to finish straightening up.

"Well, see you tomorrow." Esteban turned and left.

As his footsteps faded down the hall, Jessica realized her hands were shaking. Was it intimidation? Anxiety? Or something else?

The thing was, Jessica couldn't say no to him. Her eyes locked onto his brilliant white teeth set off by a *cafe au lait* complexion, his body like an Olympic sprinter. More importantly, he exuded a sense of self Jessica craved.

And that was the crux of it. In this California school where half the children claimed European ancestry and the other half

3

Mexican, in this hodgepodge of a community that had no obvious majority, Esteban knew who he was. Jessica (and her husband Tim, for that matter) knew themselves through facts describing their existence rather than connections weaving belonging and identity.

Was Wonder Bread the best image of herself she could conjure?

\* \* \* \* \*

Jessica opened the refrigerator to investigate a possible dinner menu, then slammed it shut, fuming. Tim refused to help, insisting her cooking was fabulous. "I can't even boil water without burning it," he would joke. Well, as far as she was concerned, praising her domestic ability was his way of placing her in a role that didn't threaten him. Then she paused. He had started to vacuum and help with laundry. She had to give him credit there.

She had met him during her sophomore year of college. One day as she walked across campus, she noticed a blue-eyed stranger gazing at her. Blushing, she stared at the ground so as not to appear to notice him back. Two days later, she found him waiting outside her English class when she emerged. Haltingly, he asked her to coffee. His stuttering invitation gave her permission to awkwardly accept. They spent the next hour laughing over high school stories, coffee forgotten.

He loved the copper pennies that sunlight sprinkled through her dark hair. She drowned in the blue of his eyes, she devoured the sandy color of his hair. Tim. A name that sounded definite. Short and to the point. They bonded over enjoyment of camping. Discovering they loved the same music (especially Jonas Brothers and Adele) and movies (they kissed their way through *Stranger than Fiction* and *Casino Royale*) felt like a message from the universe that they belonged together.

Right after their marriage, Tim quit college to start earning money for a house. College bored him; he complained incessantly about classes as though someone had chained him to a seat and compelled him to watch a series of failed auditions for some B-rated show. He took a sales job at Best Buy, which was where he was still working. He had tried, unsuccessfully, to persuade her to join him in work, to leave school. "You can always go back if you decide you want to," he would add.

But Jessica liked college. For her, every book opened a new world of ideas. She drank in concepts like epistemology, concordance rates, and Higgs' boson the way her mother had guzzled fresh vegetable juice during her heyday of health consciousness. Jessica graduated, then continued for a teaching credential.

Tim initially balked when she announced her intention to complete that fifth year. "Come on, Jess," he would say, "aren't you smart enough yet?" She gradually stopped telling him about her classes and all the new ideas dancing about in her brain like hyperactive children. Did her education threaten him? She wasn't sure. When she finally brought home a paycheck from her first month as a teacher, slim as it was, Tim helped her spend it.

But yesterday at breakfast they had a row about Esteban's presentation. She had been chatting about details of the previous day, the presentation being one such detail.

"That's another one of those ideas that's grabbing you, isn't it?" Tim remarked.

Jessica put down her coffee mug and stared at him. "What is that supposed to mean?"

"Look, Jess, you're always picking up ideas that don't seem useful to the world we actually live in. Now this guy at your school thinks it's okay not to teach Mexican kids living here in America how to be American, and you don't think that's baloney?"

"I didn't say I don't think it's baloney," she retorted. "It's just – when I walk by his classroom sometimes and see all of his students so – so – engaged ..."

"So he entertains them better than you do. Is that it?"

"I don't know. Several of my Mexican kids seem, well, tuned out a lot of the time. They're behind in reading, so I know it gets hard for them. I thought maybe I could learn something from Esteban."

"You could learn something by him making you feel bad about being American? We've both been just plain American all our lives. Is Esteban making you feel like there's something wrong with who you are?"

"No, he's not," Jessica said, clearing the dishes off the table and dumping them in the sink. "Let's just drop it, okay, Tim?"

"Fine by me. You're the one who brought it up." He stood and marched from the kitchen.

Now Jessica stomped upstairs, where she quickly changed from school clothes into jeans and a sweatshirt. Glancing around the small, cramped bedroom, she winced at Tim's aspiration to buy a house, when all they could afford was rent on this fixer-upper. That was another thing they sometimes argued about. She didn't mind the house, while he griped about not just it but the whole neighborhood. "Wouldn't you rather live in Oakridge?" he would ask, referring to a new subdivision a few miles away. "C'mon, Jess, be honest, you'd prefer that, wouldn't you?"

As she was leaving the bedroom to go back downstairs, she paused by the door to the spare room. They kept it closed to hide stacks of boxes and second-hand furniture that suggested a thrift shop stock room. Opening the door, Jessica found herself mentally rehearsing how it might feel to pack up all her things and move out. Not that she planned to leave Tim, but she liked to leave open that possibility. As long as it was within reach, she felt she could stay and work things through with him.

Entering, she surveyed the boxes of Christmas paraphernalia and college books, then spied the battered cardboard box containing what she assumed were papers, taken from her mother's apartment after her death two years ago. Curious, Jessica approached it, seeing the inscription "Precious, Save" in her mother's flowery handwriting. She had been devastated when an aneurism killed her mom at 54. She and her brother Walt had cleared their mother's apartment. Jessica had never opened this box.

Now curious, she placed it on an uncluttered corner of a table. The box itself, taped shut, was about twelve inches square and eight inches deep. Jessica looked at her watch: only a little after 4:30, not time to worry about dinner yet, since Tim wouldn't be home for another two hours.

She fetched scissors and carefully sliced through tape on the top flaps. The first thing she saw was a stack of old Christmas cards.

Opening a few, she found newsletters and pictures of children from various of her mother's friends. People actually keep these things?

She removed the Christmas cards and saw another stack of cards tied with string. She untied them and opened what appeared to be an old birthday card. The inscription read: "To my darling wife, thank you for the most wonderful 20 years together! May we have many more!" The card was dated 2001, just a year before her father had died in a car accident. Underneath was a Valentine's Day card, dated the same year, with another inscription in her father's handwriting: "Kissing you only gets better every year!"

Jessica had been heading right into adolescence when her father was killed. She had been so wracked with her own pain that she hadn't stopped to consider what her mother had lost. Lifting out the stack of cards, she saw a photo of her parents on a vacation they had taken without the children. Wearing shorts and T-shirts, they stood on a sunny beach in Mexico, holding hands and smiling like kids. Jessica remembered that trip because she and her brother had to stay with their aunt and uncle, where they spent the week bickering with an older cousin who thought it was his duty and right to boss them around.

Underneath were more documents: her parents' marriage certificate, wedding pictures from the local newspaper, her own birth announcement, and snapshots of her mother holding Walt as a newborn. There was also an old envelope addressed to Annie Hart in Iowa, postmarked August 7, 1928.

Wondering who Annie Hart was, Jessica opened it and took out a hand-written letter. She flattened it and read:

*August 5, 1928*
*Dearest Annie,*

*It has been three months now since the funeral of my dear Heinrich. I cannot get used to him not being here, even though he was ill for three years before he finally joined Gott Vater. The world has changed so much, so quickly! Is it wrong to say I hope to join him soon?*

*You, my darling sister, will understand perhaps better than anyone else how painful these past few years have been for us. I think it broke Heinrich's heart to see his life's work completely unravel right before his eyes. It is no accident his health began to fail at the very moment the St. Louis Conference succumbed to pressure on the German churches. Of course the souls he brought to Gott have not retreated from the fold. But the community of Gemütlichkeit he worked to build is gone, and he had to live to see that happen.*

*We always knew many English Americans felt threatened by us, but I never understood why. Has it made any sense to you? There were always a few who said that if we want to speak German we should go back to Germany. (BACK to Germany?? You and I have never even BEEN to Germany!) Well, maybe the English-speakers should go back to England! Of course I don't say that. But these days, sometimes I think it. In Iowa, dear Annie, we would be arrested for sharing recipes we grew up with over the telephone! How seditious is that, I ask you? We'd have to call Hasenpfeffer something else! And why on earth did people burn library books by Goethe and Schiller?*

*Do you remember when the Great War broke out, English Americans were afraid we might be plotting to support Germany? Annie, I hated them referring to us as Huns! Of course we couldn't condemn our parents' homeland, but as Americans, we sent our own sons to fight for this country. Our youngest son Albert served, as did our son-in-law. But now, even the English Methodists have turned on us, their German brethren.*

*Annie, do you think our grandchildren will remember who we were? Do you think they will remember the warmth and community, the Gemütlichkeit we shared, the old songs we so loved, the books we read, the way it felt to say our names as our parents had said them? I look at my own children and wonder. Mamie and Ralston have moved off to Oregon; will their children know who we were? What about Edward's family, now living in New York? Flora and Ada teach French in the schools here, and may never have an opportunity to teach their beloved German language and literature.*

*Ah, maybe I'm just an old woman, Annie. I remain your loving sister,*

*Mary*

Jessica was perplexed. Who were Mary and Annie, apparently elderly sisters when Mary wrote this letter? Were they her ancestors? Why had her mother kept these letters but never mentioned them? She vainly scanned the letter again for something familiar. The "Great War" must be what people back then called World War I. Who knew at the time another great war was about to break out? She tried to recall from her two years of high school German what the words *Gemütlichkeit*, *Pfarrer*, and *Hasenpfeffer* might mean.

She returned the letter to its envelope. Her parents' love was so evident in her father's inscriptions. Could she and Tim rekindle those feelings? As if she were her mother anticipating her father coming home, Jessica rooted through the refrigerator for ingredients to make Chicken Alfredo, Tim's favorite. Maybe that, a salad and a bottle of wine, would take the edge off things, at least for the evening.

As she cooked, she wondered what he would think about the letter.

CHAPTER 2

*August, 2012*

María Paz gazed at the approaching rocky hills, just bumps on the horizon only minutes ago. Then she turned to her husband, Salvador. "*¿No estás cansado todavía?*" she asked, wondering if he was tired yet. With the exception of a couple of stops, he had been driving since 4:00 a.m., and it was approaching midday.

"*Vamos a parar en Gómez Palacio,*" he replied, indicating a stop near the next town. After a quick lunch there, María Paz knew from experience she would drive much of the afternoon while Salvador slept in preparation for the evening shift. She ran a hand through her short black hair, normally styled but today flat with a misbehaving clump on one side. Glancing into the back seat of their Ford Explorer, she noted with satisfaction that the two younger children, Manuel and Jaime, slept while Marisela, about to enter fifth grade, quietly played on the iPad.

Turning back to the window, María Paz recalled tears glistening in her mother's dark eyes the previous evening as they said good night, knowing it would be months before they would see each other again. Her mother's black and silver hair, wound into a knot on the crown of her head, had displayed vivid red and yellow flowers in celebration of her fiftieth birthday. She wasn't yet what one might call old, but each time María Paz visited, signs of aging in her mother's handsome face jolted her.

Just about everyone in the village had turned out for Mamá's birthday. And had they ever eaten! Empanadas, *pan de acámbaro*, *arroz rojo*, barbeque, mangos, strawberries – it was as though the best restaurant in the state of Guanajuato threw a grand closing that would ensure its place in local folklore. María Paz thought she would never be hungry again. She treasured the preparation time in the kitchen with her sisters and sister-in-law, laughing and telling stories. Ah, she missed them so much, living now in the U.S.

But the work was better there. When Salvador was offered a job as digital publisher with a California TV station that catered to a

Spanish-speaking audience, at a better salary than he made doing much the same work in Mexico, they agreed readily to go.

*Carretera Federal* 40 north was now ascending grey, stony hills of the Sierra Madre in the southern part of Durango state. Sandwiched between highway and hills, dry brown grasses punctuated with creosote, yucca and an occasional tree reminded María Paz of a woven blanket her mother favored during winter months. A large, startlingly green swath to the right broke the arid landscape. Most likely an irrigated alfalfa field.

Normally they would make the 1600-mile drive from their family home in Guanajuato to California in three days, maybe even more if they took their time. Now, however, with school starting in the U.S., Salvador decided they would do it in two days.

"My turn!" Manuel, age seven, was obviously awake. María Paz sighed, knowing competition for the iPad was about to begin. She turned around and gave the children her "No fighting" look. Sometimes they could share without squabbling. If not, each child got it for ten minutes, with María Paz keeping time.

"Here. I'm tired of it." Marisela, reaching across Jaime, shoved the iPad into Manuel's lap, then pointedly turned to look out the window. Seconds later, the roar of a speeding car coming from the back seat prompted María Paz to turn around again and signal him to turn down the volume.

The children increasingly used English with each other. A school effect, no doubt. They had lived in the U.S. for only a year, but the English language program Manuel and Marisela experienced in their elementary school in Mexico seemed to be paying off. With most conversations involving their parents in Spanish, María Paz was confident the children would grow up bilingual, a clear asset in her view. Her own schooling in Mexico had been mainly in English, which turned out to be very useful. Maybe they will complete university like their father. Unlike her, though, since a handsome video editor swept her off her feet as she was completing her first year. She glanced at Salvador – still handsome, she thought.

"I'm getting hungry," Marisela grumbled. Breakfast of leftovers from the fiesta had been consumed hours ago.

"We'll be stopping in a few minutes," María Paz said. "I think there's another mango in here." She groped around in a plastic bag of napkins, crumpled foil, used coffee cups, and pieces of candy.

"*Por fin, la salida a Gómez Palacio y Torreón*," remarked Salvador as he spotted a sign for the exit.

"Are we there?" shouted Jaime, now wide awake. Jaime, age five, was born with two speeds: asleep and high gear, with virtually no transition time between.

"We aren't there," Marisela emphasized "there" meaning home. "We won't be there till tomorrow night. This is just lunch."

"*Tengo que hacer pipí!*" Jaime wailed.

"There'll be a bathroom at the restaurant. See? There it is." María Paz pointed.

As the car decelerated in the exit, she exhaled, her mind beginning to tick off chores she would need to do the morning after they got home. What would the kids wear to school? She wasn't sure what was still clean. She might have to do a load of laundry before taking them. Jaime would be starting kindergarten! She'd need to make sure all three were settled in with their new teachers before noon, since she was expected at her job that afternoon. Thankfully Marisela and Manuel liked school. So far, anyway.

"*¿Quién tiene hambre?*" Salvador asked as he steered toward a truck stop with a large restaurant sign.

*August, 2012*

Jessica ran a brush through her short, dark curls and adjusted her turquoise-framed glasses. She pulled on worn brown boots over black leggings, then grabbed her bag and headed for the door. Tim was still at the breakfast table in old sweats, nursing a mug of coffee while reading the news. Lucky guy, she thought, he doesn't need to be at work until almost ten. "Bye, see you this evening," she called as she dashed out to her aging black Saturn.

Milford Elementary School was a ten-minute drive from home. The quickest route wound through her small, run-down neighborhood, through several blocks of aging single-story tract housing, then alongside a new housing development and past a shopping mall. Today as she drove through the tract housing, she seemed to hear Esteban's commentary about who lived where. On one side of an imaginary line, most residents were white; on the other, Mexican. You could practically identify who lived where by the music pouring from windows and cars. Taylor Swift to the right, Juanes to the left. She wondered why she hadn't noticed any of this before his presentation.

The newer development housed mainly middle class white families. Jessica considered these houses boring – identical blush-colored mini-mansions on postage stamp lots. Like what Tim seemed to favor. At least in their neighborhood, each house proclaimed its own personality, reminding Jessica of the motley crowd that showed up at the soup kitchen where she used to volunteer. Immediately adjacent to Milford were apartment buildings inhabited mainly by Mexican families.

As she pulled into the parking lot, she wondered for the umpteenth time why the exterior of school buildings was so drab. Like most other schools in her district, Milford could have been stamped from a cookie cutter design. Outdoor covered walkways strung together several buildings, all the same beige and institutional green. Teachers joked that these colors must have been on sale when the district's facilities manager was shopping for paint.

Jessica started the morning lessons determined to avoid a re-run of the frustrating camping story earlier in the week. She relaxed as reading and math proceeded as planned. Maybe she had a better sense of the kids than she had feared.

For social studies, she wanted to assess their familiarity with locations of countries and states they would study this year. She passed out blank maps: the world, and the U.S. Using the overhead projector, she indicated a list of countries in Europe and Asia, and states on the east coast.

"You have two minutes to fill in as much as you can by yourself. No talking."

Surveying the room, she noted some students writing quickly, others frowning or gazing out the window. Two minutes passed.

"Put down your pencils. Now, working with your tablemates, identify which countries and states all of you could find."

As she walked around the classroom, she felt the beginnings of a headache. Almost everyone was able to find California and Mexico. After that, some maps were blank and several showed wild guessing. France written where Russia is located, the Philippines placed in South America. Only a handful of students had located most states and countries correctly.

Apparently reading dismay on her face, one girl said, "We didn't do very good, did we, Mrs. Westerfield?"

Jessica tried to convey encouragement. "We'll be studying all these places, I just wanted to find out what you know already." She wondered whether these kids ever travel. They probably don't even have maps at home. She would need to rework her plans for next week to get some geography down before moving ahead.

Felipe's hand shot up. "Mrs. Westerfield, I know where Michoacán is. Can I write it on my map?"

Surprised, Jessica hesitated. Then, "Yes, of course." She knew Michoacán is a state in Mexico, but wasn't sure where.

As Felipe wrote, she heard him murmur to his tablemates, "*Papá* is from there."

Unsure what to do next, Jessica glanced at the clock and was relieved that it was almost lunchtime. She announced, "Put your maps in your social studies folder, then line up."

At 11:48, Jessica sank into her usual plastic chair at a table in the teacher's lounge next to her friend Cath, a third-grade teacher who also had started at Milford last year. Although born in the late 1980s, Cath dressed as though she had come straight from the sixties, wearing long hand-made skirts topped by shirts of various tie-dye designs. Her long, frizzy blond hair was usually either braided or bunched on the back of her head with a clip. Today it was bunched, although strands had started to pop out as if proclaiming their individuality.

Cath spread out her lunch of yogurt, a banana, almonds, and rice crackers while Jessica rooted in her bag for her peanut butter sandwich, venting, "Ugh, geography, my kids don't have a clue."

Cath looked at her steadily. "That's what they have you for."

Jessica shrugged, then brightened. "Hey, I've got to show you something. I must have stuck this in here last night when I was tidying up."

Cath mixed the almonds and banana into the yogurt. "What is it?"

"An old letter I found in a box of my mom's things. It was written back around World War I. Might be someone in the family."

With one hand, Cath slid the letter around so she could read it while she ate with the other. When she finished, she slid the letter back to Jessica. "Very interesting. You found this where?"

"In a box of my mom's. Old Christmas cards, cards my dad wrote to her, birth certificates, that kind of thing. I was going to show it to Tim last night, but I kind of forgot. Well, truthfully, I don't think he'd be interested."

"Why not?" Cath asked.

"Well, he has this thing about me going off onto ideas he thinks are, well, hairbrained. If it turns out to mean something, I'll show it to him, of course. Anyway, I figure the letter must be about people in the family, otherwise why would she keep it?"

"Do you recognize any names?"

Jessica shook her head.

"You could look them up online," Cath suggested. "How far back can you trace your family?"

Jessica shook her head again. "I can name my grandparents and that's about it. My grandparents on my dad's side died a while back. On my mom's side, grandma is still alive but living in Alzheimers' land."

"You could research all this, you know. The Mormon Church keeps track of everyone. You can find a ton of information on their family history website."

"Like that TV show, *Who do you Think you Are?*"

"Yeah, but you'd have to do the work yourself. They give you a couple of free weeks to get you hooked, then start charging a membership fee. I never registered for the free trial because I get addicted to things like that and can't afford it."

At that moment Sarah Peel, the principal, walked into the lounge, making a beeline for Jessica. Only a few years older than Jessica, she worked to distinguish herself from the teachers with business suits, heels, sleek hair, and a "can-do" demeanor.

"Sorry to barge in on your lunch like this, but a new student arrived. Three of them, actually, from the same family, one in kinder, one in second, and one in fifth."

Inwardly, Jessica sighed. This would bring her class size up to 34 children, a lot to manage and teach at the same time.

Sarah noticed Jessica's half-eaten apple. "Finish eating. I'll bring the girl to your classroom after lunch."

No longer hungry, Jessica gathered her things, shoving the letter into her bag. "Well, off to face the masses."

Back in her classroom, students were returning from lunch when Sarah showed up with a girl in tow, long black hair in pigtails, sporting pink jeans with a red T-shirt. "This is Marisela," Sarah said. "Marisela, this is Mrs. Westerfield, your fifth grade teacher."

Jessica squatted down to eye level with Marisela. "Welcome," she said, wondering why the family had not enrolled their children when school started.

"Thank you," Marisela said, almost inaudibly, as she looked down at the floor.

"Thank you, Mrs. Peel," Jessica said to the departing principal. "Marisela, did your family just recently move here?"

Marisela shook her head "No," then added, "We just got home from Guanajuato. It was my grandmother's birthday."

As Jessica led Marisela to the last empty chair in the crowded classroom, she wondered why the family went all the way to Mexico for a birthday right around the start of school. Then Marisela pointed toward one of the apartment buildings. "We live right over there. We drove all the way home. It took two days."

"Oh no, you're gonna be in our class again!" hollered Álvaro as he lightly punched Marisela in the arm. Marisela stuck out her tongue.

"Young people, how are we supposed to greet each other?" Jessica asked sharply. Obviously, the family wasn't new. And, she realized, some Milford families *do* travel.

The children took their seats, and the room's energy level rocketed back up to its usual vibrant level.

* * * * *

By the time Jessica arrived home, her mind still buzzed from the children's relentless energy. She tossed her bag on the bed, opened it, and began to stack its contents on the desk in the corner. Out popped the letter. She set it aside for later.

Of more immediate concern was checking homework and finishing preparation for tomorrow. For homework, students were to write a paragraph about a character in a children's novel they had chosen, explaining why they thought that character was important to the story. Although they were reading different novels, they would complete common writing assignments.

Last year all the children were assigned Lauren Myrakle's *Thirteen*, an award-winning story about a girl's changed relationships with family and friends as she became a teenager. The school had purchased a class set before Jessica was hired, and since it was just the kind of book she had loved as a pre-adolescent, she assumed the class would enjoy it. Big mistake! The boys complained starting with page one, and several girls also found it boring. This year, she decided to fill a bookshelf with a variety of children's novels, and invite each child to select one.

This homework assignment let her know who was reading which book and how each student approached paragraph writing. Jessica sighed as she glanced through the pages spread out in front of her. A few paragraphs were well-written, some were very abbreviated, and others consisted of very long sentences that had not yet made their acquaintance with punctuation. Having added Esteban's books to the mix, Jessica noticed that all four were chosen, three by Mexican-American students and one by a white student. Then she realized these were the only novels on her bookshelf by Mexican-American authors – why had she not noticed that before? And they were the only ones she hadn't read, challenging her attempts to guide students' writing about them.

A couple of hours ago, she had stuck her head in Esteban's classroom to thank him for sharing the books. The children had left. He was sitting at his desk, absorbed in writing. She admired the contrast between his caramel-colored arms and neck, and his crisp white short-sleeved shirt.

"I'm using your books," she announced brightly.

He looked up, large coffee-black eyes puzzled. She continued, "You know, the ones you brought me to use. Well, I haven't had time to look at the history book yet, but I added the storybooks to my bookshelf."

"Oh, that's good. I'm glad to hear it," he said as though mentally marking the point in the sentence he was writing when she interrupted him. Then he lowered his head and resumed writing.

Jessica backed out, deflated, and returned to her own classroom. Well, what did she expect? She imagined him radiating, "I knew you'd get what I was trying to show everyone. You're a great teacher!"

Well, no, that isn't what he would say, even if he weren't busy. He would probably assume she had read them and could discuss them. She pictured a panicked look on her face in response to him asking which book interested her most. He might even expect her to work with the books, perhaps create a lesson about Mexican authors or plot structures.

As she dispensed with that fantasy, another took its place. Esteban rose from his desk, approached her, took her hand and pulled her into the classroom while closing the door behind her, then put his arms around her and ...

No, no, no! Where did that come from, she asked herself, appalled. The clock on the wall told her she had just wasted ten minutes. She scolded herself: Get a grip. Let's get through these paragraphs in the next hour. Concentrate, girl!

\* \* \* \* \*

It wasn't until Sunday mid-afternoon, having finished preparation for Monday, that Jessica finally had time to return to the letter from Mary to Annie. Tim was watching football downstairs with his younger brother Phil. Their running commentary about plays that were "brilliant" or "dumb-ass," and ref calls that were "outrageous, what are they paying you for, shit-head?!?," laced with the occasional roar of a crowd, filled the tiny house, even with the bedroom door closed.

Jessica's eye fell on the letter. She remembered Cath's suggestion that she might locate Annie and Mary online.

She opened the family history website Cath had mentioned, then registered for a free trial period. The process looked simple: just enter first name Annie, last name Hart, location Iowa, and hit Search. Oh, goodness! Annie Harts had lived all over Iowa in towns like Fairbank, Jackson, Union, Liberty, and Lake Pierce. She could rule out any born in the 1900s, but that still left several and no clue whether any of them might relate to her.

She decided to work backward. She entered the name, birth date, and birth location of her maternal grandfather, then hit Search. Grandpa appeared! So did numerous others with the same name, but she recognized Grandpa by birth details. She weeded out all but him, then picked the earliest census record, when he was nine years old. Opening it, she not only recognized the names of a couple of siblings, but also discovered the names of his parents and more siblings.

For the next two hours, as noise from the football game receded from her consciousness, Jessica unearthed names, birthdates, and locations of great grandparents, great-great grandparents, assorted offspring, and others who might be related. She began to construct a tentative family tree, uncertain whether she was tracing the right people. Then she opened the 1870 U.S. Census for Burlington, Iowa.

Mary, age seventeen, resided in Burlington with her German immigrant parents John and Louise, and six siblings, including eight-year-old Annie. Pieces clicked into place. This appeared to be the same Mary who Jessica had identified earlier – wife of Heinrich, a German immigrant minister, and mother of several children including Mamie. The names in Mary's letter to Annie.

She had found her people!

Using 1880 and 1900 census data, she was able to add details to the family tree. Mary and Heinrich appeared to have been married in the late 1870s, judging from children's birthdates.

Suddenly the sound of the bedroom door opening yanked Jessica back into the present. "What a game!" Tim exclaimed as he bounded in, then asked, "You still doing schoolwork?"

"No, I'm researching ..." Jessica stopped as she realized she had not yet mentioned the old letter to him.

"Good," Tim continued, "Phil's still here and asked if we want to grab some pizza with him. You haven't started dinner, have you?"

"No," Jessica said, feeling guilty that she hadn't even thought of it.

"Then get a sweater and let's go." Tim turned and headed down the stairs.

The three of them piled into Tim's battered Ford Focus and drove to their favorite pizza place. They ordered, found a table, and started on a pitcher of beer.

"So what have you been up to all afternoon?" Phil asked. How predictable, Jessica thought. Tim eventually would get around to asking the same thing, but Phil was more likely to hone right in on her preoccupations and ask her about them directly.

"I've been researching something. You'll never guess what I found in an old box of Mom's the other day. A letter dated 1928."

"Someone forgot to mail it?" Phil asked.

"No, it was mailed. Someone named Mary wrote it to her sister named Annie Hart."

Two sets of eyes simply looked at her as if she had announced that yellow replaced aqua as her favorite color. Then Tim raised his eyebrows. "So? Who was this Annie Hart?"

"Well, that's the thing," replied Jessica, "I don't know. I'm in the process of figuring out who they are. I seem to be related to them."

"Oh." Tim appeared lost for a follow-up question.

Jessica continued, "There was a lot of pain in the letter. This Mary wrote about what happened to the German Americans after World War I, but they didn't call it that at the time, they called it the Great War. Anyway, she and her husband had been part of this German-American community that was just crushed because they spoke German."

"How sad," Tim commented.

Phil asked, "Did they speak English, too?"

"Well, yes, of course," Jessica replied, taken aback. "The letter was in English."

"'Cause if they didn't, I can see where there would be problems," Phil continued.

Irritation welling up inside her, Jessica said, "They spoke English, and Mary hadn't even been to Germany. But the English speakers seemed to have canned the German church Mary's husband was pastor of, or something like that. Because it was German."

When neither brother responded, Jessica added, "If I'm related to them, I want to know what happened and who they were."

Phil shrugged. "Yeah, okay."

Tim frowned. "I get that you're excited about it and I know you liked history back in college. But I don't get spending Sunday afternoon researching this old letter."

Jessica twisted the corner of her paper napkin. "Tim, I really didn't know who my family was, beyond my grandparents. I just want to know. When you came into the bedroom after the game, that's what I was doing, researching my family tree."

Tim gave her a questioning look. "We don't know who our ancestors were either, but I don't get why it matters. Like, they're gone. And we're here."

Phil broke in, "Hey, if this is something she wants to do, I say go for it."

Jessica suspected Phil wasn't actually interested in ancestors either, but appreciated his easy-going, supportive attitude.

An order number was called out. "That's us, I'll get it," Phil said as he stood and left.

Tim asked, sounding as if he was trying to understand Jessica's enthusiasm, "So, did you find anything out?"

"Yeah, I've got names now going back about four generations. And I think I've found someone mentioned in the letter. I seem to have an ancestor named Mamie who was born in 1883 in Farmington, Iowa, wherever that is, and Mary, who wrote the letter, was her mother."

"Well that's good, you figured the letter out," he replied as if the problem were now solved.

"This is hot." Phil plopped the pizza on the table. "Half 'The Works,' half Canadian bacon and pineapple. Dig in!"

"No place else does 'The Works' like here," Tim exclaimed as he helped himself to a piece. "Grab some while it sizzles, Jess."

Jessica studied the brothers as they sank their teeth into pizza, Tim mopping melted cheese off his chin and Phil scooping up pieces of sausage that fell onto his napkin.

Phil asked Tim, "Want to bet on next Sunday's game? Loser buys pizza?"

Tim said, "I'll take the 'Niners."

"No can do, we have to flip for it."

Sighing, Jessica took a piece of Canadian bacon and pineapple while pondering why neither her husband nor her brother-in-law saw the point of her tracking down her past. But she couldn't just let it go. They were her people, and she wanted to know who they were.

*May, 1883*

MARY'S FAMILY TREE

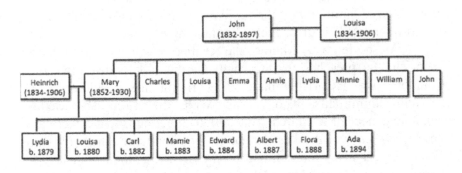

Mary glanced out the window, uttering a brief prayer that the Lord would see fit to get spring underway. May in Farmington normally enticed her to throw open windows, welcoming in the clean, flower-scented air. Farmington, a small Iowa town of roughly a thousand, was perched between the Des Moines River and a backdrop of hills formed by receding glaciers. As Mary knew, while May could be glorious, it could also present a tug of war a dying winter refused to concede.

During cold springs like this one, the mud of melted snow and rain gave way only reluctantly to new green shoots. Although gradually losing its hold, winter periodically howled in protest. The farmers planted their corn and other crops, knowing any delay meant losing precious summer growing time. But every night before retiring, they reviewed with God their pledge that they would attend church more regularly if only He would hasten along the change of seasons.

Mary, too, prayed for warmer weather so she could shoo her children out of their small home, a stand-in for Farmington's parsonage, without hearing, "It's too cold!" Days earlier, she had given birth to her and Heinrich's fourth copper-haired child. They named her Mary Elizabeth after Mary, but quickly took to calling her Mamie to avoid confusion.

At times Mary felt exhausted caring for the baby plus the other three youngsters. But she knew she took after her sturdy Prussian immigrant mother. She had her mother's even disposition, thickening waist, and frizzy auburn hair, now pinned up in braids. She also discovered she had her mother's drive to create a home where a large family might thrive, like the diligent farmer cultivating bountiful crops. This drive fueled her lagging energy.

As she fed baby Mamie, she recalled how she came to marry Heinrich, the preacher for the small German Methodist Episcopal Church. Like Heinrich, many of Farmington's residents were German immigrants who, along with their English-speaking neighbors, needed a church. But, unlike the English, the Germans knew *Deutsch* was the best language for communicating with *Gott Vater*. A year ago, Heinrich had been assigned as their preacher, so Farmington was now Mary's home.

She remembered that evening back in February of 1877, when she still lived with her family in Burlington. Every Sunday, she attended the German Methodist Episcopal Church with family members. She preferred the morning service in German because she loved old German hymns like *"Lobt Gott ihr Christen, alle gleich."* But sometimes she was so busy helping her mother with the youngest children that it was easier to attend the evening service, in English, with her father and a sibling or two.

Waiting for the service to start that particular evening, she was sitting with her younger sister Annie and their father, thumbing through the English hymnal.

"That man over there who was looking at you, who is he?" Annie whispered as she tugged Mary's sleeve.

"*Ruhig*, shush!" Mary replied, hoping desperately she was not blushing. "He's just a new *Pfarrer*."

From the corner of her eye, she tried to study the intense young man with dark hair and pointed beard, sitting on the far side of the sanctuary. This was the third Sunday evening Mary had noticed him. He usually faced straight ahead, but occasionally she could feel his brief gaze. For once, Mary did not hear the service at all; she participated mechanically while her mind kept wandering across the sanctuary. As the service ended, she thought to catch one more glimpse of him.

She turned her head, to find him staring at her. Their eyes locked briefly, then both looked away. With a racing heart and sweating palms, she sought an escape route.

The service having concluded, the crowd began to file toward the door, another peculiarity of evening service. After morning service, people lingered and chatted before slowly drifting out since church was where the German community came together, and they were in no hurry to leave. The evening service drew a more eclectic group, some of whom were not German at all.

Suddenly without warning, Mary found herself face to face with the bearded young man as *Pfarrer* Korfhage, a short round man whose spectacles routinely slid down his nose as they were doing now, was introducing her father to him: "... and his eldest daughter Mary." He explained to Mary's father, "Heinrich entered the ministry last year." Heinrich nodded silently.

*Pfarrer* Korfhage addressed Heinrich: "One of our most steadfast families, I'm sure you'll be getting to know them quite well."

Mary felt her face flame. She fell completely mute, so unlike her. Thankfully, no one seemed to notice, and her family moved on.

Heinrich was not the first young man to notice Mary. She was, after all, twenty-five. Although plain as a brick wall, she was in good health and quite eligible for marriage. Her parents, both German immigrants, occasionally had tested her reactions to young men they thought might make suitable husbands, like the way her mother often asked one of the children to taste a bite of supper before putting it on the table. But none interested her. As far as Mary was concerned, if she wanted children, she had younger siblings at home. Why leave a home where she felt comfortable to join a man she might not get on with?

That night, as Mary slept in the small bedroom she shared with her sisters, Heinrich materialized. He slowly floated toward her bed, then looked down into her wide-open eyes, his expression mixing kindness with longing. He kissed her gently – then began to fade. Not wanting him to go, she reached for him – then suddenly woke up. When she realized she had been dreaming, shame shook her for having such thoughts about a preacher!

Four weeks passed and Mary did not see him. Each week, she found herself marking time until Sunday evening, then sinking into crushing disappointment when he was not there. She was sure the Lord must be punishing her for that terribly sinful dream.

The following Wednesday afternoon, after walking three young siblings home from school, Mary was alarmed to find *Pfarrer* Korfhage talking with her parents. His visits usually meant someone was very ill or had died. As she dashed into the room, three pairs of eyes turned and talking ceased. Then her father said, "Mary, sit down. We have something very important to discuss."

Mary slowly sank into a chair, dread filling her. Not one of the children, please, dear God!

A round smile lit up the moon of *Pfarrer* Korfhage's face. "Mary, what we were discussing is beautiful, sacred, and involves you." Mary looked from face to face, perplexed. He continued, "We were considering the possibility of you becoming a helpmate of *Gott Vater im Himmel*."

Mary was even more confused. How were they envisioning her as the Lord's helpmate?

Her mother spoke: "We should be more plain. What we were speaking about involves you and the new itinerant *Pfarrer*, Heinrich. And the possibility perhaps of marriage."

*Pfarrer* Korfhage continued rapidly, "Heinrich is ready for marriage, but his work keeps him too busy to look for a wife. And, quite frankly, he doesn't know how to go about it. But he did express an interest in taking tea with you, if that would be alright."

Tea. Marriage. Heinrich. Mary looked down at her hands, noticed they were trembling and wondered how she could hide them. She nodded. "*Ja*, tea is alright."

"*Sehr gut*, excellent," said *Pfarrer* Korfhage, standing up. "I believe he can join you right here, next Monday evening."

Over tea, she found him intense but kind. She learned that after completing seminary training, he had been assigned as an itinerant *Pfarrer* in southeastern Iowa, where he provided religious services on farms too far from towns to have their own church. He lived in a rooming house in Burlington, and when possible, contributed his services to the church there.

After the third evening of tea, as Mary and Heinrich began to find their voices with each other, he worked up the courage to ask her family for her hand in marriage. Her father consented, and they were married September 20 of that same year. A year and a half later, their first child arrived.

She looked down at little Mamie, who had drifted off to sleep. The small house was quiet for the first time all day. Mary savored the peace, brief as it might be.

Yes, she had married well. Heinrich took his calling very seriously. Mary didn't doubt that he and the Lord communicated (in German, of course) on a regular basis. His congregants wanted to make sure whatever he passed on about them would get them into Heaven when the time came. Mary figured that, when his own time came, Heinrich would be there, arm in arm with *Gott Vater*, checking to see that no celestial hallelujah got out of hand. And she would be checking to make sure his cloak was clean and pressed.

#### CHAPTER 5

*September, 2012*

Monday, Jessica couldn't wait to share her research findings with Cath, especially following Tim's tepid response. She placed the folded family tree sketch neatly in her bag, next to her sandwich. First, however, the morning's lessons.

She was imagining what kind of people Mary and Heinrich might have been, while helping a table of students figure out how to solve math problems, when she felt a tap on her shoulder.

She looked up. "What is it, Chelsea?"

"They're talking Spanish at my table, and I can't understand what they're saying," Chelsea said.

Jessica glanced toward Chelsea's table, where three dark heads huddled while a blond girl worked independently. She encouraged students to help each other, and assumed Chelsea needed a peer.

"Can you work with Shannon?" she asked, referring to the blond girl.

"She likes to work by herself. They're supposed to talk English in this school."

Jessica sighed inwardly as she accompanied Chelsea back to her table. Chelsea was correct about instruction being in English, although there was no specific rule about what language students could use to help each other.

"Hey, guys, how about English, please?" she said.

Their talking stopped, and one of the boys glared at Chelsea. Then Jessica remembered that the smallest one, Tomás, was in the process of learning English and probably still thought in Spanish. But technically, Chelsea was right, this was an English-speaking school.

As Jessica moved to the next table, a horrible realization hit her: she had sounded just like veteran sixth-grade teacher Rick, who she suspected would rejoice if all the Mexican families left.

Earlier that morning, before going to her classroom she had stopped in the office to check her mailbox, when she almost bumped into Rick and fourth-grade teacher Carolyn. Engaged in a heated discussion, they didn't see her. Rick, a large man with a large voice, was saying, "I still don't think it's right to treat them any differently than other lawbreakers. I mean, anyone who's here illegally is breaking the law, correct? Ow, sorry, Jessica, I didn't see you!"

"No problem," she said, looking up and telling herself that anyone the size and shape of a military tank has an obligation to guard against running others over.

"Morning, Jessica," Carolyn said before continuing animatedly, "Rick, some of your own students are probably undocumented. Are you saying you'd deny them access to education or work?" Carolyn's shoulder-length graying hair swished in emphasis.

"I just think their families should return to Mexico and go through the process of getting authorization to be here, that's all. And their parents should all be required to learn English. Some of them talk with such a heavy accent that I can't understand them, and some don't even speak English at all."

"Oh, you're impossible!" exclaimed Carolyn. "Isn't he, Jessica?"

"Huh?" Jessica looked up from a catalog she was glancing through before tossing out.

Rick, who had been teaching fifteen years, turned to Jessica. "You're still new, but you'll get tired of some families' limited English, believe me. I'm not biased against immigrants, my own grandparents immigrated from Russia. But they went through proper channels and learned English as soon as they got here, and they made sure their kids did, too. They didn't ask for special favors like some of these people are doing."

"See, I told you he's impossible," Carolyn said.

Now, replaying her quick comment about speaking English, Jessica wondered if she was slowly turning into a Rick. She desperately hoped not. He wasn't the kind of caring teacher she was trying to become.

Math was followed by short individual book conversations with each child. Jessica carved out time for them by assigning the class a short story to read and write about, which would give her about a minute with each child.

When she got to Marisela, she saw one of Esteban's loaned books. Squatting down, she said, "I see you picked *Rogelia's House of Magic*, and you're writing about ..." she consulted the list of which child was writing about whom "... Fern. Tell me why you picked this book, and Fern."

"I like magic. That's how I picked it. The two girls, Fern and Marina, are friends. I'm more like Fern because I speak Spanish, and Marina doesn't."

Jessica glanced at a page, which appeared slightly above a fifth grade reading level. A bit more advanced than she had pegged Marisela as ready for. "Who is Rogelia?" she asked Marisela.

"Rogelia is a *curandera*. I haven't gotten very far in the book yet. But my grandmother, the one in Guanajuato, is a *curandera*. She's getting old, it was her fiftieth birthday a couple of weeks ago."

"What is a – how did you say it?" Jessica asked.

"*Curandera*," supplied Marisela. "Like a local doctor, someone who heals people. My grandmother learned from her mother and grandmother. Her grandmother was pretty well-known in her village, lots of people used to come see her for different things."

Diana, sitting next to Marisela, looked up from the reading assignment through red-framed glasses. "*Señora* Soto is the *curandera* around here. She helps me with my allergies. I want to read Marisela's book when she's done, it looks more interesting than mine."

Jessica glanced at the list to see what she was reading, but Diana continued, "I'm reading *Julia's Kitchen*. I picked it because I like to help *Mamá* in the kitchen. This book is really sad. Julia's mother and little sister die in a fire, and only Julia's *papá* is left."

"Don't they live with anyone else?" asked Marisela.

"No," replied Diana. "After the fire, there's only two of them. And her *papá* doesn't talk very much."

"So, Diana, what do you suppose Julia will do in the story?" Jessica asked as she shifted from Marisela to Diana.

At lunchtime, Jessica hurried to the teacher's lounge to share her weekend research results with Cath. Cath walked in briskly, long frizzy braids and a long green skirt flowing behind her.

"Nice outfit," she said to Jessica as she sat down and drew out her lunch bag.

Extending an arm to remind herself what she was wearing, Jessica mentally congratulated herself for having selected this particular blue and green striped tunic that complemented her slim jeans. "Thanks, I did what you suggested." She drew from her bag the family tree sketch and today's sandwich. "You were right. I could trace back a few generations more easily than I thought, once I got the hang of it."

"Interesting," Cath commented as she looked at the sketch.
"And this," Jessica pointed to the name Mamie on the sketch, "is probably the same Mamie in the letter, because her mother's name is Mary and Mary has a sister named Annie."

From the corner of her eye, Jessica saw Esteban approaching. Although he was only slightly taller than she was, his presence seemed to fill the room.

As he passed them, he glanced down at the two heads hovering over Jessica's sketch. "A little family history research?"

"Cath got me started," Jessica replied, hoping a blush hadn't yet ignited. He was such a hunk, she had trouble thinking straight when he was standing so close. She mentally gave herself a good shake and continued. "A week ago, I couldn't have told you the names of my great grandparents, and now I even know who some of my great-greats were."

"That old letter you found got you started," corrected Cath. "All I did was give you a push."

"I wish I knew something about these people," Jessica continued, setting down her sandwich. "Some of the children in my class know about their grandparents' grandparents, not just names on a piece of paper, but what they were like. This is all I have."

"I bet there's more you could find," Esteban suggested. "Old newspapers that have been digitized, plat maps ..."

"What kind of maps?" Jessica asked.

"Plat maps and other land records." He pulled a chair around and sat, the back of the chair pressed against his chest. "We used land records a lot when I took historiography in college." Esteban had been a history major. "The U.S. government ignored everyone else's land records when they took over territory. They sent out their own surveyors to draft townships that indicated land plots, topographical features, roads, and sometimes who bought which plots. That's a plat map. You may or may not find anything, but it's worth checking."

"Ben Martinez is absent again today," commented Cath as Jessica's attention shifted from Esteban to the potential of land records. "I'll call home after school."

Esteban sighed. Ben's father worked long hours in the lettuce fields and his mother was overwhelmed caring for their young children. Occasionally getting Ben off to school seemed to slip through the cracks. "Yes, call her so she knows you're concerned. If he misses tomorrow, let me know and I'll stop by to see her on my way home."

Esteban did not like acting as default home-school liaison between the Spanish-speaking families and the English-speaking teachers, but he ended up with that role anyway since no one else in the school could fill it very well.

As he left, Cath asked, "Are you going to keep researching?" Jessica frowned. "Probably. I really don't have time until the weekend, and pretty soon the free trial period will be up. But I'll see what I can find this weekend, then decide."

Cath smiled as she stood to leave. "They've got you hooked, girlie. Go for it!"

\* \* \* \* \*

Tuesday morning's sun was dispersing the night's chill as Phil pulled his 2006 black Dodge Viper into his parking space behind Goodyear Tire. The shop opened at 7:00. His boss Bert insisted the staff be ready ten minutes before the doors opened, but Phil rarely arrived before 6:55. Today was no exception.

Slamming the car door shut and locking it, he thanked his parents, as he did often, that they had the good sense to raise their family in California, although there wasn't much else to thank them for. He definitely appreciated the consistently mild temperatures and lack of rain. Even during periodic bouts of water rationing, he swore he'd rather take short showers than live in a wet climate. A lone palm tree cast its pole-like shadow across the lot as Phil dashed toward the door.

Bert scowled at him as he took his place behind the counter with his partner Jim. But Bert never did more than that, since he recognized Phil as one his most capable and reliable workers.

"I'll be right back," Jim said, scooting past Phil. A small, middle-aged white man with thinning hair and horn rimmed classes, Jim looked more like an accountant than the auto mechanic he was.

"You're going to the home-brays?" Phil asked, emphasizing deliberate gringo pronunciation of the word *hombres*. Jim and Phil had a running dispute about the shop's bilingual signage, sparse though it was. Jim, a New Yorker who had relocated to California ten years previously, spoke a smattering of Spanish and believed in what he called "linguistic accessibility," a phrase Phil mocked whenever Jim used it.

"Knock it off, Westerfield," Bert barked as he unlocked the front door. A large African American whose black hair was being overtaken by silver, Bert maintained a pragmatic outlook. If a few bilingual signs attracted more customers, he was all for them.

"I still think it's coddling them," grumbled Phil as Mrs. Lyman, first customer for the day, arrived. She approached the counter, and Phil's face suddenly broke out in a radiant, welcome smile as if assisting this elderly woman would be the best part of his day.

Right before lunch break, Phil noticed Jim bidding a Latino-looking customer "*hasta luego.*" Rolling his eyes, he mumbled, "That guy speaks English, you know."

"I know," replied Jim as he filed a receipt from the customer's two new tires. "What's it to you?"

Phil picked up a wrench from the counter and turned to put it away. "It just bugs me. It's like, we're just enabling. You're like my sister-in-law."

"I thought you liked her." Jim's eyebrows shot up above the frames of his glasses.

"I do, she's cool, usually. But Sunday night, she told us about this bee in her bonnet about digging up long lost relatives who spoke German, even though they were American. Sometimes I can't figure her out."

Phil retrieved his lunch from the cooler, then marched toward the tiny, sparsely furnished break room. "Coming?" he called over his shoulder. Despite their periodic verbal sparring, Phil and Jim worked well together, and usually ate together while others took over the counter and hydraulic lifts.

Jim pulled his lunch bag from the cooler, then joined Phil. The smell of burnt coffee announced that someone forgot to turn off the coffee warmer. Flicking the knob, then sinking into a chair, Jim announced, "Women are just strange. You don't need to try to understand some of their whims."

"That's why I'm not married," Phil agreed. "I like Jessica, but I don't know if she realizes how she puts Tim down."

Jim took a bite of sandwich, then lifted the top piece of bread to peer at the filling. "How'd this get in here?" he asked, pulling out a strip of onion. "She knows I hate onions in my sandwiches."

"You sure Millie made it?" Phil asked, referring to Jim's wife.

"Aw, I guess you're right, my daughter must have thought she was doing Mildred a favor this morning, making my lunch." Jim said. "So what does she do that puts Tim down?"

"You've met him, as I recall."

"Sure. Damn good salesman, last year he almost sold me a TV we don't need."

"Well, Tim really wants to afford one of those fancy houses in a new subdivision, like Oakridge. We grew up poor, and since he was about ten, he's had dreams of a nice big house with a yard and all. A dog and a cat, maybe even a swimming pool, the whole thing. Put our past behind us, he says. Move on up, don't look back."

"What's wrong with that?"

"Nothing. Not what I want, though. I'd rather have my baby out there," Phil nodded in the direction of the Viper he kept in mint condition. "But it's what Tim wants. He gets pretty good sales commissions working the floor, but not good enough, so he's trying to figure out how to move up into management. He tried applying for a couple of positions that came up, but no luck yet."

"Uh huh," Jim replied.

"But Jessica could give a rip about a big house. She seems perfectly happy in their dumpy little neighborhood, so she doesn't get the effort he's making. She just doesn't see it. What she does see is the weight he's gradually been putting on. Now she's got this hair-brained research project looking into long-dead ancestors who spoke German, which makes no sense to me and Tim."

"Huh," was all Jim could think to say.

"Don't get me wrong, I love her and all, she's my kid sister. But watching the two of them makes me wonder why people get married in the first place."

The door opened abruptly and Bert's head appeared. "Things suddenly got busy. I need both of you."

Bert disappeared. Phil shrugged and popped a drumstick in his mouth as he stood up.

Jim rose to his feet. "Tell him to take her out for a nice dinner and have a heart to heart. That's what Millie and I do when things start to feel rough."

Phil shrugged. "Yeah, I'll tell him. He's working most nights this week, but maybe he can find an evening somewhere."

* * * * *

Jessica was about to get into her car to go home Tuesday afternoon when she noticed a blue Dodge Viper parked by the curb. It looked like it hadn't seen a car wash in ages. Using her cell phone, she snapped a picture, then texted it to Phil with a note: "You should give the owner lessons!"

She climbed in her car and was starting the ignition when she heard a ping. Phil had texted back: "Bad case of car abuse!"

She laughed. Her easy-going relationship with Phil was like a lick of ice cream on a hot day. She wouldn't want a steady diet of it, but as an occasional treat, it often took her mind off worries.

And Esteban had just given her something to worry about. As the children were leaving for the day, he had stopped into her classroom to ask how his loaned books were working out.

"Great, all four of them are being read, three by Mexican-American kids. I thought the books would be above their reading level, but they seem to understand what they're reading."

"Uh huh," he nodded. "That happens to any of us when reading something of personal interest. I wonder if your class's overall reading level would improve if you had more books your Mexican-American kids can relate to."

She hadn't thought of that. "Geez, I don't know. Do you have more I can borrow?"

"We're using them. But the library has a bunch. Go talk to Sharon." Sharon was the school's half-time librarian.

After she finished straightening her classroom, Jessica found Sharon shelving books in the library. Sharon looked up. "What can I help you with, Jessica?"

"I'm looking for fifth-grade stories by Mexican-American authors. Esteban told me you have some."

"We do indeed." Sharon tapped on her chin as she thought. "Let me look around and I'll put together a stack for you. They aren't all in one place. Any particular topic? And when do you need them?"

Jessica shrugged. "They can be about anything, and whenever you get to it. I'm just trying some things out."

As she walked back to her classroom, retrieved her bag and locked up for the day, she stewed over the possibility that her collection of books might actually be holding some of her students back. Maybe if they were more excited about what she had to offer, they would read more and harder books.

Two new words she had learned today – *curandera*, and plat map. She wondered if Tim knew what a plat map is. She'd have to ask him when he came home for dinner.

\* \* \* \* \*

*Hot shards of glass poured down Jessica's throat. She tried to bring her hands to her mouth, but couldn't move. Blinking back tears, she watched as Mary filled the bowl again from the cauldron. Heinrich,*

*Tim, and Esteban, meanwhile, stood next to the door, arguing, but she couldn't hear what they were arguing about. Wouldn't someone help her?*

*Just then Marisela scurried by, almost knocking Mary down, shouting, "Mama, you can't get me!" Mary reached out a long rubber band arm that scooped up Marisela, while her other hand poured another bowl of hot shards down Jessica's throat. Why wouldn't Tim help her, couldn't he see what was happening? She tried to scream, but the effort made her throat hurt even more.*

Heinrich, Esteban, Marisela, and Mary faded as the room lightened. Jessica realized she was lying down, not sitting, and Tim was asleep next to her. She shook Tim's shoulder.

"What is it," he mumbled.

"I'm sick. My throat's on fire," she whispered reproachfully. After all, Tim hadn't helped her in the nightmare.

Tim dragged himself up onto his elbows and looked at her. "Ah, no. I bet it's those kids again." He slid out of bed. "Can I bring you anything?"

The previous year Jessica had battled one illness after another as her body learned to fend off children's germs. By now, she assumed she had a hearty immunity, but apparently not.

As Tim fetched cold medicine, facial tissue, and a glass of water, Jessica called the substitute office. She hoped Mrs. Porter, a retired teacher, was available. She could walk into a classroom and immediately get the kids on task while maintaining order. But Jessica was just as likely to get a newbie who hadn't yet mastered the art of acting as the adult in a classroom. Last year a couple of times busy-work and games replaced academics as the kids manipulated the sub into acquiescing to low-level mayhem in exchange for keeping the noise level down to escape notice of other adults in the school.

As Jessica drifted back to sleep, she vaguely heard Tim shower, dress, then later leave for work.

By early afternoon, she could swallow without wincing. She went to the kitchen and downed a bowl of cereal, then contacted the substitute office to indicate she would return the next day.

As she hung up, she remembered land records. Tim had been none too pleased the previous evening when she had mentioned Esteban's suggestion that she look for plat maps.

"He's giving you all kinds of ideas, isn't he?" Tim had asked, eyebrows raised.

"He majored in history, he knows more about this stuff than I do," Jessica replied. Then, unsure whether the source of his reaction was skepticism about her family history research or jealousy toward Esteban, she changed the subject. "Hey, let's go see *Cold Light of Day* this weekend," referring to a movie Tim had expressed interest in.

Now feeling better, she decided to check out land records in the family history website. After locating the link, she began to enter names from her family tree sketch.

Mary and Heinrich didn't appear at all, so she tried Mamie's husband's branch of the family. After a few tries, she got a hit with a name she recognized. Opening the link, she discovered an old plat map, just like Esteban had described. Dated 1874, it depicted Blue Mound township in Macon County, Illinois, showing plots of land around a village with the odd name of Boody.

Within each plot was a person's name and a number that must designate acreage. She located the family surname on three plots under two different given names. On the family's 160-acre plot was a German Methodist Church and Parsonage. She also found five schools, another Methodist Church, a church of some other denomination, and a railroad line.

A few minutes later, she located two U.S. General Land Office records for ancestor William's purchase of land in Macon County. One was for 40 acres in 1849, the other for 160 acres in 1853. These must be records for acreage on the plat map. A little more research surfaced information about the Preemption Act of 1841, which allowed a head of household to buy land from the U.S. government cheaply as long as he or she lived there and improved it.

She located Boody on Googlemaps. It was a tiny village a few miles outside of Decatur. Searching for some history, she found a digitized version of an old book, *History of Macon County*. In its appendix of township histories, she found Blue Mound. There, she

41

learned that the first white people had settled there in the 1820s. She wondered which Indian tribes preceded them. Most names of early arrivals suggested English or Scottish descent, like Hall, Pope, and Moffett, but there were German names as well.

Then her eyes widened. In 1855, William, purchaser of the two plots from the U.S. government, helped to organize that German Methodist church on the plat map. How interesting that this small place had two Methodist churches so long ago, one presumably for English speakers and the other for German speakers.

She used census data to flesh out births and deaths in William's family tree. William, an immigrant from the German state of Hanover, and his wife Amelia, an immigrant with her parents from Westfalen, seem to have had several children, William junior being Jessica's ancestor. William junior's wife Lydia also descended from German immigrants. As she perused census documents, filling in family trees for William junior and Lydia, Jessica marveled at the large families they had back then. That plat map enabled her to see who lived where.

Her cell phone rang. Picking it up, she saw it was Milford's principal. "Hi, Sarah."

"How are you? I gather you're planning on being back tomorrow, but if you're contagious, you might rethink that."

"It's just a head cold. The sore throat's almost gone and I'm left with a stuffy nose. By the way, who covered for me today?" When she did not recognize the sub's name, she grimaced as she pictured chaos that probably reigned. "I'll definitely be there tomorrow."

"Well, I know you don't want to start using up too many sick days this early in the year, but use your judgment."

Jessica wondered what she would use if it weren't her judgment. It's like telling someone to drive carefully in bad weather as if you expect the person to drive recklessly otherwise.

Sarah continued, "Your kids will be glad to see you back. I think things got a little disorganized. The sub looked like she was about twelve years old herself, and seemed pretty frazzled by the time she left."

"Ugh. Looks like I'm going to need to train the little devils how to behave when I'm not there. I hadn't had a chance to do that yet. See you tomorrow."

Jessica had just put her cell phone down when it rang again. Tim this time.

"How are you feeling?" he asked.

"Better. I slept all morning. I'm up now, but not dressed yet."

"Don't," he replied. "And don't bother fixing dinner, I'll pick up some Chinese on the way home."

"I would love that!" she exclaimed. In truth, she wasn't hungry. But she didn't want to have to cook, and she appreciated thoughtfulness when Tim remembered to extend it.

As she put down the phone again, she looked at the computer screen, wishing she could continue working on this jigsaw puzzle. But she needed to shift attention to tomorrow's lesson plans, or maybe a reheated version of today's plans.

## October, 1879

### WILLIE'S FAMILY TREE

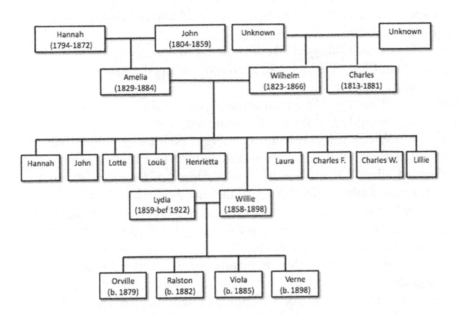

It had been a profitable morning. Golden. *Vergoldet.* As Willie drove his two-horse wagon home from Boody's grain elevator after selling the last of the summer's harvest, he whistled cheerfully. Scanning fields around him, he considered the dry stubble wheat that a month ago had been richly golden, and remains of harvested corn that had been vibrant green. His immigrant parents and their offspring had certainly prospered here in Illinois! Willie and his older brother John had inherited their father's farmland when he died thirteen years earlier. Heart attack, probably. Just six years ago, their mother Amelia, an attractive middle-aged widow, married a widower who lived near St. Louis. Willie missed having her around.

The late morning sun washed his face. He pushed his hat back from his wavy chestnut hair and briefly closed blue eyes, inviting the sun's rays to play over his forehead and eyelids. He let the reins slacken as the steady clip clop of the horses mesmerized him. Ah, at age twenty-one, fortune beckoned. He and Lydia, his wife of six months, would raise a large family. The farm would thrive, perhaps he would pilot new crops. Who knows, he might become one of Boody's prominent leaders.

"*Guten Morgen*, Willie!" Willie's eyes popped open at the German-accented voice of his father's old friend Friedrich, currently Boody's postmaster.

"*Guten Morgen*." Willie waved his hat as the wagon passed the post office. Friedrich had apparently stepped outside to inhale the sweet autumn air.

"Fine day," Friedrich commented.

"Couldn't be finer," Willie agreed.

Willie had grown up regarding Friedrich as a grandfather of sorts. He and Willie's parents had helped to establish Boody – so named after William Boody, first president of the Decatur and East St. Louis Railroad that bordered the village. Friedrich and Amelia's father had arrived from Westfalen in 1839, three years before she and the rest of her family came, and seven years before Willie's father Wilhelm arrived from Hanover.

They came to Illinois mainly for the golden farmland Willie regarded today. As a child, he and his siblings had devoured their parents' immigration stories. They pictured him arriving all alone in New York on a ship from Bremen, bravely heading west into the unknown, and stumbling by pure luck onto the fertile soils of Illinois. As they learned later, however, the process wasn't like that. Land companies collaborated with transportation companies and state governments to recruit Europeans, sometimes even transplanting whole villages from one continent to the other. Their father and a brother, fed up with Prussia's constant war and worried about impending famine, had joined an emigration party. His mother's immigration story was similar, although the part Willie liked best was the ox team that took them from St. Louis to Boody.

The wagon jerked as one of the horses stumbled and the other whinnied, then both broke into a gallop. In vain, Willie tugged on the reins. "*Halt! Halt!*" he shouted, but the team ran straight on into downtown Boody.

Two men on horseback galloped toward the team, which slowed, then stopped. "What happened?" hollered Rob, Willie's English friend.

Willie shook his head, pulled off his hat and wiped his brow with his sleeve. "I don't know. I was coming back from the grain elevator, riding along peacefully, when some animal, maybe a badger, dashed smack in front of the horses."

"*Was ist geschehen?*" Willie whipped around, to see Friedrich running up from behind. "Is anyone hurt?" he puffed.

"Just Willie's pride," laughed the other man on horseback. "See you later," he added as he turned his horse and ambled away.

Rob laughed. "Willie, I've been telling you that you need lessons running a team of horses. You aren't firm enough with them!"

"He's got his *Vater*'s spirit," said Friedrich, "he's just growing into it."

"C'mon, Will," said Rob, "let's get this wagon back to your place, and I'll stand you a beer."

"How about supper first?" Willie's eyes sparkled and his carefully-trimmed mustache dripped sweat. "Lydia should have it ready by the time we get there."

"I'll join you," Friedrich said.

The three made the short ride to Willie's farm, which abutted Friedrich's farm, passing the one-room whitewashed Zion German Methodist Church Willie's father had co-founded. Arriving at the white two-story farmhouse, they found Lydia fixing pork and vegetable stew. One hand stirred while the other tried to brush back tendrils of earth-colored wavy hair escaping from the bun at the nape of her neck. As usual, she made a full pot, never knowing for sure how many people Willie might bring home. A golden loaf of oat bread cooled near the window.

"Smells good!" Willie exclaimed as he gave her a peck on the cheek.

"Friedrich, Rob," she acknowledged. "Grab a plate, I think it's ready."

#### CHAPTER 6

As Rob helped himself, he said to Lydia, "Our boy Willie never ceases to entertain us. Let me tell you about today's adventure."

"Or, you can read about it in the newspaper tomorrow," Friedrich added as Willie playfully popped Rob on the side of the head.

\* \* \* \* \*

*January, 1884*

LYDIA'S FAMILY TREE

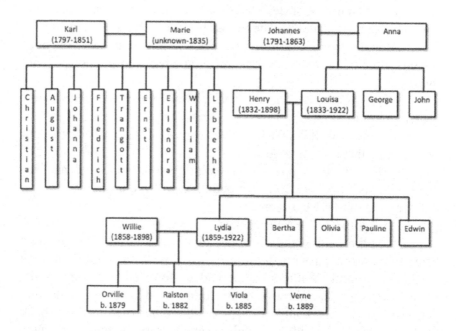

Huddled in the church, Lydia felt Willie draw her close to share body warmth. Although outdoors the sun gleamed like a giant diamond against a brilliant blue cushion, she couldn't remember it being this cold before. His mother's funeral had just concluded, and mourners were beginning to drift to the back of the German Methodist Church for hot cider before heading home through frigid temperatures. The burial would have to wait until Salem Cemetery thawed enough to prepare a grave.

Amelia's second husband Philip, standing next to Willie, stared straight ahead, seemingly oblivious to the cold. Willie admitted he had never been clear whether his mother's marriage ten years ago to Philip, a widowed lumber merchant and fellow German immigrant, was a matter of love or convenience. Philip's obvious grief suggested the former on his part, although Lydia suspected Amelia simply preferred to live as a wife rather than as a widow. In any case, Philip did not object when Willie and his brother John proposed burying her here in Boody, next to their father, rather than near his own home in St. Joseph, Missouri.

Amelia hadn't lived in Boody since Lydia turned fourteen, but Lydia had known her all her life, having grown up just two farms over from Willie's family farm. A German immigrant like Lydia's parents, Amelia had always felt like part of her extended family. What a shock to everyone when she was suddenly widowed at age 37!

As the story went, Wilhelm, a strong, hearty farmer, was moving farm equipment in preparation for spring plowing when suddenly he cried out, grabbed his chest, and collapsed. A farm hand, who dashed over to see what happened, found him on the ground gasping for air and groaning, as if an ox were sitting on his chest. He lifted Wilhelm, carried him to a horse-drawn wagon, and rushed to find Boody's doctor. By the time Dr. Douglas was located, however, Wilhelm was gone.

Poor Amelia, a pregnant mother of four, suddenly now a widow. She had already lost five children, four in one spring to typhoid and another two years later. Now her husband. Lydia couldn't imagine how Amelia had coped. Of course, these things happened, but where would you find strength to continue? And Lydia wouldn't have been able to marry someone in another state, as Amelia had done, because she couldn't imagine life apart from her extended family and friends. She glanced around the church, thankful that all these people were part of her world. Even Willie, headstrong as he could be at times, what would she do without him?

John, tall with bright copper-colored hair and beard, was tapping Willie on the shoulder. "I'll be right back, I'm taking Anna and the children home." John's wife Anna, who Lydia loved like a

49

sister, was pregnant with their fifth child. Their eight year-old daughter, who had been trying futilely to control her lively younger siblings, looked visibly relieved by this announcement. Lydia was glad one of her sisters had offered to care for their two, Orville and Ralston. Young children really didn't need to attend funerals.

Anna told Willie as she turned to leave, "Send Lottie and her husband over whenever they're ready." Willie's older sister Lottie, who had married Philip's nephew in St. Joseph, was staying with John and Anna for a few days. Anna gave Lydia a firm hug, then left with John and the children.

Lydia noticed Willie's younger sister still sobbing as she stood beside their younger brother, who was trying to comfort her. Lydia gathered the girl in her arms and held her. Her mother, Louisa, made eye contact and smiled. Louisa, like her daughter Lydia, thrived on caring for other people.

"Let's help Philip," suggested Lydia's father Henry. Philip still seemed oblivious to the movements of people around him.

Louisa said gently to him, "Come on. There's some good whiskey back at the house." She disengaged herself from her husband's arm, gently taking one of Philip's. As Henry took the other, the couple steered him toward the back of the church.

With her arms still around Willie's younger sister, Lydia slowly propelled the girl toward the door. She thought about the cycle of births, marriages, and deaths, and the family connections that enabled people to move forward when one of their own had departed.

CHAPTER 7


*September, 2012*


Jessica scanned the living room, trying to identify someone she might know. A tall, tanned man with curly brown hair and a familiar face approached.

"Tim! I was hoping you'd make it," he said. Then he noticed Jessica, extended his hand, and added, "I think we've met before. I'm Marcus." Marcus, just promoted at Best Buy, was now Tim's supervisor.

"Marcus, Jessica." Tim introduced. "Looks like a great party!"

Marcus clapped Tim on the back, "Go help yourself to drinks and snacks. Food will be out soon." He moved past them to greet the next arrivals.

Marcus lived across town from Jessica and Tim in a new subdivision. The interior of the two-story stucco house appeared newly decorated, a cut above what Jessica usually saw on HGTV when she managed to find time to watch it. She surveyed chairs and sofas, upholstered in coordinating combinations of brick, lemon, and mint on a cream background, set into conversation groupings. Area rugs in the same colors were scattered over a burnished dark hardwood floor. Not her style, but nice. From the size of the house, Jessica assumed Marcus had a wife and family whom she hadn't met yet.

Tim's blue eyes gleamed as he looked around. Jessica could read in his face a longing to be like Marcus one day. "What do you think, Jess?" Tim whispered excitedly in her ear. "And he started off without two dimes to rub together, kinda like me."

"Impressive," Jessica whispered back. Although Marcus didn't strike her as someone she would want to be married to, she had to admit he had done well for himself. Somehow he made her think of her budding impression of Willie – upwardly mobile, supportive family in the background. Was that what Tim actually wanted?

As Tim steered Jessica to the bar in the far corner of the living room, he greeted other party-goers, occasionally introducing her. He had explained that Marcus wanted to share his promotion with the rest of the staff. Hence the party and a roomful of Tim's co-workers. Acquaintances, not exactly the communities of Mary and Lydia. And not exactly the kind of community Jessica craved.

When they reached the bar, Jessica brightened as she recognized Dwight and Teri. Dwight, bland in appearance but sincere in nature, willing to lend a hand or an ear to everyone, had befriended Tim in his early days at Best Buy. Jessica and Tim had occasionally invited Dwight over for dinner until he met tiny, blond Teri, who took possession of him. Following a short, intense courtship, the pair married. Once in a while, the foursome enjoyed summertime hikes and wintertime movies.

Jessica promptly found herself seated on a couch with Teri while Tim, Dwight, and several others stood in a clump talking shop and sports as if they hadn't seen each other for months rather than hours. As they sipped wine, the two women caught up.

Teri, office assistant for a veterinary practice, was babbling about a vet's interest in tracing the lineage of dogs. "He figured out a litter of puppies someone rescued was born to a Sheltie bitch and sired by a Queensland mix. Now he's trying to trace the lineage of the Queensland mix, but since no one has identified that dog, he's seeing what he can get from DNA. Of course, Queenslands themselves are a product of mixing other breeds, it isn't that there's a pure anything. But he says it's an interesting puzzle."

Jessica replied, "That makes me think about what I've been doing. I've gotten into researching my own genealogy. I've worked out a rough family tree going back four or five generations. I'm trying to figure out what the stories would have been, who these people were."

As she dove into the subject with animation, she began to recount what she had found so far, starting with the letter, then the vital statistics she had managed to locate. She was describing land records when she noticed another couple standing by the couch, seemingly eavesdropping. Jessica stopped mid-sentence, as if caught in the midst of spilling a secret.

"Don't stop," said the male half of the couple. Jessica took in his milk chocolate complexion, wire rim glasses, and red crewneck sweater over a white shirt. "I was just interested in what you were saying." He pulled up a chair. "Mind if I join you? I'm Vic, by the way, and this is Linda."

Jessica felt like a fence post next to Linda's curves and clear, bronzed ebony skin. Linda smiled politely. "Hello," she said, then turned to Vic. "I'll be back, I need to catch up on a few things with Marcus."

As she melted into the crowd, Vic rolled his eyes. "You two weren't talking Best Buy, so you must be here with employees. I'm not one, by the way."

Teri laughed. "Yeah, our husbands work there. I work in a veterinary office."

"I'm Jessica, this is Teri. I teach fifth grade," added Jessica.

"Nice to meet you," said Vic. Then he looked directly at Jessica and said, "I was interested in what you were saying about land in Illinois. I'm from outside Chicago originally."

"Oh, well, I was talking about an ancestor in the 1840s and 1850s, not about now," Jessica clarified, as though events so long ago wouldn't interest him.

"Yes, I gathered that," he said. "I was just struck by how easy it was for him to get so many acres from the government back then."

"Well, it probably wasn't easy," she stammered. "I mean, he had to come all the way from Germany, then, well, I guess find his way to a land office, and – well, I'm not sure. But I can't think it was easy."

"It was easier for him than it was for my people," Vic said earnestly, unfazed by Jessica's sudden discomfort, "without even going into a comparison of how your people and my people got across the Atlantic. You said your ancestor bought, how much was it, 160 acres, in what year?"

"1853," she said, increasingly uncertain where the conversation was going but suspecting she wouldn't find it comfortable if it had to do with racism.

"Ah," Vic said. "This might not mean much to you, but the Illinois state legislature passed a law that year prohibiting my people from migrating into the state. So even if they had cash in hand, they were barred from buying the land your people bought."

"Oh," said Jessica as though she needed to respond but had no idea what to say, "I didn't know that." Then she added lamely, "I thought slavery was prohibited in the North."

"It was, at least earlier than in the South. But back then the good white folks of Illinois wanted to suppress the Underground Railroad, and they sure didn't want Black folks settling out and staying there. So they tried to criminalize us even being in the state. The ones who were already there kept a low profile, and they sure couldn't buy land." Then he added quickly, "I'm not trying to make you feel guilty, but since you're looking to your past, you need to realize that it's connected with my past."

"I didn't think about that," Jessica murmured. "I'm trying to find out about the German churches back then."

"German churches?" asked Teri with surprise. "I didn't know there were any."

"Yeah, my great, great – well, I'm not sure how many greats, but anyway he helped to found one, a German Methodist church, right in the middle of Illinois."

"I've heard about those," Vic said. "There were churches running on parallel tracks, you could say, the German Methodist on one track and the A.M.E on another."

"What's A.M.E?" Teri asked.

Vic gave her a look that said, *How can you not know so much*? "The African Methodist Episcopal church. It's been around since the late 1700s. Black folks started it because white Methodists in Philadelphia didn't want Black members. Maybe they didn't want German-speaking members, either."

"They didn't," Jessica said. Common ground at last. "At least not back then, or at least not if they were speaking German. I wonder if the German Methodists and the African Methodists ever joined up."

"I sincerely doubt it," Vic said. "At least, I haven't heard of it."

Jessica asked him, "How did you know about that law in 1853? It was so long ago," she added as if its distance from the present rendered it obscure.

"Most African Americans know things about the history of this country that most white people don't know, or would rather that everyone forget. Also, I'm an architect, so along the way I've paid a lot of attention to who lives where. And why."

"An architect, how interesting!" Teri said.

"Yeah, it is," he agreed.

Linda had returned with Tim and Dwight. "Okay, folks," said Dwight, "time to stop talking shop. Who wants to get a bite to eat?"

Vic, Jessica, and Teri looked at each other. Stifling a laugh, Teri said, "Yes, let's stop talking shop."

The three couples moved toward the dinner buffet in the other room. Although the rest of the evening's conversations were on a more comfortable plane for Jessica, the sense of disquiet Vic's revelations prompted remained with her.

\* \* \* \* \*

While fixing breakfast the next morning, Jessica pondered whether to share with Tim her conversation with Vic. On one hand, she wanted to process it with someone. It was embarrassing to think about her ancestors' apparent access to land people of African descent were barred from purchasing, and the fact that she not only hadn't known this, but hadn't thought to wonder about it. But on the other hand, she suspected Tim would dismiss the conversation as a race card ploy to make her feel guilty. Having grown up poor, he had little patience hearing about racism, which he viewed as an excuse for lack of effort. Jessica wasn't so sure he was right. While Vic's revelations made her feel uncomfortable, she didn't want to simply bury the issue because of it. She decided to keep the conversation to herself for the time being.

Tim entered the kitchen bubbling with excitement. The previous evening, Marcus had encouraged him to apply for a sales supervisor position opening up soon. Jessica vaguely remembered him mentioning it in the car on the way home. Apparently the idea had percolated in his brain overnight. Or she was just awake enough this morning to take it in.

"Marcus really wants me to move off the floor and into management. My sales figures have been off the charts lately. All I need to do to ace this position is spend more time on customer follow-up. A year or two as a sales supervisor and I should be ready for a position at Marcus's level."

Jessica hadn't seen Tim this excited about work for a long time. Last time he applied for a promotion and lost out to someone else, he dragged himself around the house in a cloud of gloom for a month. Marcus seemed to be taking Tim under his wing. His smiles bathed the tiny kitchen in sunlight, although her wariness of him becoming another Marcus set storm clouds on the horizon.

Deliberately trying not to see those clouds, she smiled. "I'm really pleased."

"This means some evenings I'll have to stay a little later, doing more of those follow-up customer calls."

She put down her spoon and looked directly at him. His soft tousled hair, not yet combed this morning, reminded her of how it felt when she used to ruffle it with her fingers. It had been quite a while since she had done that. Glimpsing the little boy inside Tim softened her.

"Tim, this sounds like just the kind of opportunity you've been wanting. Do what you need to nab that position."

He grinned. "One of these days, we'll be able to afford a house like Marcus's. Maybe even sign up for one of those house cleaning services so you – so we – don't have to vacuum."

"I'm okay with living here, but let's see what happens," Jessica replied, then added, "I'm proud that Marcus believes in you." Tim beamed. But Jessica asked herself what it meant that Tim wanted to model himself after someone she didn't find particularly interesting.

#### CHAPTER 8

*October, 2012*

Jessica forgot about the conversation with Vic until Thursday afternoon as she was scooping up a stack of students' writing. The history book Esteban had loaned her, previously buried, emerged as if from an archeological dig. Oh dear, she thought. She should at least open it.

She sat down at her desk, flipped back the cover, and scanned the table of contents. Right away, she was surprised to see terms like *conquest* and *colonization*, terms she was not accustomed to seeing so prominently in U.S. history books. She saw that the first chapter dove right into Anglo-American violence against Mexican people in the conquest of a large chunk of Mexico to create the U.S. Southwest. Then it described Anglos rewriting history to mask the violence and render the annexation of land legitimate.

Jessica replayed Vic's words about exclusion of African Americans from land in Illinois, and her own ignorance of that fact. Of course she had learned there were wars in the past, and whites had not always treated non-whites fairly. But what Vic had said, and what this book was describing, seemed so blatantly racist!

She also thought about the word *annex*, and how she understood annexation of the Southwest when she had been in school. As a child, the term had referred to a small building her father's business added on for storing extra equipment – a useful thing. So when she learned about annexation in school, the possibility of it involving war and injustice simply hadn't occurred to her.

Jessica thumbed through more pages, looking for discussion of culture, a topic more familiar to her. She found a section about culture clash, but it was not what she had expected. Paragraphs portrayed Anglo Americans viewing the U.S. as democratic and civilized, and Mexico as having a tyrannical and backward culture – a view that rationalized taking so much of its land.

She put the book down, thinking she should probably read it, but not liking how it made her feel. As she pondered, she heard a tap on the doorframe of her classroom. Looking up, she saw Esteban, a grin dancing across his face.

"Am I interrupting? I noticed you reading the history book I loaned you."

"Ah, well, I just started looking at it," she stumbled. "It's, uh, where did you get it?"

He came in and pulled up a chair across the desk from her. "It's one of the standard history texts for Chicano studies. I probably got it online, I've had it for quite a while."

"What I meant was," Jessica hesitated. "It's, well, different from other history books I've read. I mean, well, I just started looking at it, and it's, it's –" she felt lost for words.

"Challenging? Hard to read?" he prompted her. "It gives a different perspective than you're probably used to."

"Well, yes. Don't you think bringing up all this violence in the past will make people upset? I mean, like it talks here about Anglo Americans being hungry for other people's land. Don't you think reading that will just stir people up? It makes it seem like all the Anglos just want what belongs to other people."

"Jessica, I thought you were curious about history. I've overheard you and Cath talking at lunch about your own research."

"Yes, but that's different," she said.

"How so?" he asked.

"I'm just trying to find out about the people I descend from, that's all."

"Me, too. That's why I read books like this. Look Jessica, for Mexican Americans, these books give answers to why things are the way they are for us. They don't stir up anger, as you put it, they help to clarify things. You're trying to find out why the person who wrote that letter was hurting, aren't you?"

"Yes, but –" she began. "It's not just this book. Over the weekend, I happened to be talking to a Black architect who told me about something similar. Right when my great-great whatever was buying land in Illinois, the state passed a law prohibiting Black people from being there. I just wanted to find out the story of my relatives, and now this stuff starts popping up!"

Esteban shrugged. "It's part of the story, Jessica. I didn't make it up, you didn't either. By the way, have you tried locating digitized newspaper articles yet?"

"You're kidding. Newspaper articles from over a hundred years ago about people in a tiny out-of-the-way place like Boody?"

"You'd be surprised." He jotted something on a scrap of paper, then handed it to her. "This website archives old newspaper articles. The catch is that you have to pay a subscription fee, or find someone else who subscribes. You can probably also get old newspapers on whatever family history website you're using. It's worth trying." He stood and added, "When I was doing my senior thesis, I was amazed at what I was able to find."

"OK, thanks," she said. "Thanks," she repeated, unsure what else to say, as he walked out of her classroom.

Jessica stared at her desk as conflicting emotions washed over her. Esteban was certainly eye candy, that alone raised her heart rate. And he seemed interested in her pursuing this research. He was even helping. On the other hand, part of her felt like scrapping the foray into history if it meant unearthing events from the past that felt threatening. Maybe Tim was right, the past was best left alone and forgotten. But another part of her was curious. She really did want to know what was behind Mary's letter to Annie, and she found actually locating ancestors to be exhilarating, addictive.

She finished loading her bag with student work. As she did so, she noticed the box of books Sharon had dropped off from the library a few days ago. She would need to find time to look them over, decide how to use them. But not today. She had a date with the grocery store, then the kitchen.

A couple of hours later, just as Jessica had slipped a dish of chicken and rice into the oven to bake, her cell phone rang. Tim.

"Hi, what's up?" she asked as she pulled lettuce and tomatoes from the refrigerator.

"I'll be a little late this evening, Jess," he said. "I have a bunch of customer follow-up phone calls to make. I shouldn't be too long."

"OK, any idea when you might be home? I was just fixing dinner ...."

"Uh," he hesitated. "Probably around seven, seven-thirty. Hey, if you're hungry, you can eat before I get there."

"I'll wait, see you then."

Jessica debated whether to take the chicken and rice out of the oven, then decided to let it finish baking. She could always nuke it when he got home. She put the salad fixings back into the fridge.

This was the first time Tim would be more than ten minutes late. Even if he didn't like to cook, he was a reliable eater. She wondered how many customer follow-up calls he had to make. Couldn't he make most of them during normal working hours?

She went into the living room and turned on the TV to watch some news. More about the Obama-Romney horserace, which didn't strike her as news, exactly, since it was the same horserace every night. She realized she was getting hungry. Since Tim wouldn't be home for another hour, she went back to the kitchen, poured a glass of wine, and fixed a small plate of crackers and cheese to take the edge off.

When the news finished, Jessica returned to the kitchen. She pulled the chicken and rice from the oven, and put it in the cold microwave so it would be ready to heat back up. She made salad and set the table, then checked her watch. Tim should be home shortly. She poured another glass of wine.

Another half hour passed by the time Tim pulled into the driveway. By then, Jessica was ensconced in front of the TV, munching on a bag of corn chips and sipping a third glass of wine, muttering to herself that she shouldn't feel pissed even though that was exactly how she was feeling.

"I'm famished," he exclaimed as he burst in.

Jessica jumped up, almost spilling what was left in her wine glass. She gave him a peck on the cheek. "Let me finish getting it on the table."

While retrieving the salad and pouring water (no more wine tonight), she microwaved the main dish. When she pulled it out, she frowned. The chicken skins, having passed beyond crispness, now resembled rubber, and the consistency of the rice suggested glue as part of the recipe. He'd better not complain!

Over dinner, Tim talked about the customers he had helped that day. Finally Jessica commented, "I don't get why you had to call all of them after your shift ended. Isn't that something you usually do during the shift?"

"Yeah, if I have time. We were really busy today, Jess, and like Marcus said, it's that extra time with customer relations that will give me an edge when I apply for a promotion. I'm sorry I'm so late."

"Well, okay," she said. "It just feels like, suddenly, well, I don't know, you hardly ever get home late. Never this late."

"Jessica," he said, "If I hardly ever get home late, why are you complaining? Lots of guys get home late all the time."

Jessica felt anger well up, but needed to think before responding. She took her plate to the sink. "Your turn to do the dishes," she said as she marched from the kitchen.

*October, 2012*

"Get it, get it! OK, now run like hell!" From the kitchen, Phil heard Tim holler at the TV.

"Who has the ball?" Phil shouted as he slammed the refrigerator door shut.

"Allen," Tim replied, then continued yelling, "Run, dickhead! Go! Alright, touchdown!"

As Phil entered the living room, a bottle of beer in each hand, he saw Tim leap up, waving one arm wildly, a taco chip dripping salsa poised mid-air in the other. "Thanks, man," Tim said as he took a bottle of beer from Phil. "Looks like maybe this game won't be a wipeout after all."

Phil peered at the screen. "Twenty-one to nine. That doesn't qualify as a wipeout in your book?" The roar of the crowd drowned him out as the kicker scored another point for the Colts.

Tim grinned widely. "I know you don't care who wins this game, but I like watching the underdog kick ass."

"Well, I'm just along for the ride until the 49ers come on at 4:30," said Phil. He took a swig of beer, then asked, "How's life at Best Buy these days?"

"Life at Best Buy," Tim repeated thoughtfully. "It'll be good if I get the promotion I'm aiming for. Marcus says I need to emphasize customer relations. Speaking of, do chicks ever hit on you at work?"

"In a tire store? You gotta be kidding," Phil replied with a laugh, then asked. "Why, do they hit on you at Best Buy?"

"Sometimes. A couple days ago, this chick Marcie was shopping for a TV. She had honestly never bought a TV in her life, and she didn't know the first thing. Said her husband bought their electronics. But they split up, so she was out buying one for herself."

"And she hit on you?"

"She offered to buy me a drink when I got off work. To thank me for taking the time to help her figure out what kind of TV to get."

"Which is your job."

"Yeah, of course."

"And you said thanks but no thanks," Phil continued. "I mean, customer relations has its limits."

Tim took a swig of beer as he watched the Colts kick the ball to Green Bay.

"Let me guess again. You let her buy you a coffee." Phil's gaze remained locked on Tim's face.

Tim exhaled loudly. "Sorry I brought it up. We stopped off at the Bird's Nest and had a couple glasses of chardonnay. Then I went home."

Phil continued to look steadily at Tim. "You gonna see her again?"

"I don't know. I wasn't expecting you to be judgmental about it, though."

Phil looked at the game, then back at Tim. "I like Jessica. Just don't do something stupid, that's all."

"I like Jessica, too."

Tim *likes* her? thought Phil. She's his wife, for Chrissake, he's supposed to love her.

Tim continued, "Look, you aren't married, so you don't know what married life is like. There are times when all I want is for someone to look at me like she thinks I have something going, like she admires me. That's how Marcie looked at me, and it felt damn good."

He turned back to the game, then yelled at the wide receiver, "Don't just stand there, asshole!"

"Penalty! C'mon, call it," hollered Phil.

"Penalty!" called the referee. "Off sides."

Tim turned back to Phil. "I just don't get Jessica at times. You'll never guess what I found in the computer the other day. She'd been looking at maps and property deeds. In Illinois, in the 1800s. Not the real estate section of today's newspaper, not Zillow, she wasn't checking out prices of new houses we might think about, she was hunting down old stuff from the 1800s. What sense does that make?" Phil read perplexity in Tim's face.

So he made a show of surveying his small one-bedroom apartment, furnished through garage sales, then looked back at Tim. "It's possible to be satisfied with this, you know. Maybe she likes the house you have. It's a few steps up from this dump."

"You aren't married," Tim repeated.

"No shit."

"So you're not thinking about where you want to raise kids. Phil, I don't want to raise kids where we're living right now, and I don't want to send them to the school where Jessica's teaching. I admire her for wanting to teach those kids, but that isn't the environment I want for our kids. You hear what I'm saying? I want my kids to grow up in a better place than where you and I grew up, and I sure don't want them growing up around any gangs."

Tim turned back to the game. Phil, unable to recall specific evidence of gangs in Tim's neighborhood, shrugged. After all, he thought, wherever Mexicans move in, gangs follow. Tim has a point.

"OK, they're gonna try to convert a field goal," Tim announced. A few seconds later, the crowd roared. The Colts were now only eight points behind the Packers.

"I told you it'd be a good game," Tim grinned.

"So, back to kids. D'you have news you haven't shared yet?" Phil asked.

"Nope. Jessica keeps saying we should wait a year or two. She's been saying that for at least two years now."

Phil watched the teams line up for the next kickoff, then said, "Stay away from the Marcies."

Tim shot him a look, then returned his gaze to the game. "OK, kick the damn ball through the end zone!"

* * * * *

The house was quiet with Tim away. Jessica poured water into a tall vase of cheerful pink roses from Tim in apology for coming home so late the other evening. This was a first! Although sometimes he gave her roses on Valentine's Day, he had never done so for no apparent occasion.

Having finished school preparations, she considered going outside for a walk. She peered out the window. Tree branches flailed like an energetic screensaver. Not good walking weather. She leaned back in her chair, contemplating what to do in response to a problem that erupted during Friday's social studies lesson.

Her class had been wrapping up their unit on Native Americans, which had gone on too long, cutting into the next unit on explorers. The Native American unit coordinated with the U.S. history textbook's first chapter on pre-Columbian peoples of the Americas. During the concluding discussion, Mike raised his hand and asked, "When is the Mexican unit going to be?"

Sara chimed in, without raising her hand, "When is the African American unit?" followed by another boy blurting out, "In February, when it always is!"

Then Mike asked, no hand raised, "When's the unit on white people, like me?" He thumped his chest, prompting several guffaws. Flustered, Jessica told everyone to be quiet. Unsure how to address what she assumed was joking around, she explained that the next unit would study explorers and routes they took in big ships long ago.

Two boys near the back of the room started to pantomime Johnny Depp as a pirate of the Caribbean. Luckily it was time for lunch, so she cut off discussion, lined students up, and sent them off.

Over lunch, Jessica told Cath about the students' questions about when they would study Mexican Americans, African Americans, and white people.

"Their questions surprised you?" Cath asked.

"Well, yes," Jessica replied, wondering what Cath saw that she did not, while simultaneously comparing food value of her baloney sandwich with Cath's green seedless grapes and yogurt.

"Where else in the curriculum do we teach a unit about an ethnic group? Not just an ethnic group, really, but a whole diversity of nations lumped together as if they were an ethnic group?"

Jessica frowned. "I'm not sure. I hadn't thought about that."

Cath continued. "You know my dad is part Kiowa. He doesn't know much about his Kiowa ancestry, so I don't know much either, but I know a little bit. Maybe a better focus of the unit would be conquest, since that's what actually happened."

Jessica's mind leaped to Esteban's history book and her discomfort reading it. Then she said, "That's different from what's in the book we're supposed to follow."

"It is," Cath agreed. "But it's historically accurate. Ask your students if they think American Indians still exist. After the unit you just taught, they kind of drop out of the curriculum."

"I hadn't noticed that."

"Something to think about," Cath said as she gathered up the trash from her lunch. "Maybe I can help you work out a different approach later. Right now I have to scoot to an SST meeting. Tommy's mother is probably in the office already."

Jessica was familiar with Tommy, a frequent lunch conversation topic. On first meeting him, adults would remark what a sweet-looking child he was, with tousled blond hair and round blue eyes framed by long eyelashes. A few more minutes in Tommy's company, however, usually revealed his immaturity – he couldn't stop moving, and he blurted out inappropriate things. The other day in the hall, Jessica heard him ask an older teacher why she was so fat. Tommy struggled with reading and math, which was why Cath had called a student study team, SST for short. While her students were in music, Cath would meet with the special education teacher, Tommy's teacher from last year, his mother, and the principal Sarah. Fourth grade teacher Carolyn, who had been sitting next to Cath but engrossed in a different conversation, leaned over toward Jessica, apparently having followed both conversations. "I wouldn't take her too seriously," she said in a motherly tone. "Cath can be a little overly PC. Just stick to your Indian unit. Kids need cheerful stories, goodness knows they will learn other sides later on."

Reflecting on her students' impersonation of Johnny Depp when told they would be studying explorers, Jessica had thought: they already get happy stories on TV and in movies, at least in school they should get accurate stories.

She still wasn't sure what to make of the fallout from the Native American unit, although she could see Cath's point about how Native peoples were structured into the textbook. The explorers unit beginning tomorrow would emphasize geography (heaven knew the students could use that), and appreciation for the challenges of navigation without modern tools. Last year, a couple of students had been genuinely surprised to learn that early explorers did not have GPS devices.

But she wondered what else Cath – or Esteban, for that matter – might suggest. While the Europeans in her unit were exploring, what was going on in the Americas? Were the Incas exploring? How about the Aztecs? Or the Chinese, for that matter, wasn't there speculation they landed in California before Columbus even thought about sailing? And that Africans arrived before Columbus, as well? Would she be able to stretch her unit to include these different parts of the world if she managed to find material to work with?

And would she ever reach a point as a teacher when she felt like she actually understood her students, not just sometimes but most of the time? And not just some students, but most, even all of them?

Going into the kitchen, Jessica consulted the refrigerator for a snack. Hmmm, chicken – tomorrow's sandwich. Carrots – better save them to go with dinner. Chocolate pudding – perfect.

With chocolate pudding in one hand and a spoon in the other, she strolled into the living room and studied the roses. Beautiful as they were, they seemed like overkill for working late, unless something else caused Tim's lateness, something he felt guilty about.

With the rest of the afternoon to herself, she returned to the computer and located the scrap of paper where Esteban had written websites for old newspaper articles. Might as well give it a try since Tim wouldn't be home for a while. She opened the first website on the list. On the search page, she entered the first and last name of a member of her family tree, the date range of 1850-1900, and the state of Illinois, city of Decatur (the town closest to Boody). Then she hit Search.

Jessica was amazed that quite a few newspaper pages surfaced. She opened one. She had to hunt for the relevant article, but found it. As she read it and subsequent articles, she realized that not only had Decatur published quite a few local newspapers during the 1800s, but they had indeed been digitized. News from Boody was usually in the section so marked on the page reporting news from villages that surrounded Decatur. Here was where she could begin to find the stories of her ancestors.

*July, 1884*

"Quit dragging your feet, Orville." Lydia crossly tugged the hand of her five-year-old while Willie, a couple steps ahead, carried little Ralston.

"I don't wanna go, Ma," whined Orville. "What if that noise comes back and hurts us while we're inside the church?"

"The storm is all gone. Nothing can hurt you. Now come on." Lydia tried to sound more optimistic than she felt.

Charlie, the farm hand who lived with the family, had hitched the brown mare to the buggy, readying it to take the family to church. "Here you go, *Kerlchen*." Willie set Ralston down next to Lydia, addressing him by a favorite nickname, then climbed up onto the buggy's perch.

Lydia approached the buggy, a boy on each hand, shaking her head. "We're lucky our barn is intact. John's ..." Her voice died as words failed her.

The destruction from Friday night's tornado was seared into Lydia's mind's eye. She had come just a hair from losing her good friend Anna and her brother-in-law John.

Friday – the Fourth of July – had been celebrated as always with a church picnic. Because of the day's excitement, it took a while for Lydia to get the boys settled down and sleeping. But once they drifted off, they were so dead to the world that approaching thunder didn't rouse them. Willie and Lydia were almost asleep when a loud crack jolted them wide awake. As Lydia sprang up to check on the children, Willie said, puzzled, "A train shouldn't be running this late."

Then he bolted out of bed in panic, grabbing his trousers. "Tornado! Get the kids, I'll get Charlie, we need to get everyone into the storm cellar."

In less than a minute, the family dashed out of the house. Large raindrops pelted them as they scurried to the cellar door, fighting a punishing wind that tried to hurl them back against the house. They ran down the steps and Willie bolted the trap door shut. Although it was pitch dark, Lydia knew the cellar quite well, as she stored potatoes and canned produce there for use during winter.

The five of them huddled in the cellar for what seemed like hours, listening to the escalating roar outside. Ralston wailed, Orville whimpered. Lydia clasped Ralston tightly, while Willie held Orville.

"Sounds like a bad one," Lydia heard Charlie mutter.

"Hush," she whispered back. "Don't scare the children."

"Daddy, are we gonna die?" Orville's voice quavered.

"We're safe down here." Lydia tried not to show how violently her stomach churned.

"Let's talk to *Gott Vater*," Willie said. "Let's pretend we're in church, *Herr Gott* always takes care of his people there." He began to lead the family in German prayers they normally recited on Sundays. Ralston appeared to calm down, while Orville attempted bravely to join in.

As the noise gradually receded, Lydia felt Ralston's limp body drift into sleep. When all that remained was the thrum of rain on the trap door, Willie cautiously opened it. Although rain was falling in buckets, the tornado had passed. The family emerged, stepping into mud. Sloshing back toward the house, they found it unharmed. Lydia, knees weak, finally broke down in tears as they entered.

Charlie returned to his room on the first floor. Lydia and Willie went back upstairs, taking the children to bed with them. No one got much sleep that night.

At sunrise, after quickly dressing, Willie and Lydia went downstairs. Charlie, already dressed, was pulling on his boots. "Let's go see what happened," said Willie in a tone suggesting he wasn't sure he wanted to know.

Having grown up in central Illinois where tornados are a regular part of summer, Willie told Lydia later that he was unprepared for the destruction he and Charlie encountered. Their farm had been spared, although large tree branches were scattered all over, a couple of trees wrenched onto their sides, and one length of fence in tatters. John's artfully crafted two-year-old barn was blown clear off its foundation and now tilted precariously, its cupola missing. As Willie approached, John was standing in front of it, looking as though his mind had frozen. Thankfully, their house had been spared and their animals were okay.

The German Methodist Church on the corner of John's farm was intact, but one wall of the parsonage had blown away, taking part of the kitchen with it. Anna's parents, her father being *Pfarrer*, would have been living there had they not chosen another house better suited to their needs.

By mid-day, Lydia had a clear picture of the tornado's damage. Her uncle George lost his barn. Cousin George Junior lost not only his barn but his house as well, although by some miracle the family wasn't hurt. Willie's friend Rob lost a barn and everything in it. Another neighbor's barn, packed with recently harvested wheat, was destroyed and the wheat, now soggy with heavy rain, thrown everywhere. Willie told her that farms in the tornado's path looked like disaster zones, with trees down and farm equipment broken and scattered as if they were toys an angry child ripped apart and threw in all directions.

Amazingly, no one had been killed, although flying boards had seriously injured two small children. One family, who lost their entire corn crop, survived unhurt while their house was torn away from around them. Another neighbor, house and barn blown away, had panicked when he couldn't find his wife and baby. They turned up unhurt, lying in a hedge, the baby tucked in his mother's arms.

Lydia had cursed the afternoon's blue sky and gentle breeze that mocked the farmers, like a monster who had put away tools of destruction and donned clothing of innocence.

By evening, newly homeless families had moved in with relatives. Lydia and other neighboring women gathered up clothing, linens, shoes, and cooking utensils that could be spared for those who lost everything. Repair parties were organized. Willie was part of a team that would rebuild George Junior's house, then move on to the barns. As she delivered clothing items and extra blankets to her cousin's family, she felt almost guilty that her own home still stood.

"You're welcome to stay with us, we have room," she had offered.

"Thank you, truly," George had replied. "We'll be staying with my folks. But we'll call on you as we discover things we need."

As the buggy approached the church for its Sunday morning service, Lydia stared at the parsonage that, missing part of a wall, made her think of a woman suddenly discovering part of her dress torn away. The family descended from the buggy, tied up the horse, and joined subdued neighbors filing into the church.

The first person Lydia saw was Anna. The two hugged fiercely, as though to prevent some force from separating them.

"Your folks are doing okay?" Lydia asked.

"You know them. They're so busy taking care of everyone else that they haven't really stopped to think how lucky they were not to have moved into the parsonage when they could have."

"I keep thinking that tornado could have hit your house instead of your barn," Lydia said.

"Don't. We're all here. *Gott Vater* spared every last one of us."

Behind her, Lydia heard an elderly woman whisper loudly, "It was the wrath of *Gott*, punishing us for the sin of whiskey."

She was aware that a few neighbors considered sinful the whiskey farmers made from corn and shipped to other parts of the state. The most outspoken – not German, of course, most Germans enjoyed a beer now and then – were becoming active in the newly-created Prohibition Party. She figured a disaster like this would augment their ranks.

Anna's father, the *Pfarrer*, motioned for worshipers to take their seats, and began the service with a German hymn. As Lydia sang, she felt an even greater sense of kinship than usual with the rest of the congregation. She attended church regularly, but more out of a desire to mingle with friends and family than to worship God. Until today. Perhaps *Gott Vater* had been looking down on her community with a measure of compassion. After all, despite the violence of the storm, no one had died. And despite losses of property and homes, no one was alone.

\* \* \* \* \*

*August, 1887*

Lydia wiped another sticky smear of ice cream from the table as she gathered an armload of plates, spoons, and cups to take inside.

"Thank you so much for helping clean up," said Anna, returning from the kitchen. Hands on hips, she surveyed their husbands John and Willie as they took down the red Chinese lanterns that had graced the lawn. Behind them, John's rebuilt barn gleamed majestically in the deep sunset.

Lydia replied, "We should be thanking you for hosting! You were brave to serve ice cream in this heat."

"The children loved it," Anna laughed.

Lydia carried her armload into the kitchen where her niece Clara was washing dishes. Lydia's servant, a shy and dowdy-looking girl, was watching the youngest children, including two-year-old Viola. After a quick look to make sure all was well, Lydia returned to the tables outdoors.

"We're almost done. Let's sit a minute and let Clara catch up before we load her down again," suggested Anna. Then she added, "Pauline and Charles certainly looked happy." Lydia's youngest sister, and the youngest brother of Willie and John had recently married.

"They are indeed," Lydia agreed. "Just wait until they get bogged down with babies!"

Anna laughed. "They'll manage. Especially with all of us around to lend a hand."

When Lydia wrinkled her nose, Anna asked, "Are you thinking about Willie's comments in the debate? He was only joking, you know."

The debate capped off the evening's festivities that began earlier in the German Methodist Church, and concluded on Anna's and John's expansive lawn surrounding their freshly painted house. The church's Literary Society had organized a celebration of the new church building's first anniversary. Following a year of fund-raising, the one-room church, built twenty-four years previously and damaged in the tornado, had been replaced with a much larger stately white building that was even equipped with a modern furnace.

CHAPTER 10

Anna's father, *Pfarrer* and president of the Literary Society, had opened the service, conducted mainly in German, with a prayer. Then, to dispel rumors that the Society was some sort of secret organization, he explained that its purpose was learning and character development: "In Berlin are six thousand students, and thousands are in the universities in this country. That's very nice, but you can learn outside of the university if you study well. In the last six months the young people here have accomplished much through our means of united study. We are here tonight to show something of what has been learned, and if possible to induce those of this neighborhood who are still outside our membership to join." Various members of the Society had followed with short speeches, readings, and song.

Then came the debate, held out on the lawn. The topic for this evening was: Is the married state preferable to a state of single blessedness? Two men had argued each side. Wincing privately, Lydia had tried to show amusement as Willie argued the negative.

To Anna's comment, she sighed. "I guess he thought he was joking. But underneath, sometimes I worry Willie gets tired of the tedium of family life."

"All men do," agreed Anna firmly. "Husbands get more excited about new hay binders than diapers!"

Glancing down at her reddened hands, Lydia commented, "I couldn't say I get excited about diapers. I just can't avoid them. I wish ..."

"You wish what?" Anna asked when Lydia hesitated.

"Willie wants to be somebody, he wants to make a name for himself. Look how he's jumped into politics. He was thrilled to be elected township clerk, and now he's talking about a run for county supervisor. And that's alright. But sometimes it feels like he forgets about me."

Anna put her hand on Lydia's. "Of course he doesn't forget about you. If you disappeared, he'd be lost."

Lydia grunted. "He'd be hungry, is what he'd be. He can't cook. What I mean is, I just wish he thought more about what I want. He expects me to be there in the background taking care of our home, and he just takes me for granted."

76

"Yes, well, husbands do that. I remember the surprise party he organized for you a few years ago. Remember how much fun that was?"

Lydia smiled. "Yes, it was, wasn't it? He can be sweet, he just doesn't think of it very often. Speaking of that party, I was sorry Viola's cough last month made me miss most of Friedrich's birthday party."

Lydia recalled the community's surprise party for Friedrich's sixty-second birthday. Friedrich and his wife Adeline had been discussing plans for the evening, when a mob showed up at their door laden with gifts, food, and games.

"They were so surprised, I'll never forget the look on Adeline's face!" grinned Anna as she swatted a mosquito. "Well, Come on, let's get these last piles into the kitchen before we turn into dinner out here."

CHAPTER 11

*October, 2012*

Plat! A warm, salty drop hit the computer keyboard. Then another, and another. As Jessica returned to the present, she puzzled over splashes on the keys. Fading light through the window gradually registered. She felt tears coursing down her cheeks. How long had she been crying?

She imagined Willie and Lydia huddling in the storm shelter, wondering if their children would live to see tomorrow, baby Ralston crying with fear. She imagined their horror at daybreak as they confronted the tornado's disaster.

But no one had died. Newspaper articles, describing the destruction in detail, had been very clear about that. Sorrow welling up inside her, turning her inside out, had nothing to do with the tornado so long ago. In fact, in its wake, neighbor had turned to neighbor, everyone sharing the disaster and helping to rebuild.

And her sorrow didn't stem from whatever *faux pas* Willie had made with his remarks about marriage during the debate. His insensitivity may have hurt Lydia, but she had a trusted friend who helped her through it, a friend who listened, heard her, then made her laugh.

Where had the threads gone that bound people together like that, threads as fine and resolutely strong as silk? If these families – Lydia and Willie, and for that matter, Mary and Heinrich – if these families together with their kin and neighbors had created communities able to withstand disasters, communities that celebrated life together, supported each other through life's challenges, where had those communities gone?

Closing her eyes, Jessica felt as though she were drowning with nothing to grab onto. No net, no boat, no rescuers. Just her own waning strength resisting the powerful tug of a bottomless ocean. Was it better to glimpse that world that had disappeared? Or had she been better off stumbling along by herself, unsure where she was going and even less sure how to get there? Tim was supposed to be her partner, but he wasn't that good at listening, at actually hearing her. Like Willie, he had his own dreams that cast his wife in a supporting role as if she had no dreams of her own. Even Cath, her closest female confidant, was available to her only during lunchtime, and only Monday through Friday at that. Cath knew nothing of her uncertainties about her marriage. Cath was a work friend, not a life friend like Anna had been to Lydia. Fresh tears welled up.

Slam! Jessica started. Oh my god, Tim's home. She jumped up, catching her tear-streaked face in the mirror. She hadn't even started dinner. How would she explain why she was crying?

"Jess?" his voice came up the stairs. "You up there?"

She ran into the bathroom, then hollered, "Be down in a minute."

Flushing the toilet, she splashed cold water over her face. It removed the tearstains, but did nothing to relieve redness around her eyes. She quickly brushed her hair, grabbed a Kleenex, then opened the door and descended.

Tim looked at her quizzically. "What are you doing up there?" Then, looking at her more closely, "Have you been crying?"

"It's nothing," she said as she tried to brush by him on her way to the kitchen. With forced enthusiasm, she asked, "How about burgers for dinner?"

Tim reached out and grabbed her forearm. "Jessica, what is it?"

"I'm just being silly," she said. "You know how sensitive I am about things. I was reading old newspaper stories about my ancestors in Illinois, and a horrible experience they had with a tornado." She wondered why she was not telling him more of the truth.

Tim's expression suggested he found her completely incomprehensible.

She wrapped her arms around herself, and said, "Well, that's not quite it. Tim, do you ever feel kind of, oh, isolated? Like you can do whatever you want, but no one really cares? Well, no one except me, of course. But ..." as her voice trailed off, she felt her lower lip begin to quiver.

"What is this about?" Tim asked. "Forget fixing dinner, we'll go get something somewhere. Sit down and tell me what's going on."

He steered her into the kitchen. As Jessica sat down, Tim filled two glasses with water, then sat down across from her. "Now what is this about?"

"I don't know exactly. This afternoon after I finished preparing for school I decided to look up old newspaper articles about my ancestors."

"Old newspaper articles about your ancestors?" he repeated with a tone of disbelief. "First, why on earth would you do that, and second, why would you think there are actually newspaper articles from, what is it, the 1800s, about your ancestors?"

"But there are, I found them. I know it sounds crazy, but you'd be surprised how much old stuff is digitized. And the newspapers used to carry stories about all kinds of trivial stuff, like whose horse got loose or who plowed how many acres to plant what crop." Jessica felt strength returning as she relived the exhilaration of finding what she had read. "I can go upstairs and print them."

"No, I believe you. But I still don't get why they upset you."

"Well, it's kind of like looking in a mirror, but in reverse. What I mean is, I saw how they cared for each other, how they were born into a community for life. And I kept seeing my own life as the opposite. We're supposed to strike out on our own, do it our own individual way, not stay in one place for too long – and in the end, what does it matter?"

Tim's face looked as though he were having a conversation with a Martian. Then he waved his hand. "That's the beauty of it, Jess. You can do whatever you want, you aren't beholden to anyone, except me of course. You get to call the tune you want to dance to, who cares what anyone else thinks? If this family research is upsetting you like that, I think you should just stop. Done. Who cares what happened in the past?"

Jessica stared at her water glass as she turned it in her hand. Then she said with a shrug, "Maybe you're right." She gave a hefty sniff, blew her nose, and stood. "How was the game?"

"The game? Oh, it was, you know, an okay game. The Niners are playing now, but I'm here with you instead."

"Oh!" A smile rushed through her body. "So if the Niners weren't playing, what did you watch?"

"The Indianapolis Colts beating the Green Bay Packers in the last few minutes. C'mon, let's go eat. Burgers or pizza?"

Jessica knew they would end up in a sports bar, but that was OK. She closed her eyes in mock concentration, then said, "Burgers."

"Burgers it is."

*October, 2012*

"Everyone has their book?" Jessica asked, scanning the classroom. "OK, let's go."

Twice a week for ten minutes, students read and silence reigned. From down the hall wafted a cacophony of third grade voices attempting to "sing, please, children, don't yell" the round *Oh How Lovely is the Evening.*

Damn, she had forgotten to bring her own book. Jessica's eyes skimmed her desk for something to read. Esteban's Mexican American history book, not having been opened for days, looked back at her.

Sighing, she opened it at random. The heading *Paradox of Mexican Immigration* jumped out. Jessica began to read about the period between the 1880s and early 1900s, when Anglo Americans in the Southwest sought labor to work in mines and agriculture. Having excluded the Chinese in 1882, American industrialists were hungry for Mexican labor. At the same time, they feared that offering U.S. citizenship might enable Mexican immigrants to take over.

This was happening right around when Mary and Heinrich were raising their young family and their flock of worshippers in Farmington, and Willie's family was attending their mother's funeral, Jessica reflected. Were any of them aware of industrialists' use of Chinese, then Mexicans, as low-pay laborers? Maybe not, the Southwest was so far away. But what about freed African Americans, surely much closer?

"Mrs. Westerfield?" Jessica looked up to find several pairs of eyes on her. Marisela was asking, "Did we finish ten minutes?"

Glancing at the clock, Jessica realized the time had passed three minutes ago. She was so absorbed in what she was reading, all new to her, puzzling out why Mexicans were not wanted as U.S. citizens in territory that forty years previously had been Mexican, and how this might intersect with her own family's story, that she forgot to watch the time.

"Thanks, Marisela. OK, class, let's put our books away. We have two reports this morning." She glanced down at the list of who was reading which book. A third of the names had been crossed off as children completed their oral reports. "Álvaro and Jennifer, you're up today. Who's first?"

Álvaro ducked behind a student in front of him as he made a face at Jerome. Álvaro was smart; Jessica was becoming tired of him acting as class clown. She decided to invite Jennifer to go first, since anyone who followed Álvaro would struggle for attention.

"Now remember, in three minutes, tell us what your book is about, something you like and why, something you don't like and why, and whether you recommend it."

Jennifer approached the front of the room as a nervous blush washed up her neck. Poor Jennifer, thought Jessica. In ten years, she'll be described as statuesque; at age twelve, she's a beanpole. In ten years when her braces are a distant memory, she'll have a dazzling smile. Right now she clams her mouth shut as much as possible to avoid the epithet "railroad tracks." Jennifer took a deep breath and bravely began.

Ten minutes before noon, Jessica sank into her usual chair in the teacher's lounge just as Cath was emptying her lunch bag onto the table. "You weren't at lunch yesterday," Jessica observed. When Cath missed lunch, Jessica missed Cath, one of her few age-mates at Milford and the one she related to most readily.

"Parent conference. I ate quickly at my desk."

Jessica, watching her inhale an orange, commented, "You eat quickly all the time. I wanted to tell you about my latest research foray."

"OK, tell. What did you find out this time?"

"Did you know small towns used to publish bunches of newspapers? They must have had telegraph wire services back then because front pages had regular national and world news, like today. But they also had all this local stuff, like who went to whose birthday party, and who contributed how much to fund a new church building. Everyday details like that."

"So you found your ancestors?"

"Yeah, some of them. I got to know a little bit about their lives. Not like I was there, of course. More like getting a few seconds at a peephole, you know what I mean? You get a glimpse. Not a whole view, not action over time, but a peek you didn't have before."

"Interesting. What did you learn?"

"Well, I guess my main impression is that the people who lived in this Boody place were a close-knit group. About half seem to have been German. The Germans all went to church together and intermarried. Probably the English did the same thing. But they didn't seem segregated exactly, their farms were intermingled and they went to each other's parties. That sounds silly, doesn't it? They gave each other surprise birthday parties, and everyone would show up."

"Whose birthday is it?" Fourth grade teacher Ralph leaned over, having heard Jessica's last remark. Jessica figured Ralph must have been born smiling. In his late-thirties, with curly khaki-colored hair and bushy eyebrows, he was hands down the friendliest and most positive person in the school. Women might generally have a reputation for organizing birthday parties, but at Milford, Ralph beat everyone else if there was a party to be organized.

"No one here. A sixty-two year-old in Boody Illinois, back in 1887."

Ralph's bushy eyebrows jumped upward in surprise. "Relative of yours?"

"Just a family friend," Jessica replied. Turning back to Cath, she continued, "What intrigues me is their church. It seemed to serve as hub of the community. I don't even go to church myself, so I'm curious."

"About their church?" Cath asked.

"Well, more about how it pulled them together. It's like –" she scoured her mind for an example. "It's like they had this big swimming pool they all enjoyed playing in together. And all I've got is a little wading pool."

When Cath's face crinkled, Jessica said, "No, that isn't quite right. Of course a church isn't a swimming pool. But it was something they all belonged to. It gave them a center, a community, a sense of how they connected." She exhaled deeply. "Maybe I'm reading something into their lives …"

At that moment Sarah strode into the lounge with a stack of fliers. "Don't forget to send these home with your students. We want to get as many families to Open House next week as we can."

Jessica grabbed a couple dozen from the stack as it went by. English on one side and Spanish on the other, the flier urged parents to show up at school the following Wednesday evening. After the obligatory meetings with teachers, there would be refreshments and entertainment.

"Never a dull moment," commented Cath as she scooped up a bunch of fliers, cleaned off her section of the table, and stood to leave. "Hey, anytime you need to talk, you know I'm just down the hall," she added.

"Thanks. I'm trying to sort things out in my head. I need to get a better idea of what the question is."

Maybe Cath was more available than Jessica had assumed. She stuffed the last bite of sandwich into her mouth as she stood up. Turning, she practically knocked down Esteban, who was making a beeline for the back of the room, probably the men's room. Jessica wondered what he did about lunch, since he rarely ate in the lounge with the rest of the teachers. He was always pleasant with everyone, but not particularly close to any of his colleagues. Jessica wondered if that was just his personality, or if it might have something to do with him being the only Mexican American on an otherwise white staff.

* * * * *

Friday afternoon, after shopping for groceries, Jessica headed home. Determined to erase school from her mind for twenty-four hours, she studied passing surroundings.

To her right was a Korean Presbyterian Church. A rust-colored brick building, it could be an English-speaking church except for its Korean signage. On the next block to her left she passed *Iglesia Católica Santa Teresa*, a large adobe Mexican Catholic church. Rounded domes topped with crosses on two square towers flanked the main arched tower above the door. Some of her students' families probably went there.

Two blocks later the Kingdom Hall of Jehovah's Witnesses reminded Jessica of an incident with her mother when she was about fourteen. An African American family had just moved into the neighborhood. Jessica had accompanied her mother, a self-styled personal "welcome wagon," to their house with a basket of chocolate chip cookies, her mother's staple welcome gift. The family, boxes still everywhere, invited them inside. After briefly exchanging pleasantries, the husband commented that they were Jehovah's Witnesses. On learning they would be relocating from Texas to California, they had contacted the nearest Kingdom Hall. While they appreciated Jessica's mother's welcome, they had a community here. Jessica suddenly felt like an outsider in her own neighborhood in comparison to these newcomers, already insiders.

As she turned onto her street, Jessica considered Boody's Zion German Methodist Church. Spiritual beliefs were braided together with language, culture, and community, probably just like in the Korean and Mexican churches. What did she know of German Methodism? Nothing, really. Newspaper articles had offered glimpses into the community over a century ago, but little information about German Methodism itself. Did it even still exist somewhere in the U.S.?

How odd. She wasn't religious, and hadn't been to church since she was a child. Her parents, not churchgoers themselves, had sent her to Sunday school, believing it good for her character. They were probably also hedging their bets, in case the faith the church demanded really did guarantee entry into the everlasting. But as a teenager, once Jessica began to question Mary's virginity, her belief in Christianity crumbled, just like her belief in Santa Claus once she pondered the likelihood that reindeer could pull a fat man to every house on earth in one night.

After putting away the groceries, she decided to Google "German Methodist Church."

A couple of hours later, Tim pulled into the driveway just as Jessica was setting the table. He came in, pecked her on the cheek, and asked the perfunctory "How was your day?"

"It's Friday, doesn't get any better than that."

A few minutes later, Tim dove into tilapia stacked liberally on his plate. "Mmm, good, what did you do to it?"

"I sautéed it in olive oil, with a little garlic." This was a switch from her usual method of baking the fish with butter and lemon. "I think it's healthier this way."

Tim ate voraciously, then commented, "I noticed on the computer screen upstairs that you've been doing some church research."

She laughed, "Funny, isn't it? Me, probably an atheist, researching religion. There must be something in the blood. One of my ancestors way back was a German Methodist preacher."

"A preacher, huh? I didn't know German Methodism existed. Except in Germany, of course."

"It did, back in the 1800s, out in the Midwest. It doesn't seem to exist in the U.S. anymore. It started somewhere around 1840, when lots of Germans were immigrating. The church seems to have been centralized in St. Louis. It's kind of interesting, before the Civil War, the whole Methodist denomination split over slavery. English-speaking Methodists in the South were OK with it, but in the North they weren't, and none of the German Methodists were, either."

When Tim raised his eyebrows, Jessica realized she was starting to lecture.

"Anyway, it's interesting. They had seminaries to train bilingual German Methodist preachers. There was one in Ohio and another in Quincy, Illinois where I think my ancestor went. Hey, I got some macaroons for dessert."

As they cleared the table and Jessica opened the bag of macaroons, Tim commented, "Well, I guess after a generation or so, they wouldn't need bilingual preachers anymore, would they? I mean, once the immigrants learn English, what would be the point? That's probably why there's no German Methodism in the U.S. now."

Jessica didn't reply, suspecting there was more to what it meant for a church to be German than language alone.

"Can I tell you something about the Germans that's kind of funny?" she asked after finishing a macaroon.

"Sure." He reached for seconds.

"Well, I told you about the newspapers I found. They liked to throw surprise parties for each other, then the parties would get written up in the newspaper the next day, can you imagine? It would be like that Best Buy party we went to a couple of weeks ago showing up in the newspaper. At their parties they would do things like play parlor games and drink lemonade."

Tim lifted one eyebrow. "Parlor games?"

"Probably like charades or word games," she replied. "And they had a literary society that organized debates for their social occasions. They had this community that did fun things together all the time. It's in the Decatur newspapers. Everyone seemed to know each other really well. And when terrible things happened, like when a tornado blew down barns and houses, they all pitched in and helped."

Tim thought for a moment, then replied, "That's interesting Jess. Probably small towns all over the place were like that."

A frown slid across Jessica's face as if to say he was missing the point. Tim continued, "But it's interesting that you're finding out this stuff. Who'd have thought they would publish these things in the newspapers, and then here you are, over a hundred years later, reading about them. You might be over-romanticizing your relatives a little bit, though."

"I think they had something special," Jessica replied stiffly as she stood, picked up the package of macaroons, and sealed the top.

Tim regarded her, then said, "Well, I'd rather pay attention to what we have here and now. And what I have is a date with the computer so I can brush up on specs for the new TVs we're stocking for Christmas. You're done with it for the evening, right?"

"Sure, all yours."

He walked toward the door, then turned. "Maybe after I get a promotion, we can leave this raggedy neighborhood and buy a house in a better part of town."

Jessica turned toward the dishes in the sink. By "better part of town," Tim meant Wonder Bread burbs, which felt in her gut like capitulating to Esteban's question about who she is, rather than working it. And besides, she couldn't see how moving to a different neighborhood would deepen the quality of their relationships with people around them.

*October, 1885*

Mary balanced baby Edward in the crook of one arm as she stepped out onto the broad veranda of the parsonage in Quincy. Slowly inhaling crisp autumn air, she enjoyed this brief respite from housework before preparing supper.

When she married Heinrich nine years ago, she had no idea how often they would move. Not that it would have stopped her, but frequent moving was difficult, especially with small children. The church authorities assigned novice preachers like Heinrich to rural churches for experience, as they put it. But she suspected the real reason was that no one with seniority wanted to bounce around among churches too small and scattered to support their own preacher.

Mary noticed *Frau* Gratz approaching from the corner of Jefferson Street. A church member who had immigrated from Germany, she was now in her fifties. Short and stocky, she usually wore black. As Mary was learning, her sweet face and ruddy cheeks signaled sturdy health and an agreeable disposition. Mary noticed she was carrying something.

"*Guten Tag, wie geht's?*" *Frau* Gratz greeted her.

"*Guten Tag.* Come join me and baby Edward."

As *Frau* Gratz waddled up the broad wooden steps, Mary recognized a pan of strudel in her hands. "I thought you might enjoy something sweet for dessert," she said, proffering the pan.

"You are too kind." Mary beamed, having heard rave testimonials about *Frau* Gratz's strudel. "Please sit. Can I bring you tea?"

"*Nein, danke*, I just had some." *Frau* Gratz sat down. "How are you adjusting to your new home?" Her eyes quickly surveyed the white two-story parsonage, newly built just eight years previously.

"We are blessed. We couldn't have hoped for more."

*Frau* Gratz beamed, her husband having served on the church building committee that planned the parsonage. Then she said, "My husband was accosted yesterday by some of those English people. They called him a drunken communist. What do you make of that?"

Mary knew she was referring to harassment of presumed German unionists because of their labor organizing and opposition to prohibition. They were especially active in the Chicago area where German workers' clubs and churches co-sponsored lively and highly visible community picnics.

Mary replied, "I'm so sorry to hear that. Heinrich says there aren't many such people here, thank goodness. He says those people seem to think all Germans are socialists. I don't know I'd agree, although I don't see anything wrong with people organizing to improve their working conditions."

"Nor do I. Of course my husband, employed at the German Savings Bank, isn't involved with unions at all."

"I'm very sorry to hear he was harassed, but I don't imagine anything will come of it. Most people in Quincy seem reasonable and kind. At least, that's what I've experienced in the short month we've been here."

"*Ja*. Quincey is a good place. And the German community wraps its arms around you. We're so used to newcomers who arrive practically every day," *Frau* Graz said, referring to the constant influx of immigrants recruited to work in Quincy's various industries.

"Did you know Heinrich completed seminary training here ten years ago?" Mary asked.

"I thought he might have. Where did he emigrate from?"

"Volkerode in Hesse-Kassel, two years after Prussia annexed it," Mary replied. "Some of his relatives were already just north of here, so that's where he went. I think some land baron originally recruited Germans, that's how his cousins wound up there. His brothers and a sister joined him shortly after he arrived."

"*Ach*, those Prussians. My family left *Sachsen* when I was about fifteen mainly because no one wanted to serve in Prussia's army. When an emigration party was organized and land made available in America, we signed up to go. You were born here, *ja*? You sound more like an American when you talk than we immigrants do."

"Yes, I was. Right after they got here, my parents met, married, and then I came along." It was true, Mary thought, German immigrants like *Frau* Gratz and Heinrich never completely lost their accent.

The two women sat in silence contemplating challenges of immigration, prejudice, and childrearing.

Baby Edward whimpered. Mary stood. "I expect the younger children are waking from their naps. Our eldest, who is seven, started school here a couple of weeks ago."

Hauling herself up from the chair, *Frau* Gratz suggested, "You might look into the German School. Many German families send their children to it."

"Heinrich mentioned it the other day. We'll certainly go visit."

"Well, let me not keep you," *Frau* Gratz turned to leave. "Please call on me anytime. We're so pleased you're here."

With that, she waddled down the stairs, turned back onto Jefferson Street, and disappeared. Mary smiled as she looked down at the pan of strudel. Heinrich would be thrilled.

After dinner, Mary dismissed the children from the table for quiet playtime. She knew Heinrich relished evenings when he didn't need to return to the church for an evening service or a meeting, and could relax and catch up on news in the *Illinois Staats-Zeitung*. While she finished cleaning the kitchen, he carried on his usual commentary about what he was reading.

"Listen to this about upcoming local elections. Germans are underrepresented on both Democratic and Republican tickets."

"Well, of course there aren't many on the Democratic ticket. Who's representing us on the Republican ticket?" Mary replied as she wiped a plate dry.

Heinrich read the few names listed, along with descriptions of each candidate. His commentary then moved to latest details of Wilhem II, who had recently become *Kaiser*.

Mary had just sunk into a chair and picked up some mending to finish, when he exclaimed, "*Ach*, Mary, those eight German-American rioters were just indicted. Terrible, *einfach schrecklich*! You know, from the Haymarket Riots last year in Chicago, the Eight

Hour Workweek Association. No proof any of them threw the bomb that killed those policemen."

"Oh, no! You were afraid the English-speaking Americans would scapegoat us Germans."

"*Ja*, and they did. No matter how peaceful we are, no matter we learn the language ..." By then, Heinrich had leapt to his feet and was pacing. "The labor movement has legitimate claims, but that's no excuse for violence. I don't know who instigated last year's violence, but it wasn't Germans. And violence of hangings does not make up for violence of bombing. Violence is morally wrong."

Mary put down her mending and laid her hand across his arm. "You can't change what already happened, Heinrich," she said.

"No, of course not. But in doing the work of *Gott Vater*, I can remind people to rise to a higher level of moral behavior. The challenge is to press forward for rights, non-violently. I will speak to that Sunday."

*October, 2012*

"*Mamá*, will you be going to Mrs. Westerfield's classroom at Open House tonight?" Marisela asked as she set four white Melamine plates around the table.

"Of course, *mija*," María Paz replied. "Just because I have three teachers to meet this year doesn't mean I'll skip any of them."

"I wrote a story she put on the bulletin board. It has an A on it," Marisela said.

"Then I will certainly find it. You know I'm always proud of your good grades. You seem to like Mrs. Westerfield."

Marisela paused as if to think. "Most of the time. Sometimes class is boring and sometimes it's confusing. But she's nice, she tries to help us."

That's important, María Paz thought. Over the last year, she gradually became aware of how schools in the U.S. can be minefields for Mexican students. Some teachers make sure their students learn, but according to parents she had talked with, others seem to wish they were teaching different students, white students, like themselves.

When the three children were seated around the table, María Paz instructed, "I expect you to show respect toward Antonia while I'm at Open House. I'm sure I'll be home before *Papá*." Salvador rarely arrived home from his job at the TV station before eleven.

Marisela scrunched up her face like a prune.

"*¿Qué?*" demanded María Paz, a frown creasing her brows. "You never complain about *arroz con pollo*, have you suddenly decided you don't like it?"

"She doesn't like Antonia," Manuel explained.

"Yeah," Jaime echoed.

"What's this about Antonia?" María Paz asked.

Antonia was the tenth grade daughter of neighbors Rosa and Ysidro. When María Paz's family initially arrived from Mexico, Rosa took them under her wing. Their son was now a college freshman – aspiring to major in art, of all things, what could one do with a degree in art? Whenever Rosa vented her wish that he gravitate toward something practical like business, María Paz reminded her that at least he was in the university and not out on the streets, like too many other Mexican parents' youngsters.

Their daughter Antonia, a tenth-grader, was a marginal student with a passion for hair design. She normally wore her own shiny black mane pushed behind her ears to display gold hoop earrings, bangs poufed out and affixed with gel. On weekends, she loved styling friends' hair as though they were dolls. Rosa and María Paz periodically commiserated about how to focus Antonia on school. Giving her responsibility was one strategy. Since both families lived in the same apartment building, Antonia had become an occasional babysitter.

"She always talks to her boyfriend on the phone," Marisela said.

"On Facetime," Manuel corrected.

"That's part of the phone," Marisela defended herself.

"And she doesn't play with us," Jaime added.

"We don't pay her to play with you, we pay her to make sure you're safe," replied María Paz. Although Antonia would be nominally in charge, Rosa was just a few doors away. "What kind of homework do you have tonight, Marisela?"

"I guess I have math. It's boring. She gave us some word problems and we have to come up with three ways to solve each one. I don't get why we have to do that, what's wrong with her just showing us the right way?"

"Mrs. Westerfield is probably trying to get to you think," replied María Paz. "Remember when I showed you the way I learned long division in Mexico, and how different it is from the way they do it here? Same idea, I imagine. Manuel?"

"I have spelling words, we have to write them in sentences."

"Anything else?"

"No."

María Paz gazed at Manuel as she weighed the consistently light homework from his teacher. He was capable of working harder than she seemed to expect. Something to ask about tonight. Then she turned to her youngest. "Jaime?"

Jaime shook his head no, as Marisela announced, "They don't give homework in kindergarten, *Mamita*."

María Paz sighed. "I suppose not, *mija*. I just want you three to do well in school so you'll be prepared to go on to university later. Antonia can probably help you with homework."

"Then tell her not to spend the whole time talking on Facetime," Manuel said.

"I'll tell her I want her to make sure everyone's homework is done correctly first, including hers. Then you can watch TV and she can – well, talk to friends I suppose, as long as she keeps an eye on you."

For the next few minutes, the only sound in the kitchen was forks clicking on plates. María Paz took her empty plate to the sink, then pulled a pan of flan from the refrigerator.

"From *Señora* Hernández," she said as she placed it on the table, displaying its creamy custard and luscious golden caramelized sugar. *Señora* Hernández, a long-time member of *Iglesia Católica*, loved to cook. After her husband passed away, her two sons joined the military and her married daughter moved away. Since her home lacked mouths to cook for, from time to time, she would show up at someone's door with something freshly baked. María Paz reciprocated by treating her as an extended family member.

"Oh boy!" exclaimed Manuel, hopping up to help his mother set out dessert dishes.

As María Paz spooned out the flan, she stressed, "Our dream for all three of you is that you do well in school so you can do well in life." She thought again about the barriers and hurdles children like hers might encounter in school. Open House would give her a chance to check things out for herself.

\* \* \* \* \*

Jessica draped plastic wrap over the plate of rotisserie chicken, potatoes, and broccoli that would be Tim's dinner, and put the plate in the microwave. She slapped a sticky note onto the microwave door: "Heat on high 3 min." Then she added, as though an afterthought, "C U later, Love, J." Grabbing her coat and bag, she dashed for the car.

Open House would begin at Milford at 7:00 pm. Anticipating a room full of parents was nerve-wracking. Children, she could handle. But adults – parents, especially – showed up armed with their own expectations, much like the newspaper food critic inspecting the latest new restaurant for its faults, major or minor. And she fully expected parents of struggling students to zero in on her faults. Her stomach clenched. For a final check of her classroom, she wanted to be there before parents started to arrive.

By 7:00, the building was overflowing. The evening started in the multipurpose room with a welcome and orientation. This year, Sarah had hired a Spanish-English translator. Good idea, although without headphones enabling simultaneous translation, the crowd got to enjoy every sentence twice. Three minutes into the welcome, first in English, then Spanish, sixth grade teacher Rick, seated directly behind Jessica, muttered, "Christ, this is gonna take all night!"

Fifteen minutes later, however, the parents were dismissed to their children's classrooms. Teachers were on their own to decide how to use the time with parents. Jessica borrowed ideas from the teacher she had student taught under, who believed parents might show up at Open House if they thought it would be useful, but would definitely show up if their children, accomplishments on display in the classroom, threatened rebellion if they did not. So Jessica liberally adorned the classroom with children's best work, making sure to include at least two good pieces for each child. Shining a favorable academic light on every child was challenging, however, a bit like picking out stellar moves of every member on a crowded dance floor. But the effort paid off when she identified abilities children didn't even know they had.

After Jessica welcomed the parents, she engaged them in a brief scavenger hunt. Parents milled around finding their own child's work and visiting with other parents, in the process learning more about Jessica's curriculum and expectations. Jessica talked with as many as she could get to.

A short man with a strong Spanish accent caught her attention. "Mrs. Westerfield, I am Vicente's father." Jessica's felt nervous perspiration start to break out. Vicente was a quiet boy who found reading difficult and uninteresting. She struggled to connect with him.

"I'm very pleased to meet you," she said, trying to sound confident.

"Vicente enjoys your class," his father said. "I like the map he drew over there on the bulletin board. Very nice."

"I'm so pleased to have him as a student," Jessica replied, trying to think of something more personal to say about him.

"He's an unusual boy. Has he told you about his fascination with Mexican cowboys?"

"No, he hasn't." Jessica was surprised to learn of this interest.

"Well, no matter, as long as he is learning his reading and math. Thank you for helping my son."

Jessica hadn't felt like she was helping Vicente much at all. As his father turned in response to another parent's greeting, she pictured the box of library books she had requested, still sitting under her desk awaiting her attention. If she remembered right, one of them was about *vaqueros* – Mexican cowboys. Vicente's father just gave her an idea.

"Mrs. Westerfield? I am Marisela's mother."

Jessica turned, surprised to see a Mexican woman dressed more like a professional worker than most other parents. "Hello. Welcome to my classroom."

"I can't stay long, I have three children in this school, so three classrooms to visit. But I wanted to meet you personally, Marisela talks so much about you. I was interested in the math homework you gave the children today."

Jessica was certain Marisela had complained about it. Most of the students looked lost when she tried to explain it earlier that day.
"My daughter just wants right answers, but you seem to be asking the children to think."

"Yes, that's right. Many of them hate math because they think it's all memorizing facts. But if they realize they can figure out how to solve problems for themselves, well, I'm trying out a strategy this year to see if it helps."

"That's what I told my daughter. I can see why she likes being in your class. Now, please excuse me while I run to another classroom."

María Paz slipped out just as the father of another student happened to pick up Esteban's history book that had begun to occupy a permanent place on top of next month's science handbook and last month's professional development fliers. He asked, smiling, "You're reading this?"

"Yes, well, I've only read a little bit so far," she replied, wondering if he loved the book, hated it, or was about to quiz her over it.

"Good choice," he commented. "I read it in a Chicano studies course at the community college. Everyone should read it. Before I found it, I couldn't relate to school. This was what got me interested in enrolling in the university."

"Thank you for telling me that," Jessica said, making a mental note to spend some serious time with the book.

Time to end the scavenger hunt. Jessica asked parents to sit, then walked them through a small packet of information describing upcoming curriculum units, homework parents could expect to see, and her contact information. She involved them in a math activity and a writing activity they could do at home with their children. She stifled a laugh when Álvaro's mother reacted to the writing activity just like her son usually did. Diana looked like young version of her mother. Tall, gangly Jennifer's mother offered a hint of the beauty Jennifer would become.

Suddenly the bell rang calling everyone back to the multipurpose room for refreshments. As parents filed out, Jessica noticed a large man with brown hair and a rumpled shirt hanging behind as if waiting for a word with her alone. Now whose father is he? Jessica narrowed down the possibilities to three of her brown-haired Anglo children.

"I can see you're trying," he said quietly, "but I wish this school didn't have so many minorities. We're thinking about putting Peter in a private school, the standards here are just too low."

Jessica was taken aback. "We're teaching to the state's standards," she said defensively.

"I see that, but I'm afraid the kids here will just hold Peter back. Sorry, but that's how I feel. We're visiting a couple of private schools next week."

Unsure how to respond, Jessica just stared at Peter's father, who turned and left. A good student, although not her best, Peter was new to Milford this year. He seemed shy, but was beginning to warm to his tablemates. Too bad to move him, he'll have to start all over making friends.

Jessica gathered her bag, locked her door, and followed the last trail of parents down the hall. Ahead, Peter's father turned toward the exit.

The multipurpose room had taken on the air of a cocktail party, although lemonade was the hardest drink served. As parents washed down cupcakes and cookies with punch and lemonade, the sugar coursing through their veins seemed to amplify the volume they used in conversation.

Over the punchbowl, Jessica found herself next to Marisela's and Diana's mothers, apparently friends.

"I was curious," she ventured, "do either of you go to the *Iglesia Católica* over near Safeway?"

"Our whole family goes every Sunday," replied María Paz. "What a beautiful church. Have you been to mass there?"

"Oh, I'm not Catholic," Jessica replied, wondering if that mattered to them.

"Please join us some Sunday," Diana's mother sounded sincere, but then added, wrinkling her brow, "You don't speak Spanish, do you?"

"No, I'm afraid not, only a few words here and there."

"What a shame, you wouldn't understand what is said. But come anyway. Lots of Mexican families from around here go to that church, it's like home for us."

"Well, thank you, I may take you up on it," Jessica replied, unsure what to do with the invitation since it was true that she wouldn't understand what was being said. "I'll send word home with one of your daughters."

"Good, we will look forward to it. *Vamos a saludar a Esteban*, Graciela," María Paz said to her companion as she turned toward Esteban, who was surrounded by Mexican American parents. A loud crack of laughter burst from that group. As Jessica noticed some of her own students' parents drifting into his orbit, a pang cut into her belly. I'm their kids' teacher, she thought, but they feel more connection with him than with me.

She watched them briefly. A couple of the mothers were young and attractive. The fact that he was laughing with them shouldn't bother her, but it did. He probably wasn't flirting with them, but she wasn't sure. Although about half of the conversation was in Spanish, she caught a few phrases – *Dia de los Muertos*, which would be coming up soon; the name of a local Mexican restaurant; and the title of a *telenovela* she saw in the TV listings but had never considered watching because it was in Spanish. Maybe she should try to learn more about at least one of these things.

Suddenly a loud riff of music cut through the chatter. Performance time! Eight children marched out onto the floor clad in pioneer garb, ready to show off their square dancing skills. Jessica felt Cath approach from behind. "The Mexican kids will do a great *folklórico* piece, so why do the white kids have to parade something they can't relate to?" she hissed into Jessica's ear.

"I think square dancing is Carolyn's idea of white people's folk dancing," she whispered back.

"In California? Grooving to the Beach Boys would be more appropriate!"

It was quarter to ten by the time Jessica pulled her car into the driveway. As she entered the house, she heard the TV in the living room. "I'm home," she shouted.

Slinging her bag onto the kitchen table, she noticed the sticky note on the microwave door, still brightly announcing cooking instructions. Tim ambled into the kitchen.

"How was it?" he asked.

"I did my duty. Actually, it's fun to meet the parents. People say kids resemble them, but for me, it's like, parents resemble their kids. Hey, I see you didn't eat the dinner I left."

"Nah, since I knew you wouldn't be home, I stopped off for pizza and a beer. With some of the guys from work."

He's lying, Jessica thought, but she wasn't sure what told her that.

Tim wandered back into the living room where the TV was announcing a new episode of CSI. As she removed the dinner from the cold microwave and shoved it into the refrigerator, she realized what bothered her: a tiny red smudge on Tim's cheek. She heard him go upstairs and start the shower.

* * * * *

Tim showered before Jessica could get another look at the red smudge on his face. Had he scratched himself? Smeared pizza sauce? Been with someone? Was her imagination running in overdrive? She didn't want to interrogate him, it was probably nothing. But uncertainty gnawed at her all night.

The next morning she decided she needed to ask him, but wasn't sure how. As she poured coffee, she just plunged right in. "Tim, are you seeing someone?"

He stared at her blankly. "Why would you think so?"

"I, well, last night when you came home late with something red on your cheek, I just ..."

He put down his mug. "There wasn't anything on my cheek. What is this? You sound like you don't trust me."

"I want to," she said. "I'm trying to understand you coming home so late twice in just a few days, when you never used to be late. Okay, I'm sorry I asked."

"You're my wife, for heaven's sake. Why would I want to see someone else?"

For a full minute, they stared at each other. Jessica wasn't sure whether she had made a terrible mistake, or put him on the spot. "Now, just sit down and eat," Tim said softly. They finished breakfast in silence.

*October, 2012*

Jessica stewed the remainder of the week, wondering if she should have confronted him, why he hadn't directly answered her, and whether she should have tried to confront him again. When she had married Tim, she truly believed they would stay together for life, but now her internal conflict about their marriage seemed to be growing. Fantasies about Esteban scared her, exhilarated her, while Tim seemed to find fault with her more and more. And to be truthful, her growing attachment to her students was pulling her away from the vision he was painting ever more vigorously of their future life together.

At noon on Sunday, as she pulled into the driveway after spending the morning in her classroom preparing for the week, she noticed Tim's car was gone. He must have already left for Phil's to watch football.

Entering the house, she imagined Marisela's and Diana's families just coming home after being surrounded by friends in church. Once again, Jessica tried to imagine being connected to a dozen or so people by invisible elastic strings that pull you back in if you stray too far out. Would that feel claustrophobic or comforting? Hard to say, that kind of web not in her experience. Maybe she should take her students' mothers up on their invitation to visit the *iglesia*, even if she wouldn't understand a word being said. Hmm, but then she would feel very much an outsider.

Jessica slapped a tuna sandwich together, then took it out into the weedy little yard behind the house. She flopped into a tattered lawn chair, surveying a would-be garden ringing the cyclone fence. When she and Tim had moved into this house, she had intended to cultivate flowers. Petunias, dahlias, and impatiens had briefly graced her first attempt in the arid, sandy soil. But by August, the dahlias resembled small, dry corn stalks, and the few surviving petunias and impatiens displayed leggy stems with shriveled blooms. Last summer wasn't much better. By August, the hydrangeas had lost most of their leaves, and the lavender, better suited to California's dry climate and still surviving, nonetheless stood gray and flowerless.

Just like my life, Jessica thought.

The gentle October sun bathed her face and arms, inviting her to play. But play with whom? Not Teri, who as always would be spending the day with Dwight. Not Cath. Their friendship, while secure at school, had never lapped beyond that. Her college friends all lived somewhere else.

No better idea in sight, Jessica decided to surprise Phil and Tim with a snack suitable to football. She jumped in her car and swung by the grocery to pick up tortilla chips and salsa.

A few minutes later she was knocking on Phil's door, sharply to be heard over the din of the TV. Footsteps, then the door opened, revealing barefoot Phil dressed in ancient plaid shorts and a faded T-shirt coming apart at the neckline.

"Hope you two don't mind company," she announced, entering. "I brought some goodies."

Phil stared at Jessica in surprise as she set the bag down on the second-hand dining table. "Where's Tim?" she asked, not seeing him.

"I don't know," Phil said as he shut the door.

"He must have stopped somewhere on the way," Jessica said, then added when Phil didn't respond, "He said he was coming over here to watch the game."

"I haven't talked to him since last weekend."

Jessica felt blood drain from her face. She sank down into a chair. "Then where is he? What's going on, Phil?"

With the remote, Phil turned down the volume, then swung a chair around to face her. "I don't know," he replied. "Tim isn't here, and as far as I know, he didn't have plans to be here."

Jessica stared at the puzzle on Phil's face, lost for words.

"Jessica, what's up with the two of you?"

"What do you mean?"

"Look, Jess, I'm not blind. You and Tim remind me of roommates rather than lovers."

Tears jabbed at her eyelids. Phil sprang up. "Let me get you a beer, you look like you could use one." From the kitchen he retrieved the Kleenex box along with beer.

Setting both in front of Jessica, he said, "Jessica, tell me what's wrong. The last few months, being around you two has felt like – I don't know, being around my dentist and his assistant. Polite and perfunctory."

Tears began to course down Jessica's face. Thankfully, Phil wasn't the kind of guy who balked at tears, he just handed her a tissue.

"I think he's having an affair," she mumbled. "A couple weeks ago he came home from work really late. He said he was calling customers, but it didn't seem like that to me. Then this last Wednesday, I had Open House at school. When I got home, Tim said he had stopped for pizza with some guys from Best Buy, but I think he was with a woman, and he wouldn't flat out deny it when I asked. Was he, Phil? Is he seeing someone?"

"Damn," Phil exhaled. He reflected for a moment on Tim's description of Marcie. "I have no idea where he was Wednesday. But the thing is, Jessica, it's like – well, I know Tim feels frustrated. He can't seem to impress you."

"Impress me? What are you talking about?"

"What do you admire about Tim?"

Jessica looked at Phil as though he had grown another head. Then anger welled up. "Tim may be having an affair and you're asking me what I admire about him? Like this is my fault?"

"I don't know if he's having an affair or not, Jess. You're the one that said he is, not me. All I know is, Tim's big dream is to buy you a fancy new house in a swanky neighborhood, and you could give a shit about that. Right?"

"But – that's what he thinks I should want. It isn't what I want, not really." Loudly, she blew her nose into the tissue.

"So, would you admire him if he were an intellectual like you?" Phil asked, then shook his head as if to erase that question. "Let me rephrase that. Tim isn't an intellectual and never will be. How do you feel about the fact that he can't compete with your brain?"

"Compete with my brain? Marriage isn't a competition!"

Phil exhaled. "I'm not saying this very well. Let me try again. When Tim left college, he wanted to provide you – and him as well – with a nicer house than the one we grew up in, then start a family."

"What does that have to do with anything?"

"Well, look at your life from his point of view. So far you aren't in a house that's much better than our parents', and I don't see any progress on the babies front. And some months, you're the one bringing home a bigger paycheck. Now here you are, moving right along from studying for university to studying for fun, I guess, with that research you're doing on your family. It's like, you aren't going in the same direction. You don't even need him. At least, that's what it looks like to me."

For a moment, language seemed to evaporate from Jessica's brain. Even the tears, unsure what to do, stopped dead in their tracks. She took a deep breath, then felt words returning, wrapping themselves around anger.

"I've always been curious. I like learning things, I shouldn't be penalized for it, for God's sake, I shouldn't have to ask for permission. And I'm just starting to figure out teaching, I'm not ready yet for kids. And I don't see what that has to do with anything. It seems like Tim is always at work. On weekends, he works Saturday. Sunday is football. Monday through Friday we're both at work, or at least I am, he gets some Mondays off. And now he's spending more time at work doing God knows what so he'll get promoted, or at least that's what he says."

"Do you and Tim ever talk about any of this?"

"I tried to."

"Touchdown!" Even with the volume down, the crowd's roar was hard to miss. Phil turned toward to the TV to see who scored.

Jessica stood. "I need to go think this through."

"You don't have to leave, I'm not pushing you out."

"I know you aren't." Her voice softened. Angry as Phil's words had made her, she liked him. "Thank you for talking to me. You've thrown me some curves I didn't quite see coming. I just need to think."

After returning home, Jessica went out for a long walk. But somehow the day, warmly inviting earlier, had turned cold. As she tried to sort out where things had gone wrong, she bristled at Phil's accusation that she was too much of a bookworm – or maybe computer-worm would be the better term.

By the time she got home, Tim's car was in the drive. She found him in the living room, beer in one hand, TV remote in the other. A different football game was on.

"How was your walk?" he asked.

"Where were you?" Jessica blazed.

"I told you I was going over to Phil's to watch the game."

"*I* went to Phil's." She snatched the remote and clicked off the TV. "Now where were you?"

Without answering, Tim stood and walked toward the kitchen. Jessica grabbed his arm. "I said, where were you, Tim? Who is she?"

Tim shook off her grip. "If you must know, Jessica, I'm getting tired of all this."

"All what? Is it me you're tired of?"

"I'm tired of what our life has become. It's like your mind is always somewhere else. In books, in schoolwork, with your German ancestors as if you'd rather be living with them, God knows why. It's like, it's not good enough for you anymore to be just plain American like me, trying to get ourselves to a better just plain American neighborhood. You'd rather stay right here in this dump, but be hyphenated, like those kids you're teaching or that Mexican teacher at your school who you seem to think is so great. I'm not interesting enough for you, am I?" By then, he was shouting.

He stormed to the coat closet and grabbed a duffel bag from the top shelf, then sped upstairs, two steps at a time. When Jessica entered the bedroom, she found him shoving shirts, socks, and a pair of slacks into the bag.

"What are you doing?" Suddenly she was afraid. Things were escalating too fast.

"Going to Phil's. For real this time, you can check up on me again if you want."

"Tim, I, I ..." she stammered. "Don't you think we should talk?"

He shoved a pair of shoes into the bag, then went into the bathroom for his toothbrush, deodorant and shaving supplies.

"Talk about what?" Tim faced her, angrily. "Your latest research findings? That seems to be all you want to talk about these days. Or maybe that Mexican teacher you could be banging behind my back, for all I know."

"Where did you get that idea?" How could this be happening?

Tim zipped up the duffel, then said, "Look, Jessica, I need to get some distance. It feels like we aren't going in the same direction anymore. I'm not sure you want to stay with me, and I'm not sure I want to stay with you. Right now I need space to get a little perspective."

He grabbed the duffel, then dashed downstairs and out to his car. As Jessica heard the engine spring to life, she crumpled onto the bed in tears.

* * * * *

*In freefall, Jessica jerked the strap frantically, but the chute still didn't open. Glancing toward her chest, she realized she wasn't wearing one! Nothing would stop her but the ground below, where groupings of people were coming into view. On the lawn behind the small white church was Boody's German Methodist Literary Society; German folk music drowned out Willie and Friedrich's debate. And there was a roofless Iglesia Católica where Jessica could see families clustered, singing Spanish hymns. In a park an extended family picnicked. While a grandfather bounced a baby, the mother played softball with children and the father helped his daughter grill hamburgers.*

*No one seemed to notice Jessica hurtling toward her death in their midst. She tried to cry out, but couldn't.*

Jessica jerked awake, blinking. Rolling over, she saw Tim wasn't there. Funny, all the times she had fantasized leaving, she never actually expected him to be the one to leave.

When she turned on the bathroom light, the mirror displayed eyes swollen like heirloom tomatoes. Since she didn't need to be up for another hour, she went back to bed with an ice pack on her face.

The ice pack, along with her glasses, rendered her face presentable. By the time she got to school, her bloodshot eyes prompted only a couple of comments about apparent lack of sleep or allergies maybe? Jessica went through the morning on autopilot. The part of her everyone else could see carried on as usual, while another part, visible only to herself, churned, trying to figure out what to do next and who to talk to.

She had never been especially close to her brother Walt, who lived with his family in Colorado Springs. She saw him only once every couple of years, and couldn't imagine calling him to discuss a personal crisis. He always seemed to view Jessica's problems as her own making. Even her marriage to Tim showed lack of judgment, as far as he was concerned. Walt would say, Good riddance, now stand on your own two feet. End of discussion.

In high school, Jessica had been close to cousin Verna, her same age. But college took them in different directions both geographically and academically (Verna became a civil engineer), a distance phone calls and texts never quite bridged. Their communication had shriveled to the occasional Christmas card.

The few couples Jessica and Tim socialized with were "their" friends who she didn't dare ask to choose sides. That pretty much left Cath as sole prospective confidante. How pathetic, two and a half decades on this earth, and not a single person she could count on for support in a crisis.

At lunch, Jessica was trying to figure out how to broach her need to talk without making a spectacle of herself in front of her co-workers, when Cath set the topic for discussion: her third graders' struggle to memorize the multiplication table beyond 8.

"They bombed the timed quiz I gave. Too many are still working out multiplication by adding, which makes them really slow when they have two and three digit numbers." Cath jabbed a packet of pine nuts at her salad as if to scold the lettuce's computational failings.

111

"Well, you could give them short timed tests everyday," Jessica ventured. "Maybe reward everyone who beats their own score from the day before."

"The kids who are slow hate quizzes. Joey and Margie don't even try. I need more ideas."

Jessica rooted through the attic of her brain for every credible idea she could find. Then she piled them on the table, one at a time, between bites of sandwich. Cath, in turn, brushed most aside, but picked up two ideas that had worked when Jessica tried desperately to move her kids from sounding out long words to recognizing them by sight.

"Now it's my turn," Jessica finally said. "Not here, but I need to talk."

Cath studied her face for the first time that day. "After school, my room or yours?"

"Doesn't matter. I'll come to yours." Jessica gathered the trash from her lunch. "Thanks," she said as she stood, turned, then left the lounge.

Jessica didn't wait to straighten up her classroom after the children left before heading down the hall to Cath's room. As she entered, she found Cath kneeling on a table, stapling labels onto a bulletin board that had two columns: "What we Heard" and "Our Fact Checks." Down the left side Cath had stapled: "Proposition 30, taxes to fund schools" and "Proposition 33, auto insurance." The stapler thwacked, and "Proposition 35, human trafficking" was up.

"What on earth are you doing?" Jessica asked as Cath slid off the table and shook her skirt, which had bunched around her knees.

"Teaching critical thinking. The kids hear about this stuff on TV and sometimes from their parents. All they really hear, though, is either 'it's good, vote for it,' or 'it sucks, vote against it.' This week, everyone's supposed to bring to class one thing they've heard about one of these ballot propositions, then as a class, we do some fact checking." Cath brandished one arm toward six small boxes on the table, similarly labeled, apparently awaiting the children's checked facts.

Jessica stared at her. "Your third grade kids are struggling with multiplication tables, and you're teaching them the finer points of ballot propositions?"

"They don't have their math facts down as automatically as they should. That has nothing to do with their ability to reason. And before you point out that studying ballot propositions isn't in the standards, you're right about that. But reading, writing, critical thinking, and research are in the standards. Sarah agrees that as long as I'm hitting what the kids will be tested on, it's OK to do this."

Cath pulled two chairs opposite each other and sat in one, motioning for Jessica to take the other. "Now, tell me what's bothering you."

Jessica took a deep breath, then exhaled like a balloon. "Tim left me yesterday."

"Ouch. I'm surprised you made it to school today."

"What else would I do? At least being here is distracting."

"So tell me what happened," Cath invited.

Jessica recapped her suspicion that Tim may be seeing a woman, then the preceding day's events that culminated with him walking out the door. "I just really need someone to talk to." As tears welled in Jessica's eyes, Cath retrieved a pack of Kleenex.

Then her eyes narrowed slightly. "I'll have to say that I'm a little surprised you're so upset. I could have sworn you had a thing for Esteban."

Jessica felt her face go crimson. Cath added quickly, "Don't worry, it isn't that obvious. Esteban is probably oblivious, anyway."

"And he could be taken, for all I know. He never talks about his personal life here. But yeah, I think about him when I probably shouldn't."

"Well, with Tim gone for the time being and you now being a free woman, how would you like to see all this unfold?" Cath swept her arm through the air as though "all this" referred to her third grade curriculum.

Jessica looked about as if to locate an answer somewhere in Cath's classroom. Then she replied, "I don't really know. Tim and I have some big problems, maybe they're just too big. But for the last few years, he's been my closest friend and companion, in spite of the problems. The really depressing thing is that I don't feel all that close to anyone, including Tim." Fresh tears popped into her eyes, and she continued, "I mean, for the last few years, I've spent more time with him than with anyone else. We get along great around some things, but not others, like my own intellectual curiosity."

"Not an uncommon story for women," Cath agreed. "That's probably why I'm still single."

"Yeah, well. And Esteban, he encourages me to learn. He's given me some of his books to read, not that I've read much yet. He's also given me suggestions for my family history research."

"And he's a hunk," Cath added.

Jessica nodded in agreement, then continued. "Of course, over time, he might get on my nerves in some way, but at the moment he doesn't, so I sort of imagine he'd always be perfect. Which of course is pure fantasy. But I know how Tim grates on me, like putting down the neighborhood we live in and not taking good care of himself physically."

"Says the lady who eats Wonder Bread every day at lunch," Cath replied. "At least switch to whole grain, it doesn't turn into sugar in your bloodstream as fast as bleached processed grain. Look, I'm not warm and fuzzy, Jessica, you know that. I doubt I can comfort you and I sure can't suggest how to fix a marriage, not having been in one myself. I have an idea, though."

"What?"

"You're gonna think I'm changing the subject, but I'm not. I've been volunteering on weekends for the local Democratic Party. You don't even have to be a Democrat, but we could use help getting out campaign material for some key propositions and local candidates. You could come pitch in this Saturday."

Jessica's mind struggled to connect political volunteer work with a solution to her marriage problems. "I don't get it. You did change the subject."

"No, I didn't. This will give you something else to focus on. It sounds to me like you need time to sort through things, and you don't need to sit around by yourself from now until Doomsday doing that. Come for a while on Saturday. You'll meet some folks, and your mind will get a break. I usually work out problems better when I'm doing something else than when I'm obsessing over them."

"How about if I tell you Friday? I'm not at all political, I can't see how this will help."

"If you get a better offer, go for it. But don't sit home all weekend stewing." As Jessica started to leave, Cath tossed out, "What would Mary or Willie or one of those folks do?"

*April, 1889*

"*Prost!*" Rupert hoisted a beer to toast Willie, newly elected to Macon County's twenty-two member Board of Supervisors, having soundly defeated his rival 127 to 95.

"*Prost!*" "*Zum Wohl*!" "To Willie!" others responded in kind. Beaming, Willie surveyed the group, mainly farmers, filling tables in the outdoor beer garden behind Boody's two-story wooden General Store. Many were his friends, but he realized he also had followers he barely knew who had voted for him.

"You'll be spending a lot more time over in Decatur, now, I see," commented a gaunt man Willie knew only slightly, his well-worn hat pushed back exposing a pale forehead the sun rarely saw.

"No more than I need to," replied Willie. "I'm still first and foremost a farmer."

"But a farmer who's found his way into politics! You do us proud," insisted a robust man seated near Willie.

"Hear, hear! Three terms as county clerk under your belt, now Supervisor, what next?" hollered Rupert, organizer of the celebratory fete.

Suddenly, a lively German hunting march burst into the beer garden in the form of the cornet band Willie's brother John had formed a couple of years earlier. A dozen young men, most still clad in denim trousers and work shirts they had worn all day as they prepared their fields for spring planting, belted out a popular number as they strutted around the tables. The crowed joined in singing.

More beer glasses appeared, more toasts were proposed. Then Friedrich inquired with his deep German accent, "So, Willie, what issues do you plan to take up first?" The usual business of the Board of Supervisors consisted of county transportation, taxes, construction and maintenance of the county courthouse, use of the fairground, appointment of the grand jury, and assistance to the poor.

"Lower our taxes," shouted Jim, one of the farmers.

CHAPTER 16

Willie began, "Now, all of you know why I ran for office, and just because I won doesn't mean I've changed."

Someone yelled, "Willie, stand up! Can't hear you back here!"

Willie set down his beer as he stood, then continued, "As you know, I'm a farmer at heart, and I'm mainly interested in representing us farmers." A smattering of applause and a few supportive hoots rang out. Willie's predecessor had been criticized as bowing too much to party bosses and attending too little to farmers.

"No unnecessary taxes." Willie continued, tipping his head to Jim, then grinned. "But I've got a vested interest now in making sure our roads are maintained, since I'll be using the one to Decatur on a regular basis."

Laughter and someone yelled, "Hear, hear!"

"Obviously I'll make sure we improve the county's land use and water policies. Some of our friends who live in Decatur really don't understand what we farmers need."

More applause.

"I also want to make sure our kids keep getting a good education. Our new school building now has plenty of space for our youngsters." Willie felt good about the new building, which three years earlier replaced a small one-story school that stood on John's farm, on land their father donated years ago when he co-founded it.

"Mr. Donahey over here," Willie tipped his head toward a cleanly-scrubbed, youthful looking man wearing a white shirt and necktie under his coat, "Mr. Donahey's doing an exemplary job of making sure his seventy-odd youngsters behave themselves and learn their sums. My sons Orville and Ralston say he's too strict, they prefer the ladies who assist him." Laughter. "I want to make sure Mr. Donahey keeps getting the tools he needs, and a few more assistants, without more red tape from the city."

"And without wasting our tax money on them colored kids in the city," grumbled someone loudly.

"Andy, shut your mouth. Those colored kids have a right to education, just like our kids do," chided the man sitting next to him.

"They can pay for their own schools," Andy replied.

118

Willie intervened, "Communities mostly do pay for their own schools. Only a little bit comes from the state. Here in Boody, our taxes pay for our own kids' education."

Someone barked out, "Is it true a colored man is on the Board?"

Rupert responded with exasperation, "Read the paper, you *Trottel*! Rogan was elected a year ago."

"I've met him, he seems like a good worker," Willie said, bewildered at the conversation's turn.

"I hope they don't start moving out here," someone else grumbled.

Willie was relieved when Friedrich stood and glared at the group. "This is our Willie's celebration. Shame on all of you for turning it into a forum for complaints."

In the distance, Willie heard a bird chirp gaily as men looked sheepishly into their beers. Then one lifted his glass and belted out, "To Willie!" Other beer-holding fists shot up. "To Willie!" they hollered.

When Willie arrived home, he found Orville hauling in firewood as Lydia, four months pregnant, pulled roast pork and potatoes from the oven. Ralston was drawing a picture on old newspaper, while four-year-old Viola napped.

Willie hung his coat, then peered over Ralston's shoulder. "Cows?" he guessed.

"Pa! These are our horses. Wait, let me fix the tail." Ralston scribbled a thicker tail on one of the animals.

"Of course, how could I not see that?" Willie remarked. Kissing Lydia on the cheek, he murmured, "Smells good!" As Lydia's morning sickness had abated over the last month, her interest in meal preparation had returned to normal.

"How'd it go? Did John's band show up?" she asked.

"In full force. The beer was on the house, I hadn't expected that."

"Don't know why not, James has always been your supporter," she remarked, referring to the General Store owner.

"Rupert and Friedrich kept everyone in line. After the toasts, some of them got off onto their own issues. Less taxes, keep the coloreds out."

"What do the coloreds have to do with us?" Lydia asked with surprise.

"Friedrich said as much. You know how some people worry about their women getting raped. As far as I can see, the Negroes are minding their own business in Decatur. Anyway, it was a good celebration. I'm famished!"

\* \* \* \* \*

## September, 1889

Willie and Rob were enjoying an afternoon of fishing in a nearby creek that empties into the Sangamon River. Autumn, approaching stealthily, had lengthened shadows and brushed once-green grasses with gold. Willie was using the occasion to vent about tedium on the Board of Supervisors.

"Take the Committee on Fees and Salaries," he said as he attached a new fly to the hook. "When I was county clerk, I'd get lists of people to pay who had worked for the county. Simple. But I had no idea how many hours the committee could spend just debating how much to pay them! Five people to pay in July, and we probably spent three hours on it!"

He cast his line, pulled his hat down to shield his face from the slanting rays of the afternoon sun, then continued. "Roads and Bridges, now you'd think that committee would take up a lot of time, 'cause, hell, there are lot of roads and bridges in this county. But no, it's Fees and Salaries."

Rob reeled in an empty line, then fixed his gaze on Willie. "You were the one who decided to run for office. You having second thoughts?"

Willie watched his fuzzy yellow and red fly bob in the gentle flow of the creek, sun sparkling like spilled diamonds. Then he replied, "No, it's just testing my patience, that's all. I've got to complain to someone. Or someone other than Lydia all the time. I figured the Board's issues would be fairly straightforward, but I didn't figure on making straightforward things complicated."

Rob cast his line. "So maybe Lydia would rather you had stayed out of politics?"

"Nah, she always supports whatever I do. She's happy cooking and taking care of family."

Rob cast his line again, then asked, "Say, did you see where today's newspaper compared you to a rose?"

"A rose? What are you talking about?"

"You didn't read the *Morning Review*? Anyway, this wasn't on the front page, it was one of those little stray scrap articles in the middle somewhere. 'One by one the roses fall,' it said, commenting on your apparent move from the Republican Party to the Prohibition Party after you attended their congressional convention."

Willie turned to stare at Rob, shook his head, then slowly reeled in his line. "I guess they have to find something to write about. Back in April, it was speculation that I'd jumped over to the Democrats because of my vote for board chair. My brother John is the true believer, he actually joined the Prohibition Party. Personally, I'm all for keeping beer flowing."

Rob grinned. "That's good to hear, I was afraid maybe we lost a potential farm boy to represent us in the state legislature."

"No way! Board meetings might be tedious, but I can handle them." Willie fingered the fly on his line as though admiring it, positioned the pole to cast again, then stopped midair, a sly look crossing his face. "Maybe mayor of Boody. What do you think?"

Rob guffawed. "It has a ring. Mayor Willie. Or how about Senator Willie?"

Willie cast his line, then continued, "I only went to the Prohibition convention because I get tired of Republican big-shots making unnecessary rules. I like to keep them guessing."

"Speaking of unnecessary rules," said Rob, "what do you think about that law Moffett wants, making it illegal to fish along here?"

"The one that's supposed to protect fish by making what we're doing now illegal?" asked Willie.

"Yeah." Rob pretended to study the water. "I don't see a fish shortage, do you?"

121

"The fish population is doing brilliantly," Willie declared, ignoring his empty fish basket. "Moffett's just getting back at folks who don't support him. Not me, of course, I helped get him on the grand jury."

"An honor or a curse?" Rob laughed.

"One could say the same about three-day Supervisor meetings. Thankfully they only come around once a month."

"And you think you'd like Boody's city council meetings better?"

Willie molded his face into seriousness, eyes dancing. "Of course. They're here, and I'd be running them." He cast his line into the river again. "Our tax-cutting advocates aren't going to like an item on next month's agenda. The board is supposed to build a new courthouse, but the only way we can fund it is to raise taxes."

"Oh, you vote for that and they'll run you out on a rail. Your family will have to subsist on fish!" Rob looked pointedly at their empty fish baskets. "Or not subsist." Then, stroking his beard as he thought, he suggested, "I've got an idea. Let's form a protective organization. For fishermen."

"A society that protects fishing farmers! Brilliant! I've been fined, so have you, and so have several others when we've shown up with our poles near someone else's farmhouse," Willie exclaimed, slapping Rob on the back.

"We come along looking to feed our families, and wham, we get fined!" Rob jerked his line out of the water. Seeing it empty, he cast it again.

Willie laughed. "We'll have founding principles, membership, the whole thing! And when Moffett comes along, we fine him!"

A week later, the newspaper announced the founding of the Mutual Protection Society for Farmers who Fish, Rob being president, and Willie, secretary.

*October, 2012*

Saturday morning found Jessica and Cath walking into the local Democratic headquarters. "Wasn't that clever? Farmers who Fish, it was right there in the newspaper." Jessica knew she was babbling, but she was nervous about her first-ever stint of political volunteering.

Cath steered her to a table in the corner where a middle-aged man with ruddy cheeks and thinning hair sat. After a brief introduction, Steve, in charge of volunteers, showed them what to do. "You see, these labels endorse specific local candidates and ballot initiatives." Looking at Jessica over the tops of his glasses, he demonstrated, "Just place the label here. Next week, we'll hang them on doors of registered Democrats."

Jessica and Cath took their stacks of labels and door hangers to a table where other volunteers were already working, sat down, and got started. At first Jessica, trying to be neat, carefully lined up each label as if this were an art project. But after a few minutes, she began slapping them on like everyone else. As she developed a rhythm, she started to pay attention to two women across the table who apparently knew Cath. Their hands moved rapidly as they chatted.

One woman, whose silver hair, weather-beaten face, and hooded eyelids suggested she had passed sixty, was saying, "I don't know who this Mark Samuelson is," referring to a name on the label. "I don't live in his district."

Cath said, "He's new to politics, a strong environmentalist. He's also a Democrat, that's why we're endorsing him."

The other woman, perhaps in her fifties, bobbed hair as blond as a bottle can get it, said, "I'd support him as a strong environmentalist alone, even if I didn't know anything else about him. Another housing development is proposed for east of the freeway, can you believe it? It's the last thing we need!"

"Pull up the ladder, I'm up. That's what you sound like, Barbara," chided the older woman.

"That's not what I mean." Barbara's hands stopped as she considered her reply. "It's just, there's too much traffic, and too little water to support all the people trying to move here. By the way, we haven't met, I'm Barbara." She extended her hand to Jessica.

"Sorry, I forgot introductions. This is my friend Jessica. Jessica, this is Barbara, and this is Theresa." Cath motioned who was who.

"Hi," said Jessica, uncertainly. "I'm new at this, I've never been very involved politically."

"Oh, that doesn't matter, we're happy for anyone who comes and lends a hand." Theresa turned back to Barbara, "As I recall, you weren't born in California."

"Well, no, we moved here fifteen years ago." Barbara turned to Jessica. "We came from Montana when my husband was transferred here." Then to the table at large, "We came with a job, we weren't like all these people coming and then trying to find a job."

A loud rattle announced the front door opening. Jessica looked up to see two men enter. One reminded her of the Forty-Niners' linebacker Patrick Willis. The other, of medium build with wire-rim glasses, looked familiar.

The door slammed behind them. "Hey there, Gerald, I see you brought more help," greeted Steve, looking up from piles he was sorting at his desk in the corner.

"Steve, this is Vic," announced Gerald. "What's the work today?"

Vic, the architect from the Best Buy party!

Steve showed the new arrivals the day's work. As they took chairs at the volunteer worktable, Vic, who hadn't yet paid attention to the other volunteers, happened to sit next to Jessica.

"Vic? I'm Jessica, I think we met a couple of weeks ago."

Startled, he turned to look at her, then broke into a broad grin. "The family historian! What brings you to these parts? Where's your better half?"

"You two know each other?" Gerald's voice resonated like an operatic tenor.

124

"We met at a party for Best Buy employees about a month ago. You know, where Linda works," Vic replied.

"Politics isn't Tim's thing," Jessica said, not wishing to haul out her personal problems for public inspection.

"It isn't my thing either, but there's too much at stake here to stay home." Vic carefully lined up a label, then affixed it. Having started the same way, Jessica grinned watching him.

Barbara leaned over Gerald's stack of labels. "Looks like Steve gave you a different batch. I recognize the names on yours. We were just talking about this Mark Samuelson person on our labels. I hadn't heard of him before."

"He's the one who opposes development of any kind." Gerald shook his head. "We're supporting him?"

"He's a registered Democrat," Cath pointed out.

"The thing is," continued Gerald, "this area needs more affordable housing, you know what I mean? Workers who need a place to live have a hard time finding something here within their means. Developers don't make much profit building housing for poor people."

Jessica asked Vic, "What kind of architecture do you do?"

"What I enjoy most is designing small affordable homes that are visually inviting and don't fall apart as soon as a family moves in." Probably not a Mark Samuelson fan, she thought.

"So how's the research coming?" Vic asked Jessica.

"What kind of research are you doing?" Theresa asked.

"I'm looking into the German side of my family tree, I've become intrigued by these people who lived in Illinois and Iowa around the 1880s." She turned back to Vic. "The biggest thing I've learned so far is that the Germans created these close-knit communities centered around the church, whichever German denomination it may have been. Their communities were like big extended families. People intermarried, so I guess they really were family. Anyway, people were connected to each other at a deep level, like, they looked after each other, they enjoyed being together."

Smiling, Vic commented as if to himself, "They knew who they were in the world."

"Yeah, that's it."

"How on earth did you find out all that?" asked Barbara.

"From reading old digitized newspapers and other articles about the German churches and German immigrants."

Theresa mused, "It's funny. I was born right after World War II, and grew up hearing terrible things about Germany, like they were all savage Nazis. My father fought in the war, so he hated them."

"Well, ironically for all you know, you could be part German. Germans are the largest ethnic ancestry in the U.S.," Jessica said.

"Hmmm, could be," said Theresa as she stood. She took her completed stack of door hangers to Steve, who was talking quietly on the phone. Without interrupting his call, he tossed it in a box and handed her more hangers and labels.

"These were just ordinary people," Jessica continued. "They weren't Nazis, they weren't even military people. I think some of them came here to avoid the draft when the Prussians were taking over everyone."

"German draft-dodgers, who would have thought," Gerald said.

Jessica continued, "The thing is, I didn't grow up with many stories about my family. A few about my parents' generation, hardly any about my grandparents, and none before that. It was almost like they didn't exist, like we don't have a past."

As Theresa spread out her next batch, she said, "I didn't grow up with many stories, either. I heard a few about how hard my parents had it when they were young, but they didn't seem to want to talk about their past."

"Mine neither," Barbara said. "I figured there wasn't much of anything worth telling us. And as we grew up, well, the attitude was, who wants to hear about the old people when their ways are out of date, and everything has changed?"

Vic shook his head. "Why is it that a lot of white folks don't grow up with stories in their families? Hell, I grew up with all kinds of stories. Aunt Hazel was the family historian, she knew everything about everybody, and made sure we all learned what she knew."

"Same for me," added Gerald. "Even though my folks split when I was young, my mother made sure we knew who we were and where we came from. Where we fit in to a larger picture."

Jessica replayed her earlier conversation with Tim and Phil. Neither could see the point of her family history research. Their disinterest pained her. Now, here were people she had just met taking up the topic as worthwhile, a conversation starter rather than stopper. Jessica said, "That's just it, Gerald. Without the stories, you don't learn where you fit. Instead, you see life as something you improvise as you go, more or less in a vacuum. I guess that's why these German ancestors are pulling me in. They're my past. They seemed to know who they were. I must be part of them, but all that got lost along the way."

The door rattled open. "Can I register to vote here?" A young woman with spiked black hair, large silver earrings, and a tattoo down one arm addressed the room at large. Several sets of eyes took her in.

Looking over his glasses, Steve announced, "Dorothy's working registration, she'll be back in a minute. Have a seat." He indicated a chair next to the desk by the door. Jessica realized Dorothy must be the nondescript woman who had been sitting there when she and Cath had arrived, and who had quietly vanished.

"Some of our past gets buried out of shame," said Cath. "At least that's what happened in my family. My folks were convinced my dad's Kiowa ancestry would ruin their ambitions to become respectably middle class, so they erased his family from their memories as best they could."

"I'm really surprised to hear you say that," Jessica affixed her eyes on Cath as if seeing her for the first time. "You always seem so together."

"No thanks to my family, God love them. Peace Action has been my main community since college, when I joined to protest U.S. military involvement in the Middle East."

From the corner of her eye, Jessica noticed that Dorothy had materialized soundlessly, and was now registering the woman with spiked hair. There must be a back door somewhere.

Theresa was saying, "Mine is the Unitarian Church, and volunteering here. But I can relate to what you're saying. I really don't know much at all about my roots. And personal isolation, well that can just creep up on you when you aren't looking."

Jessica fell silent as she listened to the conversation move on to another topic. She found herself relaxing in a way she had not expected. When Cath initially invited her, she had imagined a room of people arguing stridently about political issues, who would judge her as woefully naïve. But these were ordinary people, different from each other, yet willing to spend several hours on a common project while exchanging views about any topic that happened to roam across the table. A little like informal discussion groups she had enjoyed as a university student.

By mid-afternoon the door hangers had all been labeled. The volunteers, minus Barbara who had left earlier, stood and stretched like cats emerging from a deep nap.

"I guess we'll see each other next Saturday?" Theresa asked.

Steve ambled over to the group. "I've got about eight more folks who've agreed to distribute these things next week. I'll need you to either help with that, or work on our get-out-the-vote campaign."

Jessica tried to look as unnoticeable as Dorothy. She wasn't yet sure she wanted to commit another Saturday. The work itself had turned out to be pretty monotonous, although the camaraderie was refreshing in a way that surprised her. She smiled to herself as she realized she sounded rather like Willie.

As the volunteers trailed out into the afternoon sunshine, Vic asked Jessica, "You gonna be here next Saturday? Maybe I can convince Linda to come pitch in if she knows there will be another familiar face."

"I haven't decided," said Jessica, doubting that her short conversation with Linda at the party qualified her as a familiar face Linda would want to see next Saturday. "I never had a political bone in my body. Cath thought this would be a good way for me to get out and meet people."

He stopped and looked at her. "It's none of my business, but you seem kind of lost. Your husband still at work?"

"He left," Jessica said so quietly she wasn't sure Vic heard her, so she repeated, "Tim left me last weekend. I don't know where he is."

"I'm so sorry to hear that. Do you have family around?"

"No. I have Cath. I know some people, but –" Jessica let what was unspoken hang in the air like bitter smoke from a cigarette. Then she inhaled deeply. Vic was asking her to join the group again next week, why would she even hesitate? Isn't this exactly what she had been looking for? "Tell Linda I'll be here, and I hope she's here as well."

They had reached Cath's car. Jessica slid inside, waving goodbye to Gerald, Vic, and Theresa. "See you next Saturday."

\* \* \* \* \*

"Thanks for agreeing to help me this morning," said Jessica the next day as she poured Cath a cup of coffee. "A few days ago, I thought I'd be spending this morning in the *iglesia* with some of my students' families, but when Tim pulled the rug out from under me, I couldn't manage to get that idea together." Peering into the oven, she announced, "Looks like the frittata's almost done."

Cath winced slightly with her first sip of coffee. "Woo, hot! Just how I like it." Gingerly, she took another, then set her mug down. "Now tell me again, exactly what I'm helping you with? I know it has something to do with your family history research, but I didn't quite follow you yesterday afternoon."

"And you came anyway. Wow, thanks!"

"You bribed me with frittata," Cath reminded her.

"That I did, and it worked. Okay, here's the deal. One, we're taking my mind off my problems with Tim. That's the main thing."

"Have you talked to him, by the way?" Cath asked.

"I called him last night." Jessica's lower lip quivered. "Yesterday he looked for a place to rent on a month to month basis. He said Phil's place is kind of cramped. We talked about how to split next month's bills on this place."

Cath put her hand on Jessica's, murmuring, "I'm sorry, honey."

"Yeah, thanks." Jessica turned back to the oven. As she removed the frittata, she added, "I told him he could come back here anytime, but he just said he needed space."

"Well, if I'm not mistaken, you do too. I'm no expert on relationships, but I think it would be a mistake just to jump right back into where you were. Even if your interest in Esteban were to evaporate, the fact that you think about him is telling."

"I suppose." Jessica set the frittata and whole wheat toast on the table, then sat and offered Cath the serving spatula, while wondering why Tim leaving was so upsetting when she had entertained her own fantasies about leaving him. Maybe what was upsetting was being alone. "Help yourself. Number two, why you're here. A question that's been bothering me is whether, after the Civil War, former slaves and European immigrants were on the same playing field in the job market."

Cath raised her eyebrows as she slid a slice of frittata onto her plate. "You're not messing around with small questions." Inspecting her plate, she added, "This looks great, by the way.

"Thanks."

"And very good," Cath proclaimed after the first bite. "You're a veritable cookbook! I should take notes."

"Glad you like it," said Jessica as she scooped up a forkful. "Anyway, I was reading the Chicano history book Esteban loaned me. I learned about industrialists recruiting Chinese, then Mexicans, as low-wage workers, and I wondered where newly freed African Americans and European immigrants fit into the picture. The question just sat in the back of my mind, though, I was too busy with other things. Then yesterday, seeing Vic reminded me of him pointing out advantages my European ancestors had, when I first met him." Jessica reflected on her German American ancestors' apparent desire to keep the "coloreds" out of their community, a new insight she had not considered earlier.

"So how to you propose looking into this?" asked Cath.

"My idea is using the occupations people reported in the census, comparing jobs of African Americans and German immigrants in places where my ancestors lived."

Cath considered Jessica's project, then said, "Okay, and you need me for …?"

"I mostly need you to think with me while we do this. Sometimes you're just more systematic than I am. I plow ahead and you stop to ask questions, to analyze things."

Cath nodded once, as if to compliment Jessica on knowing how to win her over. "Well, we'll see what we can do. You're the one asking the deep questions, though. Mind if I have another slice?"

"Help yourself!"

A half hour later, the two were seated at Jessica's computer. "Let's start with Muscatine, Iowa in 1880," Jessica proposed. "My great greats Heinrich and Mary, along with their kids, moved there in the 1890s, but since there's no 1890 U.S. Census, 1880 will do."

"What happened to the 1890 census?"

"Most of it was destroyed in a fire in Washington D.C. in the 1920s," Jessica replied as she called up the 1880 Census from the family history website. "Okay, let's start with Blacks in Muscatine, since there were fewer of them than German immigrants." She showed Cath where to designate race in the website window, then hit Search. The term Black yielded 58 people, and Mulatto yielded 78; Negro and colored, used in some census records, didn't give any results.

"So that's 136 African Americans in Muscatine. Now let's scroll through all of them and list occupations," Jessica directed.

"'Working at home.' That doesn't count," Jessica said, pointing to an entry.

"Housework is work," Cath emphasized. "Not paid labor, but labor nonetheless."

"Agreed, but it's paid labor I'm looking at."

Silence as they scanned census documents and made notes. Then Cath laughed. "What's a corn doctor? See right here?" she said. Jessica shrugged, adding "corn doctor" to the list of occupations. When they finished, they had eighteen day laborers, five farm laborers, nine washer women, five servants, five cooks, and assorted other kinds of work.

"What did white washers do? We've got two of them," Jessica asked.

"You know, they white washed buildings. I think it was a mixture of lime and something. And look, they had an A.M.E. church, here's the pastor," Cath said, pointing.

"I wonder if Heinrich knew him. Anyway, let's take a look at the German immigrants." Jessica opened the 1880 Census search page again. "This time we want people born in Germany but living in Muscatine." She entered the terms, then hit Search. "Whoa, there are hundreds of them! This is gonna take the rest of the morning."

"No," Cath said, "they're listed in alphabetical order. If we take the first 136, that would be pretty random in terms of work, don't you think?"

"Good idea, I knew you'd earn breakfast."

They used the same process tallying paid work of the first 136 German immigrants. "Sister of St. Francis," read Jessica. "That would be a nun?"

"Yep," replied Cath as she wrote it down.

Jessica said, "Hey, here's a capitalist! Look, that's what this guy told the census taker!"

"Capitalist," Cath repeated as she wrote.

"Another sawmill worker. Looks like the sawmill in Muscatine refused to hire Blacks."

"As did the lumber yard and the wagon maker," Cath said.

They studied the two completed lists. "Oh, shit," exclaimed Cath, "We forgot about something. We're gonna have to do this over."

"What?" Jessica asked, puzzled.

"When you look at these two lists of work, do you notice anything strange?"

Jessica studied the lists. "Well, it looks like Black women took in a lot of laundry, and Germans didn't. There were German merchants but not Black merchants."

"Right, but that's not what I'm getting at. Which list is longer?"

Jessica looked again. "The list of jobs the Germans had. It looks like they had more access to work?"

"Maybe, but that's still not what I'm getting at. The 136 African Americans were whole families, including kids. The 136 German immigrants were mainly adults. Most of their kids were born in America, so they weren't on the list."

"Oh, shit. You're right." Jessica sighed, then stretched her arms. "I guess we could start with the African Americans and only count the people doing paid work, then do the same with the German immigrants." Jessica looked down at their notes, then added, "I don't want to go through Muscatine again, let's try Decatur, Illinois. That's near Boody, but Boody's too small to show up in this kind of search."

"Then why don't we just do the whole county Boody is in?" Cath suggested.

A riff of music punctuated the air. Surprised, Jessica grabbed her cell phone. "I forgot, I changed the ring tone last night." Then she said into the phone, "Hello?"

Walt's voice replied, "Jess, how are you?"

Momentarily flustered, Jessica replied, "Uh, great! What's up?" It had been months since Walt had called her; she was more likely to call him. And of course he didn't know Tim had left.

Walt's voice marched through the airwaves, "Just calling to see if you and Tim would like to join us in Colorado Springs for Thanksgiving. We haven't seen you two for a while, and would love it if you wouldn't mind flying out here."

"Gee, uh, that's really nice of you," Jessica stammered as she stood and ran one hand through her hair, wondering what prompted this invitation. Walt's wife Jan had probably redecorated the house and wanted to show it off. "Let me get back to you later this week."

"Sure, any time. But don't wait too long, the planes are probably pretty full already."

"Yeah, well, let me, uh, talk to Tim and I'll get back with you."

"Great. Talk soon." Walt rang off.

Without opening her mouth, Cath's face broadcast curiosity. Jessica said, "My brother, Walt. He was inviting us to Colorado Springs for Thanksgiving. He doesn't know about Tim and me."

"Ah. It doesn't sound like you two talk a lot."

"We don't. Walt usually doesn't approve of me, so I try not to give him anything to criticize. Let's get back to this project, okay? I'll figure out what to say to him later."

"Sure. But it just strikes me as paradoxical that you're spending hours getting to know ancestors who aren't alive anymore, while holding your brother at arm's length."

Jessica studied her fingernails. "Hmm, you have a point. Maybe it's because the ancestors can't hurt me, and my brother can. I'll need to think about that."

"Right. So, how about switching places? I'll do the computer thing and you take notes."

About twenty minutes later, they had repeated the search process, this time for Macon County in 1880, comparing 140 African American workers with an equal number of German immigrant workers.

"This is striking," Jessica exclaimed as she examined the two lists. "Almost all the laundry was done by Black women, just like in Muscatine. Most of the servants were Black, and most cooks were Black. Hmmm, almost all the barbers were Black. Looks like jobs serving white people, kind of like slave jobs but now for pay."

"Yeah, and a lot more laborers were Black. It's obvious who had access to land – there were way more German immigrant farmers than Black farmers," Cath noted.

"And access to factory jobs, like the sawmills in Muscatine. Nine German immigrants worked in factories, zero African Americans," Jessica added.

"Same with skilled trades. Carpenter, shoemaker, cabinet maker, tailor. A couple of African Americans, but a lot of German immigrants. I'd be willing to bet folks got into these through apprenticeships, unions or guilds that admitted only white men."

"Hmm, I wonder why all the butchers were German immigrants, or at least why none of them were Black. German sausage, maybe?"

"And I see different access to money," Cath continued. "There were nine German immigrant merchants, like these three who sold dry goods. Only one African American was a merchant."

Jessica thought a moment. "What this says to me is that African Americans came to Macon County to make a living, like everyone else, but then ran into limits on what they could do, at least compared with German immigrants. The average German immigrant not only had more financial resources, they also got jobs that seemed closed to African Americans. In fact, the Germans seem to have been recruited for jobs some of the African Americans might have wanted but couldn't get."

Cath added, "And, although we didn't look specifically at gender, off the bat you can see Black women taking in other people's laundry as a way of making ends meet. The German women didn't do that. Probably didn't need to, maybe even sent their dirty stuff to the Black women to wash."

Jessica leaned back in her chair and studied the ceiling, as if it would reveal more patterns in the data. Then, brow wrinkled, she looked at Cath. "I wonder if any of my ancestors had a clue that opportunities were stacked in their favor. I noticed as we looked at the African Americans, none of them lived in Blue Mound Township."

"Maybe the white people of Blue Mound kept them out."

Jessica sighed. "Yeah, Illinois already had a history of doing that."

"You've been kind of misty-eyed about your long lost family," Cath commented. "But along with their strong sense of community, they may have also been playing exclusionary race cards."

"Yeah, I was afraid that might be the case. When Vic first mentioned how white people in Illinois had access to land Black people couldn't buy, I started wondering what my people thought. I guess they probably just considered that normal."

"Probably so," Cath agreed, then glanced at her watch. "It's almost two, I should get stuff ready for class tomorrow."

"Yeah, me too."

"Hey, thanks. This was eye-opening," Cath said. Jessica gave Cath an unexpected hug. "Thanks, Cath, you've been great."

"No problem." Cath hugged her back, then the two headed downstairs to the door.

After Cath left, Jessica decided to browse old Decatur newspapers, "just to get more of a feel of the place," she told herself. She wondered if there might be clues as to how her ancestors thought about the racial patterns she and Cath had just uncovered. In the website of digitized newspapers, she entered the date range 1890-

1895. Then, because she had to enter some sort of search term, a glance at the lists she and Cath had just compiled led her to type in "colored carpenter."

Up came the *Herald-Dispatch* for July 1, 1893. Surprised that there actually was something about colored carpenters, Jessica located and read the article in question:

> What the colored people need more than anything else is an opening in the industrial world. Of the hundreds in domestic service for instance there are a number who are capable of learning skilled trades and of receiving the larger pay which awaits those who have skilled labor to sell. Why do not more of them learn skilled trades then? Simply put, because they have not the opportunity, simply because they are not given a chance. The labor unions are almost all against them. In one way or another nearly all the colored race in our city are directly serving white men. Where do you see the colored carpenter, stair-builder, painter, plumber, iron or brass molder ....

The long-ago writer continued to list skilled trades from which the labor unions blocked African Americans. Labor unions consisting of white men. And some of those white men were probably German immigrants. And the German churches – churches that had abhorred slavery – they didn't appear to have been agitating for post-slavery justice, at least not as far as she knew. For them, community was both sustaining and exclusionary, a way of thinking about community she hadn't considered before.

Jessica scanned the rest of the page. She saw a diagram for building a chicken coop, an article about a bank failure in another county, and an article about a grand jury – for a lynching case!

Schoolwork forgotten, she began to pore through digitized newspapers to figure out how her German ancestors, and especially Willie who had been elected into a position where he could do something, figured into race relations in Macon County during the latter part of the 1800s.

## June, 1893

Samuel craved water. The June sun, blasting down on him since morning, showed no sign of relenting, and he still had days to go before reaching his sister's home in Tennessee. Maybe there he'd be safe from pursuit since robbing that store near the Iowa border. What a stupid thing to do! Gainfully employed as a farm hand, there was no reason to steal. There was only the temptation of an open cash register drawer while the clerk fetched a box of canned goods from the stock room.

Samuel spied a farmhouse ahead. Maybe they'd give this dusty Negro some water. They might even be persuaded to give him a plate of food, his first and probably only meal of the day.

As Samuel approached the two-story farmhouse, which resembled a painting in a hotel where he had worked briefly, he wondered why the air was eerily quiet. Not a soul in sight.

He knocked on the door. Silence, then footsteps. A white woman, black hair drawn back into a knot, cautiously peered out. "C'n I help you?" she asked.

"Ma'am, I'm traveling to my sister's house, and wonder if you can spare me some water," he said.

She glared at him. "Just a minute." She shut the door. A few seconds later, she cracked the door open again and handed him a dipper. "Well's over there," she pointed.

Samuel went to the well, filled the dipper, and drank deeply. Returning it to her, he said, "Thank you, Ma'am. You wouldn't have any food to spare a hungry man, would you?"

"Get away from me! Get out of here!" she yelled.

Instinctively, he touched her arm. "Ma'am, please, I won't harm you. I'm just hungry."

"Don't touch me! Help!" she shrieked.

"That's alright, Ma'am, I'm leaving." He withdrew his hand, backed up, turned, and fled.

Samuel scrambled down the road, then dove into a clump of bushes, his heart pumping wildly. In the distance, he heard men's voices and the clip-clop of horses. He remained as still as possible as the voices approached.

"That nigger's around here somewhere," a voice said. "He can't have gone too far."

"We'll teach him to touch our women," another said. "He'll be sorry he was ever born."

Samuel tried to control his trembling as they neared his hideout. They didn't stop, however, but continued on as they discussed where he might be.

He stayed in the bushes for what felt like hours. Finally, as dusk approached he crawled out, then ran as fast as he could. He gradually slowed, knowing that a running Negro would look suspicious to any passer by. Presently, he heard the clatter of a horse-drawn wagon behind him.

"C'n I offer you a ride?" Samuel turned to see a white man, about his age. The man's relaxed face suggested he was unaware of Samuel's pursuers. "Where're you staying?"

"I'm bound for Tennessee, sir, to stay with my sister," Samuel replied.

"Tennessee, you have a long walk ahead of you. Hop in. You're probably hungry. That's my farmhouse just up ahead. Let me give you a little supper and you can sleep in the barn if you like."

As Samuel jumped into the back of the wagon, the man said, "My name's Anderson."

"Thank you, Mr. Anderson, sir. My name's Bush."

When they arrived, Anderson showed Samuel into the barn, then disappeared into the farmhouse. A few minutes later, he reappeared with a tin plate of stew and a cup of water. Samuel thanked his benefactor, inhaled the food, then curled up on the hay and fell asleep.

The sharp barking of a dog awoke Samuel. Blinking, he realized the sky was beginning to grey with the early light of dawn. Then he heard voices. Unsure what was happening, he jumped up, grabbed his shoes, and was about to flee when a large man threw open the door. Samuel dashed to a window and jumped out.

"Over here!" he heard someone yell from just a few feet away. Suddenly, two men grabbed him.

"We got the rapist!" one of them hollered, then said to Samuel, "We're not gonna string you up here, boy, we're sending you on to Decatur where you'll be dealt with right proper. You'll get everything coming to you there."

\* \* \* \* \*

Willie trudged through the door, grateful to be home. "Daddy!" Like a homing pigeon, eight-year old Viola bolted into his belly, sandy curls dancing. Willie dropped his suitcase on the floor, looping an arm tightly around her. "How's my girl?" he murmured.

Four-year old Verne scurried from the kitchen where he had been "helping" his mother make supper, and folded himself into the arms and legs of father and sister.

Lydia emerged from the kitchen, wiping her hands on a towel. "How was the meeting?" she asked as she kissed Willie's cheek.

"Not one I'd want to repeat. I'll give you details after supper. Where are the boys?" Orville, who had survived diphtheria three years previously and was now in his early teens, matched Willie's height, and Ralston wasn't far behind. But to Willie, they were still "the boys."

"They're out mending that hole in the fence by the black oats, the one you noticed last week. They should be along any minute, they know supper's about ready. Viola, come help set the table." Lydia's efficient orchestration of the children reminded Willie of a band conductor he had enjoyed watching in Decatur last summer.

Willie took his suitcase upstairs, washed his face, and returned to the family.

Later that evening when the two younger children were in bed and the older boys were outdoors doing who knew what with neighboring cousins, Willie unburdened to Lydia what happened at the Supervisors' meeting in Decatur.

"It would have been an ordinary meeting, except for that lynching," he began, referring to a white mob from the village of Mt. Zion, about ten miles away over dirt roads, having lynched Samuel

Bush two weeks previously. "And the fact that, being white, I almost felt guilty about it when I talked with Hugh." Hugh, a former barber and current owner of a successful Decatur restaurant, had succeeded Rogan as the sole person of African descent on the Board of Supervisors.

"What did Hugh say to you?" Lydia asked as she pulled a thread on the sock she was darning.

"The first day, he didn't say anything about it. We just did our usual business." Willie twisted the hem of his shirt restlessly with one hand as he held a glass of whiskey in the other. "But we all felt it. The grand jury was meeting in the courthouse, and we kept wondering if they were going to indict anyone, maybe announce it while we were there. Hell, everyone knew who led the break-in and lynching, they hadn't worn masks. And every time I looked at Hugh, there was this unspoken question: Will white people do anything about it?"

Lydia bound off her stitching, clipped the thread, tossed the darned sock into a basket at her feet, and picked up another one, then prompted, "And?"

"Wednesday, after Roads and Bridges, I ran down the street for a beer and bumped into him. Lydia, he looked like he had aged about ten years just in the last month. I didn't know what to say, so I just asked how things were going at the restaurant."

Pausing, Willie gulped whiskey as if it might clear his thoughts, then continued, "He looked at me kind of funny. Then he said, 'The restaurant's fine, I'm just coming back from there. But the community's not fine. Not fine at all.' I didn't know what to say. I'm hardly ever at a loss for words, as you know, but I just didn't know how to react."

"Newspapers say the colored folks have been meeting. I imagine Hugh's been part of it," Lydia said.

"He has, and he was frustrated. He told me the colored folks had tried to prevent this kind of thing from happening in the first place."

Willie had joined Hugh on a sidewalk bench, foregoing his anticipated beer since Hugh was a tee-totaller. Hugh shook his head wearily, then said, "When we heard they'd found a suspect, Jacobs

140

and Gray – you know who Jacobs is, he works at the newspaper office, and Gray's a day laborer. Anyway, they went round to the Sheriff and offered to guard the prisoner. All the talk that was going around about lynching the rapist, we figured anyone brought in would need guarding. But the Sheriff, he just told them to go home, said they have everything under control."

As Hugh paused, Willie watched passers-by stroll peacefully as though nothing out of the ordinary had happened. He wondered which of these Decatur residents had witnessed the lynching.

"Woodford offered to serve as Bush's attorney," Hugh continued, referring to Decatur's only Black lawyer. "Bush kept insisting he was innocent, that he'd been to the white lady's house but only to ask for water. I don't think Woodford believed him, but he does believe in the right to a fair trial. Then the state Attorney General met with two Mt. Zion leaders to explain that if Bush was found guilty, he'd get life in prison. But that wasn't enough for them, they wanted blood.

Hugh had not learned of the lynching until the next morning, and Willie, not until he read about it in the newspaper. By then, although hundreds of white people had witnessed it, very few admitted to having been there. Nonetheless, word spread like a swarm of mosquitos.

As the story went, after Bush was in the Macon County jailhouse, a white crowd anticipating a lynching formed outside, swelling to perhaps a thousand by nightfall. In the wee hours of the morning, twenty-five Mt. Zion men, armed with guns, sledge hammers, pick axes, and crow bars, arrived. The deputy sheriff on duty refused to give them the keys, so the men broke down doors to the cells while the guards looked on and the deputy just yelled at them. The men grabbed terrified Bush and hauled him out to the street, where the white mob cheered and whooped, "Lynch the bastard!" They dragged him to a nearby street corner, where a noose had already been hung. Only one law officer tried unsuccessfully to stop them. One of the vigilantes invited Bush to pray before dying, but someone shouted that the woman he raped didn't get a chance to pray. Then someone else pushed him into the noose and hoisted the rope, which broke. Another was quickly found, and this time held.

Bush's body dangled from a tree for about an hour until the Coroner arrived, cut him down, and proclaimed him dead.

Hugh continued, "The next morning, a group of us met with the Sheriff as soon as he returned from Chicago, offering our services once more, this time to help locate suspects in Bush's murder." He shook his head as though trying to reconcile sense with senselessness. "Once more, he said they could handle it. They hadn't even handled it in the first place, and I don't think they intended to. D'you know, the Sheriff even told a reporter that he was glad no one had been killed in the melee."

Willie sat mute as Hugh detailed how Black leaders attempted to help. "The state Attorney General wouldn't meet with us either. And all we were requesting was that the law be followed. By Monday, when it looked like nothing was going to happen, over a hundred of us met. I don't know if you know this, but lynching's becoming more common in these United States, as a way to return us to subservience. Anyway, we discussed a range of things we might do, but settled on sending a resolution to the governor and the legislature, condemning lawlessness – both rape and lynching. You see, we value upholding the law."

Willie nodded, mumbling, "Yes, I understand," when, in fact, he didn't. He felt guilty realizing that he, like many other white people, assumed most Blacks disregarded the law.

Hugh continued, "When the resolution reached the legislature, the Black representative from Chicago tried to introduce it, but the Democrats objected, and the Republicans just capitulated, like they really didn't care."

"I didn't know that," Willie murmured.

"I know you didn't," Hugh replied. "The Governor has offered bounty money for Bush's killers, but hell, everyone knows who they were. Now the grand jury's debating whether to indict anyone." Hugh sighed heavily. "I thought Decatur was a good place for Blacks folks. Our kids can go to school without a fuss, our people have work – maybe not the kind of work white folks get yet, but the city had been making progress. Now this."

Willie had sat mutely as Hugh slowly hoisted himself up, turned, and trudged away. One of the lynch mob leaders operated a grain elevator in Mt. Zion. Although Willie didn't know the man well, he recalled swapping jokes with him last fall as they slapped each other on their backs while comparing grain sales. Willie knew he could urge the grand jury member he had appointed to vote for an indictment, and he could even contact the Governor's office with names.

But he didn't. He just sat until he had to return to his meeting.

Willie's attention returned to Lydia and the whiskey in his hand. Lydia was saying, "You can't feel guilty, you weren't involved."

"But people like me were," Willie replied. "I know one of the ring leaders. Look, what if one of Boody's women was raped? What would we do? I'd hope we'd uphold the law, but I'm not sure. That posse in Mt. Zion, they weren't hoodlums, Lydia, they were town leaders, like me. I can identify with them. Listening to Hugh, his frustration was plain as this glass in my hand. It's easy to sit here and say the posse shouldn't have taken the law into their own hands, but I keep asking myself, what would I have done?"

"You don't even know if Bush was guilty. He never got a trial," Lydia reminded him.

"I know that." Willie twirled his glass, watching what was left of the whiskey. "There's what you know, and there's what you feel in your gut. And now the grand jury's grappling with the difference between the two. They know who led the break-in and hanging, and they know what the penalty is – either life in prison or death. So, do they condemn Mt. Zion's leaders to death? If they do, the whole town will go after them, the law be damned. If they don't, the coloreds, who I'm learning value the law a great deal, will know it won't protect them."

Willie stared into his whiskey. "I used to think colored folks' business didn't have anything to do with us. Now I don't know, Lydia, I just don't know."

Two weeks later Willie learned the grand jury's decision: no indictments.

*November, 2012*

Esteban noticed that the more Jessica talked, the more animated she became. "What happened next," she said without stopping to catch a breath, "was that another grand jury was impaneled to investigate the lynching, but they didn't indict anyone either. So the African Americans got really disillusioned. I mean, here they had migrated to Decatur from the South after the Civil War, hoping to become ordinary citizens of this community, and what happens? Bam! They find out the laws don't apply to them."

Inwardly, he marveled at how emphatically white people just discovering racism talk about it.

"But then, just one year later, another white lady got raped and another Black man got arrested. This time, the mayor and the sheriff's brother guarded the jail, and they didn't interfere when a bunch of Black men patrolled the neighborhood near it. So there wasn't a second lynching. But the African Americans never trusted the authorities after what happened to Bush. Their whole view about white authorities in the North had shifted."

"I can see you've been busy." Jessica had more guts than he had realized to be asking these kinds of questions about the past. He wondered if she would also begin asking them of the present.

"Yes, well, it's kind of kept me from preparing for my classes as much as I should, except I'm learning tons of history I can bring in. But it bothers me that my ancestor didn't do anything when he could have."

Esteban glanced at leftovers from Day of the Dead celebrations that would have to wait until Monday to be cleared away. A corner of his classroom still housed an altar complete with photos of assorted deceased people, candles, marigolds, fruit, and candy. Brightly colored skeletons danced along the back bulletin board. His desk was piled with materials from yesterday's afterschool activity when children created memorials of dead loved ones to take home. He would come in early Monday. Right now, he had a meeting to get to.

He noticed Jessica holding his Chicano history book in one hand while the other fingered paper marigolds on his desk. "You've been reading it?" he asked.

"Yes! I'm seeing patterns in how people with darker skins have been brought here to work for low pay, while white people got to move up the opportunity ladder, like the Decatur employment patterns I told you about earlier."

He smiled. "You have courage, Miss White Bread." When Jessica wrinkled her nose, he suspected she didn't like that nickname.

He glanced at his watch. It was almost 4:00, and the meeting he was helping to lead across town was supposed to start at 4:30. While he enjoyed watching Jessica dive into issues new to her and important to him, her presence in his classroom most afternoons this week was – well – not annoying, Jessica was too likable to be annoying. But didn't she have a life of her own?

"Look, Jessica. I've gotta run to a Raza Studies meeting across town."

"Oh! I'm sorry, I won't keep you." She moved toward the door, then turned. "Raza Studies?"

"Chicano Studies. Like that book. A bunch of Mexican parents have been getting frustrated with the schools here. By the time they hit high school, a lot of their kids are so alienated they don't see the point of school. We've been meeting to think about what to do. I'm working with some other teachers to try to get a Chicano Studies program going."

"Oh!" Jessica repeated, turned, and left.

Esteban quickly shoved a pile of papers and books into his backpack, flipped off the lights, left the room, and locked it. Then he dashed to his old green pick-up truck.

Normally it wouldn't take a half hour to get to Jefferson High School, but Friday afternoon traffic was a logjam. He pulled into the parking lot just after 4:30, a bright red Miata right behind him. It screeched to a stop next to his pick-up, and out stepped Brenda. In an instant, he took in her slender legs and sensuous lips.

"Traffic's terrible!" she greeted, then gave him a quick kiss on the tip of his nose.

"What kind of kiss is that?" he laughed as he slid an arm around her waist and gave her a lingering kiss on the lips. He gazed into her dark eyes, then took her hand. "Come on, the meeting's about to start."

They entered the school and walked briskly to the classroom of one of Esteban's good friends. Donaldo, a history teacher, was piloting a Chicano studies version of U.S. history this year. Esteban had been working with him, two of his Jefferson colleagues who wanted to develop a broader Raza Studies program in the school, and a handful of teachers from other schools. This would be their first meeting bringing in parents from their different schools.

Donaldo met Esteban and Brenda at his classroom door. "We're gonna need to go to the cafeteria or someplace like that with more space," he said by way of a greeting. "Wait here, let me go get Jorge, the custodian who can help us." Esteban could see all the chairs occupied and people beginning to stand along the back wall.

Tall, gangly Donaldo trouped down the hall as more parents arrived. A few minutes later, he returned with Jorge and announced loudly, "We're moving to the music room. Everyone, come this way, *vamos*!" Turning to Esteban, he remarked, "This is great! I didn't know how many people would turn out, I didn't expect this many."

"We hit a chord," replied Esteban, buoyed by the turnout.

Once resituated, Donaldo introduced the Core Planning *Junta*, as he called them – himself, Esteban, and middle school teacher Dolores, a stocky, bespeckled fifty year-old with short grey hair and a radiant smile.

Then Donaldo asked, "Everyone registered to vote next week?" He looked around, adding, "*¿Todos van a votar?*"

Judging from reactions, it appeared everyone understood English. With meetings like this, one never knew. Some families might be recent immigrants, while most could be second, third, even fourth or fifth generation, many having lost Spanish entirely.

Donaldo stroked his goatee and continued, "We have too much at stake in next week's election. If any of you aren't yet registered, or if you need help getting to the polls, see one of us before you leave." A few people clapped and someone exclaimed, "We're on it!"

Donaldo's voice then took on a timbre that reminded Esteban of Dr. Martin Luther King recordings. "Our African American colleagues have broken the color barrier into the White House, we Latinos haven't done that yet. But in our classrooms, we might have the first Latino President of these United States! But ..." he paused briefly for a few enthusiastic hoots. "But, *señores y señoras*, first we have to nurture the brilliance of our *hijos* and *hijas*. A lot of the teachers and the curriculum in our schools aren't up to doing the job. Too many of our kids lose heart as they go through the school system without seeing people like themselves doing significant things for the world. They look around, and every day see cops surveilling our *gente*, parents scrambling to find jobs, tests telling them they aren't smart enough, and in some of our *barrios*, the only people they think are actually in charge run the gangs. Well, you know and I know that what our youth need is a good education, one that really ed-u-cates them." Donaldo emphasized each syllable with his hands.

He went on, "They need to know people like us aren't foreigners here. This is our country, too. Many of us have been here longer than the *gringos*!"

Applause broke out. Esteban stood back, watching Donaldo preach, as it were, as though a million sermons, stored inside, finally had a place to go.

"Our kids need a history that helps them situate this place where we live, this American place, in a story that includes Mexico. They need to know that Mexican Americans are Americans, and America is part Latino. They need a history that helps them make sense of their everyday lives, they need to know what people like themselves have been working for, fighting for, since way before they were born."

Heads nodded. "They need to know our *literatura*, they need to read Rudolfo Anaya and Sandra Cisneros, they need to know the brilliance of Luis Valdez and Alurista. Many of our kids don't see the point of reading Shakespeare and Hemmingway until they know Chicano writers, Latino writers!"

Most clapped enthusiastically, although a few puzzled expressions suggested unfamiliarity with names Donaldo had listed.

Esteban felt Brenda tap his arm. He leaned over and she whispered into his ear, "There's a plan coming, I hope?"

As Esteban nodded, Donaldo beckoned him and Dolores forward. "Many of you know," Donaldo said to the crowd, "that I'm teaching U.S. history from a Chicano perspective this semester. It's a college prep class, I've got our youth doing very serious reading and research. And they are doing it, very few absences, very few tardies even. They're into it. Now's the time to get the district behind us, and expand the program. Dolores here teaches language arts at Washington Middle, just down the road, and Esteban teaches fifth grade over at Milford. We've got about eight other teachers here as well. Teachers, would you stand up and introduce yourselves?"

The teachers stood. One by one they gave their names and schools.

Then Esteban took over. "We've drafted the skeleton of a Raza Studies program for the district." Holding up stapled papers, he added, "Donaldo and Dolores are handing these out so you can take it home, read it, think about it. The next school board meeting is Tuesday the thirteenth, the Tuesday after the election. Got that? Next Tuesday we'll all be voting. Next Wednesday we'll be celebrating. Then we get to work again, and we show up at the school board meeting to explain this plan. We're on the agenda, and we need some of you to come support us."

A weather-beaten looking man who looked older than he probably was raised his hand. "I appreciate what you are doing," he said with a tone of respect one would use when addressing elders. "I've got four kids in the schools here, and I understand what you're saying about them losing interest. My concern is, will this plan help them succeed? I understand needing to know our history and all of that, but will it help them pass their tests and graduate?"

A few other parents nodded.

Dolores adjusted her purple-rimmed glasses. "*Gente*, that's why we need this plan. We teachers don't intend to ignore the tests our youth have to pass. On the contrary, we think they will not only pass, but surpass what the district expects of them, if we can get their intellects awakened. That's the challenge."

Esteban added, "It isn't just a curriculum problem, it's a bigger teaching problem. This curriculum will require teachers who understand our *jóvenes*, who understand what they're capable of when they see a purpose and when their teachers are willing to know them and stick with them through the hard stuff."

"Where do we find those teachers?" someone asked loudly.

"Yeah, there's a couple teachers like that in my daughter's school, but we need more," said a mother sitting near the front, still wearing a waitress uniform, obviously having come directly from work.

Esteban replied, "One of the things we need your help with is encouraging any of your *hijos* and *hijas* who are in university to consider becoming teachers. We can grow our own, but we need to be intentional about doing that."

"My son is thinking about it," someone remarked uncertainly. Someone else said, "My niece is majoring in ethnic studies, maybe she might want to become a teacher."

"Good," Esteban encouraged them. "We'll start a list of our young people who might want to teach in this community, and build some support for them. We'll also help the district find teachers who have the background to teach Raza Studies."

Dolores nodded and added, "The other thing we plan to do is identify teachers who are already in our schools, who might want to become more relevant to our kids, even if they don't become Raza Studies teachers themselves. Maybe some of them will want to get involved and help."

Esteban heard someone murmur, "Like Mrs. Westerfield at Milford." A couple other parents chimed in with names of more teachers.

Donaldo stepped forward. "The most immediate thing is that you read this plan and let us know what you think. We'll be at the district board meeting Tuesday after next. Come if you can."

From the back of the room, another teacher announced, "And next Tuesday we all vote!"

Several people applauded. Then one by one, parents began to stand, collect whatever they had brought with them, and talk as they milled toward the door.

As the room emptied, Esteban squeezed Brenda's hand. "Thanks for coming."

"Thanks for opening the meeting to an immigration attorney," she replied.

As they approached the parking lot, Esteban said, "Let's talk. I've been doing some hard thinking." He opened the door of his truck and motioned her inside.

When the door closed, he turned to her. "You know why I've been keeping you at arm's length."

"Yes, I do. And you know I've matured a lot over the last four years. I'm no longer that headstrong girl who thought she could romp around the country while you sat home waiting for me."

He fingered her dark, wavy hair. "I finally understood that you had to get out of L.A. You couldn't spend your life where you grew up, and you had every right to find the best law school for what you want."

"So now, here I am back in California. Esteban, I shouldn't have just expected us to pick right up where we left off four years ago. That was stupid on my part."

"And I shouldn't have just expected that we would walk straight from graduation to the wedding chapel. I should have paid more attention to your dreams than I did. When you left, well, there's no way I can explain how badly that hurt. It's taken me a long time to pick myself back up."

"Yeah," she said, "when you stopped answering my calls, replying to my texts, I knew things were bad. Now that I'm back, you have every right to be wary."

"Do I, Brenda? Should I still be wary of you?"
She looked deeply into his eyes. "I'm not going anywhere without you, ever again, Esteban. If I have to follow you around for the next fifty years to prove that to you, then that's what I'll do."

He laughed. "It won't take fifty years. Let's take it slow, and this time we don't move in together unless we're married first."

He pulled her close and kissed her deeply. He felt her trying to move closer, then break off the kiss, laughing. Placing her hand on the stick shift, she said, "Making out in this truck is too much like college! Can we go somewhere else?"

\* \* \* \* \*

María Paz was clearing dinner dishes from the table when the phone rang. "Marisela, *contesta*," she called out.

She was running hot water into the sink when Marisela appeared in the kitchen doorway. "*Mamá*, it's Diana's mother, she wants to talk to you."

Inwardly, María Paz sighed, wondering what kind of trouble the girls might have created this time. Although Marisela had been a relatively easy child to raise, as she approached adolescence there were days María Paz wished she could turn the clock back to diapers.

"OK, you can finish washing up here." An expression suggesting exasperation flitted across Marisela's face before she approached the sink and took the washrag.

María Paz went to the telephone. "Graciela, *¿qué tal?*" she greeted, intentionally trying to sound as though she had not a care in the world.

"*Muy bien*," Graciela replied. "Listen, something very interesting is happening with our schools, and I wanted you to know. This afternoon I attended a meeting over at my son Roberto's high school. Had you heard about the Raza Studies plan?"

"No," María Paz said uncertainly. "I guess I'm not sure what you mean by Raza Studies."

"It's what they call Chicano Studies, Mexican American Studies. Anyway, a group of teachers is planning an exciting Mexican American studies curriculum for our young people." Graciela sounded as if she had just discovered a wonderful new *mole* recipe.

María Paz sat down. "I don't understand," she said. "Why would they do that? I want my kids to get a good education so they can go on to the university."

"That's the whole point," said Graciela. Silence for a few seconds, then she continued, "You came to this country because your husband got a job with a TV station that has a large Mexican American audience, right?"

"Yes," María Paz said slowly, wondering where Graciela could possibly be going.

"TV stations like that are popular with us because most Anglo stations don't carry what we like to watch. You know, news about what's happening with Mexicans here, news from south of the border, our *telenovelas*, our music, things like that."

María Paz smiled to herself as she remembered being hooked while still living in Mexico on the wildly popular *telenovela* "*La Fea Más Bella,*" then being pleasantly surprised to learn it had been shown here in the U.S. as well.

"Well, what I'm learning is that it's the same thing with school. As our kids get older, a lot of them tune out. Roberto says school is boring. You've probably heard that."

María Paz frowned. "They don't go to school to be entertained, they go to learn." But as she spoke, she reflected on sons and daughters in families she had met at church who had quit school. She had assumed the parents weren't stressing education hard enough.

Graciela continued, "The Mexican American teachers at this meeting were saying school bores our *hijos* and *hijas* because too much of it isn't relevant to them. Our kids should be learning where they fit in as Americans, but instead they seem to learn how foreign they are. Maybe I'm not saying this clearly."

María Paz thought for a moment. She and Salvador considered themselves Mexicans temporarily living in the U.S., intending to return to Mexico one day. But what of their kids? What if they were to stay and eventually become U.S. citizens? And even as kids, she noticed Marisela bringing home books she particularly enjoyed that were written by authors with Spanish surnames.

"You're probably saying it clearly, it's just a new idea for me. I'd have to know more," María Paz replied.

"Of course. The plan as I understand it is to create four new classes, two for middle school and two for high school. In one of the middle school grades, instead of taking an English class where they read mostly Anglo literature, they could take a class where kids read literature by Mexican American and other Latino authors. Same at the high school level. It would be an option. And U.S. history, rather than studying it through Anglo eyes, they could study it through Mexican-American eyes. Something like, starting the story with Mexico and the *conquistadores* rather than starting it in Massachusetts."

"You seem excited about all this."

"I'm very excited, because the main thing I heard was their concern that our *hijos* and *hijas* do very well in school, get preparation for university. Esteban was clear about that."

"Esteban was there?" María Paz liked him, even though none of her kids had him as a teacher.

"Yes, he's one of the group's leaders."

Suddenly from the kitchen, "Move, *tonto!*"

"I just want another cookie!" Apparently Jaime was trying to take advantage of María Paz being occupied on the phone.

"Excuse me," she said to Graciela, then put her hand over the phone. "Jaime, come here. And Marisela, I don't want to hear you talk to your brother like that."

Jaime emerged, a victim expression on his face. María Paz placed her hand firmly on his shoulder, then said to Graciela, "I think I'm needed here. *Gracias por informarme*, you've given me something to think about. You'll tell me about any new developments?"

"*Por supuesto*," Graciela promised to keep María Paz in the loop. "*Hasta pronto!*"

After hanging up, María Paz looked at Jaime's downcast face. "No extra cookies, *mijo*. Period. *Nada*."

Jaime continued to study the floor, then nodded his head. "OK," he said.

"*Bueno*." María Paz lightly squeezed his shoulder, then released it. "Now, take out the garbage and then I'll read you a story."

*November, 2012*

Jessica's cell phone announced an incoming text. Hearing it bleep, she opened her eyes, rolled over, and glanced at the clock on the nightstand: 8:05 a.m. She rolled back over, throwing the blanket over her head. Volunteer work at the Democratic Headquarters didn't start until ten, she could sleep a little longer.

The cell phone bleeped again. Realizing she had already begun the climb from slumber to consciousness, she threw back the blanket and reached for it.

"Good morning, how R U?" she read, then saw it was from Tim. She sat up, wondering how to interpret his message. Maybe he wanted to talk. After all, it had been a week since they had communicated. Jessica smiled at the thought of Tim missing her. Then the smile retreated as she wondered whether she missed him.

Another thought – maybe he wanted reassurance that she hadn't thrown herself headlong down the stairs in despair over losing him. He might feel guilty – good. Or, he might think she was enough of a flake to kill herself – not good. Or, more mundane, it could be a question about this month's bills.

"OK, just woke up. U?" she texted back, then waited.

"Getting ready for work. New address 444 St Ambrose Ave apt 6." Jessica rolled her eyes and hurled the cell phone sharply toward the blanket at the foot of the bed. Damn, Tim was just letting her know he found an apartment. He didn't care at all how she was.

She slid out of bed. Might as well start the day.

An hour later, having showered, dressed, eaten breakfast, and perused the newspaper, she still felt annoyed. Tim kept popping into her brain like an unwelcome song taking up residence there. Had he moved in with someone? Surely he was seeing some woman or another. On the other hand, she knew he would have a cow if she talked about the research she and Cath did last Sunday. He wouldn't understand. So maybe whoever he was seeing could just have him.

She picked up her cell phone to call Phil, who felt more like a brother than her own flesh and blood brother Walt. Walt! She had totally forgotten to get back to him about Thanksgiving.

She hit Walt's home number, Walt being one of that dying breed of people who turned his cell phone off when he wasn't making or expecting a call.

"Hello?" Jan's voice rose up over the line. Walt's wife Jan, plump with henna-colored hair severely sculpted with hairspray, always started a greeting the second she picked up the receiver.

"Hey there, Jan, it's me, Jessica," she began, but was cut off by Jan's throaty gush. "Jessica, honey, how grand to hear from you. Walt tells me you two will be joining us for Thanksgiving. I can't wait to show you how we've redone the guest bedroom."

"Well, that's what I'm calling about. We decided to save some money and stay here for the holiday. Besides, you sometimes get a lot of snow by Thanksgiving," she said, hoping this excuse didn't sound lame.

"Oh, that's too bad." Jan's voice conveyed relief rather than disappointment. "I was hoping to see you. Maybe summer? Summertime is so nice here, you know, and of course you and Tim enjoy hiking. There's a new winery we must take you to, and by then I'll have our kitchen completely redone. You'll love it." Jessica wondered what in their spotty history together had given Jan the idea that she enjoyed seeing other people's home improvement projects, or that she and Tim craved winery hopping.

As soon as she concluded the call, she punched in Phil's number. He answered on the third ring.

"You're up earlier than I'd have expected," Jessica said.

"Jess!" Phil's voice conveyed enthusiasm at hearing her on the other end. "I'm going to work in the shop this morning, so I was up already. What's happening?"

"Just calling to see if you have any time to get together this weekend." Jessica paused, then added, "Tim texted me his new address a little while ago."

"He texted you? He didn't call?" Jessica heard exasperation in Phil's voice. Of the two brothers, Phil was often the more communicative, less likely than Tim to dodge difficult subjects. "Sure, how about getting a bite this evening, say around seven?"

"That works, I'm not doing anything. What happened to Samantha?" Samantha was a girl Phil had been seeing periodically since July. Emphasis on girl, not woman. To Jessica, Samantha might as well have been fifteen, although Phil swore she was in her early twenties.

"She's history. Not really my type. What did it was that she started dropping marriage hints."

"Ah," Jessica replied. Phil just gained back most of the points he had lost in her book when he started bringing Samantha around. "You're learning."

"I don't like admitting you were right, but you were right. Pick you up at seven."

Jessica spent the remainder of the morning and early afternoon at the Democratic Headquarters, working a phone bank for the first (and last) time in her life. On arrival, she learned that the door hangers had already been distributed. Vic and Linda, conspicuously absent, must have known what today's work would be.

Hating to receive political phone calls prior to elections, Jessica was leery about making them. Steve, however, explained the strategy research found effective. (Who knew this was something researchers actually studied?) Volunteers would call only registered Democrats in swing states. Rather than asking whether they planned to vote and who they planned to vote for, or pitching specific candidates, the intent of the call was only to get voters to the polls. So, they were to ask voters who had not already voted by mail where their polling station was, what time the voter anticipated going, whether the voter would be at work that day, and what route the voter planned to use to get there.

"All we want them to do is verbalize a plan to get from wherever they'll be to the polls. Research finds people are more likely to go vote if they've thought out a plan than if they haven't," he explained. "Your job is to be friendly. Just stick to when and how they plan to get to the voting booth. If they need a ride, write that down so we can pass the information on. Got it?"

Almost a dozen volunteers had shown up, armed with cell phones and chargers. Steve handed everyone a rough script to follow and a list of names and phone numbers, telling volunteers to mark who they reached so those names could be taken off a master list.

Jessica spent about four hours, minus a quick lunch break, making calls, feeling more like a mechanical robot with each one. Most people she reached were civil, a few even pleased to have someone to talk with about the election – or maybe just to talk with, period. But she also got several angry responses. One woman screamed, "Why can't you people leave us alone?" then hung up, leaving Jessica momentarily frozen.

After working her way through two lists, she had enough. Her phone was almost dead, giving her an excuse to leave. She gave the second completed list to Steve, then signaled to Cath that she was leaving. Cath, in the middle of a call, just waved. As she left the Headquarters, Jessica resolved this would be her only experience with phone banking. She realized she had looked forward to visiting with other volunteers, like last Saturday. But today's only conversations had been on the phone with strangers, which hardly worked as social interaction. Maybe after the election there would be volunteer opportunities of a more social nature.

It was a little after seven when Phil rang the doorbell. "This is like a date," Jessica joked.

"If it were, I might have put on something less ragged." Phil looked down at his old T-shirt under a grey polar fleece jacket. "So what are you hungry for?" He steered her out to his car, hand under her elbow as if she actually were his date.

Jessica liked riding in his Viper. The small, sleek two-seater propelled by a powerful engine turned heads on the road like a movie star at the beach. While most other people Jessica knew saved up to buy a house, Phil saved up for wheels. He had bought the Viper several months ago on Craig's list, selling an old Porsche through the same venue. Although Phil's dress style was sloppy, he gave his Viper as much care as first-time parents give their newborns.

"What do you feel like eating?" he repeated as he buckled his seat belt.

"How about Italian? Fantini's, where they have those great raviolis."

"Fantini's it is," Phil said as he gunned the motor. Doing that before backing down the driveway announced the Viper's presence, but Phil watched where he was going and rarely broke the speed limit. Jessica appreciated that even though he loved showing her off (the Viper was a "her," he had explained the first time Jessica referred to the car as "it"), he was a careful driver.

Fantini's was a small, unpretentious family-owned restaurant on a busy street. Whenever it was full, like now, finding parking was challenging since the restaurant's parking lot had enough spaces for only about half its customers. Inside, tables were squeezed together cozily, but Jessica didn't mind since the food made her feel like she had been suddenly whisked off to Tuscany.

Over ravioli, bruschetta and wine, Jessica opened up the subject of Tim. "So who's he seeing? Did he move in with her?"

Phil smiled wryly. "One thing I like about you, Jessica, you don't beat around the bush."

"Neither do you. So tell me."

"I've only actually seen him with a lady once, a couple of weeks ago. They were having pizza when I stopped in to pick up an order. I don't even remember her name."

With a tone of disbelief, Jessica probed, "Come on, Phil, if he left me for someone, there's more to it than that. I can take it."

Phil popped a piece of bruschetta in his mouth as he waved a hand pleading innocence. "That's it, Jess. That's my one and only encounter with Miss What's Her Name. He's not living with her, if that's what you wonder, I helped him move on Wednesday. I've seen the place."

"OK, well, what was she like?"

"Blond." Phil thought a moment. "Short, I think, but it was hard to tell because she was sitting down. Lots of make-up, too much, if you ask me. Wearing a ruffly blouse."

Jessica wondered why men were clueless about relationship signals. Who cares if her blouse had ruffles, what Jessica really wanted to know was whether Tim was in love with her. Taking a more direct tack, she asked, "Could you tell if Tim loves her?"

"I have no idea," Phil said. "He did tell me a month ago about someone named Marcie who hit on him at work and looked at him with goo-goo eyes, but this chick wasn't named Marcie."

Then he shifted gears. "Now be honest with me, Jess. Do you wish you two were back together? You haven't struck me as a happy couple for some time."

"Well, I just didn't think we were about to fall off a cliff. Even though you did warn me. Sure, I used to think about what it would be like if we split. I just wasn't expecting it to happen."

"You weren't expecting him to do the splitting, that's my guess." Phil said.

"No, I guess I wasn't."

"And you weren't expecting him to think you have the hots for someone else. You're worried about who he might be seeing behind your back, but it went both ways, you know." Phil managed to accuse her without sounding accusatory.

"But –" Jessica wasn't sure where to go with this observation. Yes, she certainly had a crush on Esteban, but no, that relationship hadn't gone anywhere. Yet.

Phil continued, "But here's the other thing you don't pay enough attention to. Tim really does not like that historical research you're into. Do you have any idea why?"

"Because I'm too much of a nerd?"

"There is that. I'd call it bookishness, not nerdiness. But there's more to it. How much do you know about our family?" Phil leaned back in his chair.

"I know you grew up poor. I've only met your folks twice, you know. I had the feeling Tim wants to keep me away from them."

"OK, well, let me add some details." Phil took a deep breath. "Our mom was a product of rape, abuse, whatever you want to call it. An uncle sexually abused our grandma in her early teens. When she turned up pregnant, her folks tossed her out. She hooked up with a gambler, I never heard much about him. They lived somewhere over near Fresno. They didn't get married or anything. He helped our grandma and Mom survive, more or less, except our grandma got tuberculosis and died way before we ever came along."

Jessica was stunned. "I never heard any of this."

"No, Tim would rather forget it. I would too, for that matter. Anyway. Mom couldn't wait to get away, so she married the first thing that came along. That would be our dad." Phil paused to gulp down some water, then continued.

"Dad came out to California from Georgia, probably looking for place to surf. After he and Mom got married, he just drifted from job to job. Then we came along. As we grew up, we vowed not to be like him. We used to kid around and say we were going to college and then become Wall Street bankers. We did it to get his goat, neither of us wanted to work on Wall Street. Hell, we didn't even know what that meant, we just said it to get a reaction out of Dad."

Jessica couldn't visualize Phil on Wall Street, but she could picture Tim wearing a charcoal grey Armani suit, tasteful silk tie over pale blue shirt, crisp hundred-dollar bills in a snakeskin wallet.

Phil continued, "Dad always seemed pissed about the idea of us going to college. He called it expensive and 'prissy,' that was his word for it. He said the only people to get into places like Berkeley were either the rich, prissy kids or the affirmative action kids."

Jessica didn't know what to say. She was beginning to understand why Tim stayed away from his parents.

Phil continued, "So, you see, our grandparents on Mom's side included a rapist – or a gambler, depending on which one you consider her dad – and a lady who never really recovered from sexual abuse. On Dad's side, they were shit-poor and lived about three thousand miles away. We only saw them once when somehow they managed to come out to California to visit. They didn't stay long. I was about ten, and all I remember was that they seemed really disappointed that Dad hadn't become a pharmacist or a lawyer or something like that. I thought they were money-grubbers. Maybe that isn't fair, but I never saw them after that."

"Your grandparents are all dead, aren't they?" Jessica asked, trying to connect what Phil was saying with the little she knew of their family.

"Far as I know," he replied. "But here's the thing. Neither of us wants to look back into our past. I mean, why would we? For us, the best thing to do is turn the page, chart out a new course, look to the future. For me, that course is pretty simple. For Tim, it's not so simple. The Wall Street banker was a joke to me, but not to him, as I gradually realized. He wants to be looked up to, and he wants to raise a family in a flash place people envy."

Jessica nodded.

"So here you come along, falling in love with the neighborhood Tim's working to get away from, and digging up all the stories you can find about your own family's past. It's disconcerting, to say the least. And instead of finding the kind of dirt that's all we have to show, you seem to have these cool ancestors who got written up in the newspapers, lived in nice little loving families, on nice little farms ..."

"With tornadoes, babies dying in epidemics – it wasn't all idyllic, Phil," Jessica interrupted. "Besides, the history part is helping me think about things. Like, I'm starting to get why the Mexican families don't want to just Americanize and dump all things Mexican. And I'm starting to see this community tradition in my own family's past that I wish hadn't gotten lost." Jessica felt emotions welling up as she came close to verbalizing her own loneliness.

"OK, I take back what I said about nice little families on nice little farms," Phil backtracked. Then he looked directly into Jessica's eyes. "But do you see why Tim gets this knee-jerk reaction every time you talk about your latest findings? Do you see why he feels like he's losing his dream the more you identify with that school you're teaching in?"

Jessica looked away as tears sprang up in her eyes. She bit her lip. Then as anger welled up, she turned to Phil and declared, "Well he sure wouldn't like me looking at advantages white people had back then."

"Advantages white people had?" Phil was taken aback.

"Well, yeah. I mean, I had assumed European immigrants came here at the same rung on the ladder as Black people after the Civil War, but it turns out, at least where my ancestors lived, the immigrants could ascend a bunch of rungs on the ladder that were closed to the Black people."

Phil dropped his head onto the table, then raised it. "Why would you open up all of that? What does that have to do with you, or with anything here and now? Jessica, can't you see what you're doing?"

"Well, I grew up hearing that our immigrant ancestors came here with nothing but the shirts on their backs and worked their way up. I wanted to know if that was the whole story, and I'm starting to see it wasn't." Jessica stared back at Phil defensively.

Phil grimaced, then fired back, "So what you're saying to us is, Hey guys, you might come from slime, but the game was actually rigged in favor of white slime, so get over it. Is that what you're saying?"

"I'm not sure, that doesn't sound good ..." Jessica mumbled.

"You better believe it doesn't. There might be a history of racial discrimination, but those days are over, Ma'am. They were over at least fifty years ago. We've got a Black President now, which proves my point. If you ever want to think about reconciling with Tim, don't go talking that shit to him."

Jessica studied her plate as if it would advise her what to say next. Good thing she finished most of the raviolis, since her appetite had vanished. She glanced at Phil, his face now a cold mask, eyes like ice. Then, gradually the ice softened.

"You can lift up stones and see bugs crawling around underneath, but just think about why you're doing that. Some stones are better left alone," he said.

"Dessert menu?" Their tense silence was broken by the waitress, who had been chatty when they first sat down, but now looked harried as she scurried from table to table.

"Nah, just the bill please," said Phil, his easy-going expression returning.

*November, 2012*

The day after Barack Obama defeated Mitt Romney in the Presidential election turned out somewhat differently than Jessica had anticipated. It wasn't the election outcome that was different, nor her colleagues' varied reactions, but rather the attention her class gave to it. Or, to put it more accurately, the lack of attention.

Three weeks previously, she had planned a research and writing project that would focus on the election. Students would brainstorm six key issues to gather opinions about. Six small groups would each develop interview questions about one issue, then every student would interview someone. Students would write up their interviews and make copies for their group. They would analyze and synthesize their own group's interviews, each student drafting a multi-paragraph, well-organized expository paper (Jessica's attempt to breathe life into the fifth grade writing standards). Groups would exchange papers for feedback, then use it to revise their own papers. If all went well, she pictured the class creating a newspaper to distribute to the rest of the school reporting pre-election opinions in light of election results.

But that wasn't what happened. When Jessica had proposed the idea, students responded with comments like "That sounds boring," and "We've been hearing about the election since third grade. Can we do something else?" When she asked what they would like to research, she had been surprised by the topic they selected: school.

"But you've been hearing about school since you were in, well, preschool," she countered, puzzlement written all over her face.

"Yeah," said Mike, "but there are things about school no one ever really explains to us."

"Like what?" Jessica asked.

"Like our lunches," grumbled Marisela. "Who plans them, anyway?"

Tall, thin Jennifer elaborated, "Sometimes they're pretty good and sometimes they're terrible. But we don't know who decides what we will eat, or why they make certain decisions."

Jerome added, "We aren't even supposed to share food. Like if Álvaro has an apple and doesn't want to eat it, he's supposed to toss it out instead of giving it to me." At this, Álvaro stuck his tongue out at Jerome, who continued, "Is that a law or something?"

"OK, school lunches," Jessica conceded, writing "School" on the board, and "lunches" underneath. "What else?"

"What all do principals do?" piped up Timmy. "I mean, we see them in the halls, and in the office when we get in trouble, but what else do they do all day?"

Jessica forced a straight face, laughing inwardly – Timmy was no stranger to trips to the principal's office.

"Yeah, and how do they become principals?" Jana added. "Do they have to go to school and take a class in how to be a principal?"

"How come we don't use iPads in our classes?" Diana asked. "I saw this TV show where everyone was using iPads, and all we have is the stupid computer lab."

And so it went. Jessica shifted her plan to the new topic. There were still six groups, each with an area for investigation, and each student responsible for interviewing someone. Last week students shared write-ups of their interviews with group members. Monday she walked them through analysis: identifying commonalities and differences among their interviews. Yesterday she helped students make outlines based on their analysis. Today, while some students had begun to draft papers, she helped others who were still unsure what it means to analyze.

By lunchtime, Jessica felt the beginnings of a headache, mainly from repeated efforts to get three boys to find commonalities among their interviews rather than simply reporting each one separately. As she locked her classroom door, she saw Esteban approaching.

"Great that we didn't have to stay up all night to find out who won," he greeted her with a big grin.

"And great who won," Jessica replied, falling into step as they headed to the teacher's lounge.

"I wanted to catch you for a minute," he said.

Jessica felt her heart lurch. Might he ask her out? She wasn't even sure he knew she and Tim had separated.

He continued, "You know that Raza Studies meeting I went to last week? We're planning a curriculum for the district. Next Tuesday, we'll be presenting our proposal to the school board, and the Saturday after that we're holding a rally. We're trying to get as much support as we can, and I thought you might want to participate."

The music that had begun to play in Jessica's heart abruptly vanished. She quickly retrieved mental duct tape to affix her smile in place, hoping he wouldn't sense her disappointment.

"Ah, well, yeah, uh, maybe," she stumbled, then regained composure. "Can you tell me a little more?"

"Sure. The rally will be held from noon to two at Cesar Chavez Park. There will be lots of parents and some teachers. I think someone has organized a Mariachi band as well. We'll have signs for people to hold, and we plan to have an information table."

They stopped, having reached the door to the teachers lounge. Two teachers behind them scooted by, on the way in.

Esteban continued, "At that meeting, a mother of one of your kids mentioned you as a great teacher who might want to help us out."

Jessica felt a brief surge of pleasure. "Wow, that's nice to hear."

"I'd really like to see you there, if you can make it."

"No flirting with ladies in the hall," joked fourth-grade teacher Ralph, as he came up behind them on the way into the lounge.

"At least I have good taste," replied Esteban with a laugh as Jessica felt her cheeks burn. Turning back to her, he said, "Put it on your calendar," then turned and walked away.

Momentarily confused, Jessica froze in place. He said he'd really like to see her at the rally. He'd like to see her. Put it on her calendar. But then why didn't he offer to pick her up? If Ralph thought he was flirting with her, perhaps he was. Or perhaps he wasn't.

"So are you going in or coming out? Or just standing there as a greeter?" Cath's sudden appearance shook Jessica back to life.

"Going in." Jessica followed Cath into the lounge.

Jessica's students may not have been interested in discussing the election, but the topic dominated conversations in the teachers lounge. Jessica and Cath passed four Romney supporters in a huddle that resembled the aftermath of a funeral, while another group relived election returns as if they were last night's winning basketball game. As they sat, Cath commented, "Phone banking paid off."

Marge, sitting across the table, beamed, "Whatever it took to get people out. Wasn't it grand?"

"You phone banked?" asked Ralph.

"We both did," replied Jessica, launching into a description of their experience the previous Saturday. For the first time in Jessica's memory, Ralph frowned without responding.

As they returned to their classrooms fifteen minutes later, Cath suggested, "Want to stop off for a celebratory toast on the way home?"

"Sure. Meet you at your classroom?"

Quarter to four found Jessica and Cath seated at a table in a café that doubled as a coffee house and microbrewery, sipping local brew and sharing a large order of sweet potato fries. The café, located in a renovated warehouse, was furnished with well-worn wooden chairs and tables, currently unoccupied; old stuffed armchairs and small sofas, tucked into corners, were occupied at the moment by people who looked like university students, studying quietly or working on laptops.

Jessica and Cath took one of the tables. They toasted the election results and their satisfaction at having played a small role.

Thinking about phone banking led Jessica back to her dinner with Phil. She recounted his reaction to her mention of research on race and the job market during the 1800s. "He texted me the next day to apologize for over-reacting. He said I hit a raw nerve when I talked about white people having advantages."

Cath shook her head in agreement. "When you grow up poor, it's pretty hard to see yourself as having any kind of advantages at all. Even if you do, the problems you face are so big."

"Yeah. He went on to say that he and Tim always felt burned hearing about affirmative action because they felt like they were the ones penalized because of their race. So then here I come along saying they're wrong. At least, I think they are, but I guess I'm not sure."

"Who'd they vote for, do you know?" Cath asked.

"Phil said he was voting for Obama, but 'not because he's Black.'" She pantomimed quotation marks. "Can you believe he said that? I mean, do you ever hear a white person say they're voting for someone 'but not because they're white?'"

"I think having a Black family in the White House is forcing people to grapple with race in a way they haven't had to before."

Jessica sighed. "Yeah, and I don't even know who Tim would have voted for. He often votes Democratic, but this time, I really don't know. And obviously I haven't compared notes with him."

The two sat silently, then Jessica asked, "Did you hear about the Raza Studies thing Esteban is working on?"

"The Raza Studies thing," Cath repeated, clearly having no idea what Jessica was talking about.

"Raza Studies is Chicano Studies," Jessica explained.

"I know that, but what 'thing' are you referring to?"

"A group of teachers is working on a Raza Studies curriculum for the district. I don't know much about it yet. They're having a rally, not this coming Saturday, but the one after, and Esteban asked if I'd want to participate."

"So, are you going to?" asked Cath.

"Probably. Well, I don't know." Jessica frowned. "He said he'd really like to see me there."

"Oooh, this sounds promising!"

"Well, but he didn't say anything about picking me up. So I don't know if he wants to see me personally, or if he's just trying to boost turnout. The other thing is that I should find out what the curriculum is like. I don't want to just show up without knowing what I'm supporting."

Cath smiled without commenting.

"In my classroom, I can see some of the Mexican kids getting excited about books they can relate to. Esteban loaned me some books written by Mexican authors, and I got more from the library. A lot of the kids, white kids as well as Mexican kids, really do get into it when they can connect with what they're reading," Jessica said.

Cath prompted, "So you would show up to support a curriculum the kids can relate to. And the question is?"

Jessica twisted the corner of her napkin. "Well, it's one thing to shift a few things in my own curriculum a little bit. It's another thing to step out in public with mostly Mexicans to support big changes in the district's curriculum. And I keep thinking about Phil and Tim. It's like, what I'm doing right now in my classroom is just making a few adjustments for my own students. But is Raza Studies too big of a change? Is it putting Mexicans ahead of everyone else?"

"And what do you think?"

"Stop sounding like a psychiatrist, Cath!"

"Sorry, I was just trying to prompt you because I thought you needed to think out loud," Cath apologized. "Given the dropout rate of Mexican students in our high schools, and the low test scores of so many of them from second grade on, it's a little hard to see where something that directly addresses them is putting them ahead of everyone else."

"Yeah, that's what I was thinking," Jessica agreed. "I just don't know if I'm ready to step out at a rally."

"Are you asking me to go with you?"

Jessica brightened. "Great idea! Want to?"

Cath rolled her eyes. "You aren't even subtle."

"Really, I wasn't thinking about asking you, but it's a great idea," Jessica beamed.

"I'll get more information from Esteban about the proposal, so we know what we're holding up signs supporting. Let me know if he offers to pick you up." She gave a knowing wink.

Blushing, Jessica drained her glass as the waitress put their check on the table.

\* \* \* \* \*

Saturday morning, as Jessica sat at the kitchen table with her third cup of coffee, she studied the bright orange flier Esteban gave her about next Saturday's rally. The background featured a muted gray raised fist, like the Black Power fist, but clutching a pencil – a variation Jessica had noticed of a logo on a teacher activist group's website. The flier boldly announced the time and location of the rally, inviting all interested in Mexican American studies to participate. At the bottom were the names of three teachers organizing the event, one being Esteban.

She wondered what he was doing this weekend. She rinsed breakfast dishes, emptied the last of the coffee into her mug, and retreated to the patio where the morning sun was gently shoving aside the night's chill. She stared at the garden, which stared reproachfully back as if she were a negligent stranger it knew a long time ago, but whose name it could no longer recall.

Jessica would be going to the rally next Saturday with Cath. Although she had fantasized Esteban offering to pick her up, he hadn't. She wondered what he wears on weekends. At school, he always looks sharp – freshly ironed shirt, khaki pants rather than jeans. She wondered if she should call him, let him know Tim left, ask him for coffee. What if he said no? What if he said yes?

Jessica's ringtone abruptly shattered her fantasy. Picking up her phone, she saw it was Tim. Darn, not Esteban.

"Hi there," she greeted him.

"Hi Jess, what are you up to?"

"Just sitting here on the patio contemplating my existence on the planet. What's up?" Maybe she wasn't supposed to ask him that, maybe that's why he wants space.

"Not much. Getting ready for work. Best Buy's going full out into Christmas this weekend," he replied.

Jessica shook her head, murmuring "Amazing." Tim would know what she meant, as they had often discussed the lunacy of forcing everyone into Christmas when Thanksgiving hadn't even happened yet. Business owners swore Christmas music and decorated trees made people feel like opening their wallets. Jessica swore it drove away people like her, but there wasn't much in her wallet anyway, so she probably didn't count.

"Phil told me he enjoyed seeing you last weekend. He said you've been keeping yourself busy. I didn't know you like political work," Tim said as if she had been keeping a big secret from him.

"It was news to me, too," she replied. "Cath's the instigator. But to tell you the truth, it feels kind of good knowing I might have made the tiniest bit of difference in the election outcome, even if the work itself wasn't exactly thrilling."

"Yeah, well, I decided to sit this one out."

"You did? Why?" Jessica was genuinely surprised.

"I just wasn't excited about either candidate. I couldn't identify with them." Jessica could picture Tim running his hand over his hair, like he often did when thinking. "I just have this feeling Obama can't get away from racial preferences and giving handouts to people, but Romney seems to have the spine of cooked spaghetti, so I couldn't vote for him either."

"Romney's the one with racial preferences, and they're all white." This just popped out before Jessica could look at it carefully, edit it, weigh its possible impact on Tim. His silence on the other end told her the impact wasn't good.

"Well, I won't keep you from your research or your political work, or whatever else you're doing these days." Tim's voice suddenly sounded edgy, distant.

"Tim, wait, that just jumped out," Jessica said, although she also knew she meant what she said.

"Even if you just thought it rather than saying it, you seem to be changing, Jessica. And it's hard for me to relate to the new you. Sorry, but that's how it is."

"Maybe we could meet and just talk," Jessica ventured while wondering whether she really wanted to "just talk" with Tim, since their talking seemed more and more to lead to arguments.

"Talk about?" Tim asked.

"Well, I don't know. But talking on the phone doesn't seem to bring out our best."

"If you can figure out what does bring out our best, as you put it, let me know. Anyway, I've gotta run."

"OK, bye," Jessica said, her insides feeling hollow. The line went dead.

She stared at the dried out garden, wondering when it was going to finally start raining, and why her eyes were filling with tears. She missed him. And it was true that she was changing. She wished she could talk with him without feeling the need to edit out this or that. They used to be able to talk. Or maybe the things they used to talk about weren't very deep. Maybe what she craved wasn't their old relationship, but one she hadn't yet experienced.

She jerked herself to her feet. If she didn't have a husband anymore, and didn't have a best friend, at least not one who was free this weekend, she could leap back in time and spend part of the weekend with the ancestors.

As she hauled herself upstairs, she wondered what it was about the ancestors' families that seemed to keep everyone together. Did couples ever drift apart, finding themselves stuck in the same house and bed with someone they didn't relate to anymore? Or maybe never really related to in the first place?

Maybe they simply expected less of marriage since their nuclear families were nested within extended families and communities. Take Lydia, for example. She might become pissed with Willie – she probably was, on a regular basis. She probably got tired of waiting on him, doing the same routine of housework everyday. But her life was also populated with sisters, cousins, and church members. Maybe growing up with all those people around, functioning as a large extended family, buffered the jagged edges of individual relationships.

And what about Mary, spending half her young adulthood pregnant? Uprooting her family every couple of years because her husband was transferred was probably hard, although she seemed to move seamlessly from one tight church community to another, welcomed in each new place due to her status as the preacher's wife. However, Jessica knew she would not want to get stuck with all the cleaning, cooking, and diapers, just because of her sex. She liked her job and wouldn't want to have to stay single to keep it, like women teachers did back then.

When she reached her desk, Jessica noticed a large padded envelope, still unopened, that arrived in yesterday's mail, probably a book she had ordered. She ripped it open, finding a Xeroxed copy of

173

a memory book put together by a Boody family. She had seen it referenced on a website maybe a month ago, along with an order form. She had forked over $15 because she recognized the German family surname from the Blue Mound plat map, then promptly forgot about it.

Opening the book, she found a wide variety of items – personal reflections by the oldest still-living family members, passed down recipes, photos of family members including the family patriarch Johann, and old church records. Perusing the church records, Jessica realized some were minutes of committee meetings of Boody's German Methodist Episcopal Church, dated as far back as 1895. Although she didn't see Willie's or Lydia's names, John popped up here and there, as did Friedrich and Lydia's father Henry.

She wondered what Willie did after the grand jury refused to hold anyone accountable for the lynching. Had he done anything, and would either this book or Decatur newspaper articles reveal anything?

*August, 1895*

"Willie's your son-in-law, Henry," Johann remarked in his deep German accent one sweltering evening, shifting discussion away from plans for construction of a preacher apartment, during a weekly meeting of the church's building committee. "Why is he following his brother to Iowa? It was bad enough that John and his family left."

Henry liked Johann, who had emigrated from Germany a few years ago and owned a 300-acre farm about a half-mile east of his own. An imposing man with a full beard, blue eyes, and a gregarious personality, he dove right into church business as though he had always lived in Boody. At the moment, he was waving a copy of *The Evening Bulletin*, pointing to a paragraph announcing the impending move of Willie and family to Storm Lake, Iowa.

"John and Willie have always done things together," Henry replied, as he thought about the brothers' close on-going partnership. Wrinkling his brow, he continued, "Whenever I ask, he just tells me how much more land he'll be able to buy there."

But Henry, too, was puzzled. The brothers' farms were thriving, Willie's work as a supervisor was well-regarded, the four children were doing well in school. Willie and Lydia enjoyed the company of good friends and family. Why leave?

"I was surprised as anyone when John sold me his farm last year. I don't trust the land agency that's been coming in here, I think our boys are being sold bad *Äpfel*," Johann continued, referring to the Northwestern Land Agency, a firm of speculators that had recently purchased acreage in Storm Lake to sell to Illinois farmers. The agency had been actively distributing pamphlets describing the land, located in Iowa's Great Corn Belt, as cheap but potentially prosperous.

Friedrich said, "*Ja*, and now Willie's about to sell those very same 160 acres his father bought from the government almost fifty years ago." Then he sighed and declared, "I just might buy 'em from him myself, and keep 'em in the family."

"We'll arm wrestle for that!" Johann boomed.

"You're just trying to expand your empire, Johann," teased Henry, whose own farm had never grown beyond forty acres.

"I just want to leave each of my boys his own forty acres and my girls a good bit of cash for their households when they get married," replied Johann.

Henry shook his head. "If Lydia had her way, they'd probably stay put right here. But Willie gets hold of an idea and you can't stop him."

"Maybe he's tired of those colored problems over in Decatur that come to the Board of Supervisors," Johann suggested.

Henry shook his head. "No, I never hear him talk about what's going on the city. He's a farm boy, and just concentrates on the interests of us farmers. I think he sees this move to Iowa as following in his father's footsteps. His father came here from Germany and made good, and now these two sons are trying to get even farther up in the world."

"Well, I don't trust that land agency," Johann repeated.

"I hope you aren't writing all this down in the minutes, Johann," said *Pfarrer* Kies, who was chairing the meeting. "Um, can we get back to the matter of the preacher's apartment?"

While the business of the meeting resumed, Henry recalled that Lydia had, in fact, initially opposed the move, and was angry that Willie seemed so determined, despite her opposition. But then she visited Storm Lake herself, joining one of the excursions the land agency arranged in collaboration with the Illinois Central Railroad. When she returned, she reported liking what she saw.

Storm Lake, as she explained to her parents, was the name of both the lake and the picturesque village perched back from its northeastern shore. She described clouds breaking, slivers of sun glimmering off the lake like swarms of summer fireflies. Two- and three-story brick buildings lined the village's main street, still muddy from spring rains when she visited. Budding trees dotted the landscape, and prairie grasses determinedly thrust green shoots through the mud.

She found John and his family, having already relocated, bubbling with optimism about the land's potential. John and his boys were beginning to drain swamp water so they could start spring planting. Lydia liked the fact that the Land Agency offered temporary housing (of which John's family was making use), assistance with land records, and assistance draining swamps.

Although she returned to Boody still vacillating, she told her parents she had gained a new sense of possibility. This would be an adventure for them. She was drawn to the idea of working closely with Willie again, like when they were first married, without the distractions of local politics. And since the train directly connected Storm Lake with Decatur, they wouldn't be all that far away.

As Henry rode home after the meeting, however, he felt a sense of foreboding. Boody might be small, and Willie might want to stretch beyond its bounds, but for people like them, Boody was safe. It was home.

*November, 2012*

"*Papá*, can I use your computer?" María Paz heard Marisela ask her father Friday evening, one of his evenings off work.

He looked up from *El Observador*, the newspaper he was reading. "Of course, *mija*, what for?"

"I'm doing a report on this lady." Marisela studied the cover of a book in her hands as she struggled to sound out the author's surname. "Louise Erd – Erd-ich, Erdrich."

"May I see it, *mija*?" María Paz asked. Marisela handed it to her. *The Birchbark House*. After briefly studying its cover, she asked, "What's it about? What's a birchbark house?"

"It's an old-fashioned Indian kind of house," Marisela said.

"Is it a story book?" Salvador asked, craning his neck to see the cover.

"Yeah," Marisela replied. "It's about this little Indian girl more than 200 years ago who lived with an adopted family in Minnesota. Her real family died of some kind of disease." She retrieved the book from her mother, opened it, and scanned a couple of pages. "Small pox. That's what it was."

Salvador and María Paz exchanged a smile. "Sounds interesting," María Paz said.

"Oh, it is," Marisela replied. "She does cool stuff, like she learns how to tan a hide and make shoes with it, and she learns how to drive crows away so they don't eat up the corn."

"So what do you need to look up on the computer?" María Paz asked in her 'let me help you' tone of voice.

"Umm, let's see." Marisela pulled a folded piece of paper from between pages near the end of the book. "OK, here's the questions. Number one. When and where was the author born? Number two. What is the author's ethnic background? Number three. Describe the author's education."

María Paz looked down at the rumpled sheet and read along with Marisela. "Number four, Why do you think the author wrote this book? That's a very interesting question!"

"*Mamita*," Marisela said in her 'I can do this myself' tone of voice.

"Alright, but let me at least find out who this woman is that you're researching for a report. We'll do question number one together, and then you'll have to figure out the rest by yourself." María Paz glanced at Salvador who, having witnessed these kinds of exchanges many times before, looked as though he was trying to maintain a straight face.

A few minutes later, María Paz emerged from the bedroom and sat down across from Salvador. "I'm letting her do her own work."

Salvador just raised his eyebrows and smiled. María Paz continued, "This woman is a very well-known Indian author. Her ethnic group is Ojibwa. But Ojibwa people call themselves something else, a long word that starts with A. They live in the north part of this country, near Canada."

"That sounds like question two," Salvador observed.

"I was interested, I wanted to know about her." María Paz smiled sheepishly as she recognized her tendency to help the kids when they didn't want help. "She writes novels for adults as well as children. Some of her books have won awards. A very interesting person for Marisela to research, I think."

"Maybe one day our little girl will write books," Salvador said, then pointed to the newspaper. "Or become a reporter."

"Kind of like her *papá*," María Paz kissed his cheek lightly. "I'm glad her school is teaching about people like this Louise woman, something that makes children excited about learning. Salvador, what would you think of a program in the schools that focuses on Mexicans?"

"Is this a way of segregating Mexican students?" Salvador asked.

"No, I don't think so, this seems to be a way of broadening things for all the students. Graciela told me that some classes in middle school and high school would focus on Latino Americans rather than just plain Americans."

"*Pues*, if you mean something like adding my TV station into the mix of TV stations available to everyone, that's probably a good idea."

"I didn't think so at first, but I'm starting to think so now." With that, she picked up pages of *El Observador* Salvador had finished, and began to read.

\* \* \* \* \*

Holding a plate of steaming microwaved pasta, Jessica sank into a chair in front of the TV and clicked on the news. She was bushed, as usual, on Friday. She was about to dive into the pasta when she heard the news headline: "… oil rig explosion has killed two platform workers in the Gulf of Mexico." Only two years since the huge oil well explosion in the same general area. This one apparently was smaller, but still worrying. As the news moved on to the latest David Petraeus story, Jessica ate.

When the weather report came on, she realized she had tuned out the news while reflecting on the literature assignment's successful beginning. Her students were starting new children's novels. Working with Sharon, the librarian, Jessica had further diversified her classroom collection. She added novels by a few American Indian authors and several African American authors. Novels set in the past and novels set in the present. Several award-winning novels. Novels about athletes, artists, chess players, children in wheelchairs, and children who didn't fit in.

The first writing assignment was guided by research questions about the author. Next week they would write about the author from a third-person point of view, then use the same information to try writing from a first-person point of view. She was used to someone complaining whenever she introduced a new assignment, but this time the children were so engaged picking out a book that no one murmured a peep. Although she knew they would dive into material related to their interests, until the last month or so, she hadn't considered a book's cultural context as something they would notice or care about.

The meteorologist, looking like a fashion model for Ralph Lauren, announced tomorrow would be sunny. A good thing for the Raza studies rally. The rally! Jessica's stomach flipped every time she thought about it. The only reason she could identify for being nervous was that this would be the first time seeing Esteban away from school.

She pried herself away from that thought, then went to the fridge in search of a next course. Dessert – chocolate ice cream directly from the carton. As she licked the spoon, she wondered why Willie and Lydia decided to leave Boody. They had everything there, right? Family, friends, prosperous farm. Maybe Willie wanted to avoid the county's racial issues, or at the very least, he had the luxury of being able to turn his back and walk away from them. Maybe it was plain and simple greed, since they seemed to think they could sell the old farm to buy a bigger one. Maybe adventure. Surely they figured there'd be a German church in Storm Lake that would take them in, like Heinrich and Mary always found.

Jessica realized she had not checked on Heinrich and Mary for a month or so, when they were recent arrivals in Quincy and Mrs. Gratz's husband had been harassed, regarded as a socialist agitator. She tossed out the empty ice cream carton, then went upstairs to the computer. Hunting through census records, she found that Heinrich and family had moved yet again, this time to Muscatine, Iowa.

#### CHAPTER 24

*September, 1897*

Farmington, Wapello, Quincy, St. Louis, and now Muscatine. Mary knew uprooting the family every couple years would be difficult indeed if the German community didn't welcome them in each new location. Would it be so if Heinrich weren't a *Pfarrer*? Hard to say.

Spread out on a blanket, she and the family were enjoying their usual Sunday afternoon picnic with the church congregation. Or, more accurately, Mary held dozing three year-old Ada and visited with her friend Anke while the rest of the family scattered like crickets. Fifteen-year-old Carl, who thrived on kicking or throwing any kind of ball, was pitching baseball in a game that included his two younger brothers. Eighteen-year-old Lydia had drifted off to share whatever gossip enticed other eighteen-year-olds, and Mamie, at fourteen, let younger sister Flora join her church choir friends as they harmonized songs learned at school. Heinrich was off commiserating about politics.

Anke's husband Klaus worked in a lumber mill, one of many bustling industries in this Mississippi River town. What a dear pair they were! When Mary first met them, their relationship as a married couple escaped her. Tall, slender Klaus, hairline rapidly receding, boasted a full beard and mustache, and eyes as blue as the river on a June morning. Anke, on the other hand, reminded Mary of a typical schoolmarm – short and plump of stature, graying straight hair pulled sternly into a knot at the nape of her neck. While Klaus laughed readily, one had to gently coax a smile from Anke.

Suddenly Anke cried out as a small rock zinged past her head. Both women ducked reflexively, then looked up. Two unfamiliar boys, perhaps age ten, were yelling at them.

"Get out of Manila!" one shouted in English.

"German Catholics, go home!" the other yelled.

A man, possibly their father, grabbed their arms, while a woman, perhaps their mother, looked on with an alarmed expression.

"They aren't Catholic," said the man sternly as he shook one of them.

"But they're German, and the Germans are interfering with the Americans," the boy wailed.

"In the Philippines, not here in Iowa." The man pulled the two boys next to him, then all four continued on.

Anke's eyes trailed after them. Then she turned back to Mary. "We could have been hurt," she said in German, the language she usually used.

"Even worse, our children could have been hurt. That father didn't even scold them for their behavior."

"Or apologize to us. That English element sometimes worries me. Those children were just repeating what they hear adults say."

The two sat silently. Mary gazed toward Muscatine's sturdy brick buildings, some vaguely reminiscent of French estates and others of German breweries. Church steeples graced the skyline, German denominations mingled with English. The Germans and English usually lived peacefully side-by-side, but ruffians periodically shook up that peace.

Anke brightened, changing the subject. "Your daughters always look so cute together on the parsonage porch! Klaus just bought a camera, would you mind if I sent him over to take a picture?"

"What a treasure that would be!" Mary replied. "Thank you for thinking of it. The girls do indeed love sitting out there and visiting with whoever passes by."

As Mary contemplated a photograph of her daughters, she overheard snippets of Heinrich's conversation. The U.S. impending war with Spain, U.S. imperialism in the Philippines, imperialism generally, and German distrust of deepening ties between the U.S. and England punctuated the air like fireworks.

Reinhold, short with graying hair and bushy eyebrows, exclaimed, "It's the British stirring things up! They just want to convince the Americans that *Deutschland* is trying to take the Philippines, so the Americans will view the British as their loyal friends and the Germans as their rivals!"

"*Verdammt!*" swore Ulrich, a tall, bony man recently arrived from Bremen. "Germany is being scape-goated to excuse American imperialism."

Heinrich shook his head. "We German Americans can see right through what the British are doing. The problem is that English Americans don't trust us. I oppose war, but feel almost helpless to do much about it except preach."

Meanwhile, another cluster of men, among them Klaus, enjoyed beer as they swapped stories and listened to a band play traditional German tunes. When it struck up *In Rüdesheim in der Ziegelgasse*, they hoisted their glasses and belted out lyrics.

Mary observed, "Looks like Ulrich and Reinhold read the same *Deutscher Anzeiger* news stories as Heinrich. He reads it from front to back whenever he can find the time."

"Look, Mary," Anke was pointing toward a street intersection in the distance. Several women holding signs marched, trailed by young men jeering at them. Mary could hear something like chanting coming from the women, who ignored everyone around them. Mary and Anke stared until they were no longer visible.

"More of those English ladies out protesting alcohol and demanding the vote," Anke commented. "They act as if they were heads of their families."

While Mary had seen German men protesting things like war and low wages, she could not imagine German women doing so. Anke continued, "When I see those ladies, I wonder about their families. Instead of taking care of their husbands and children, there they are, out in the street, marching. And they look even more earnest than Heinrich!"

Mary laughed and shook her head. "They're church ladies like us, you know. But you're right, in a way they aren't like us. The Women's Christian Temperance Society, they call themselves. I've wondered about their families, too."

"Well, it's no wonder their men drink too much, with their wives out on the streets."

Mary said, "I just hope they don't turn on us. Like those little boys a few minutes ago. You've heard English whispers about us Germans, haven't you?"

"You mean that American Protective Association that thinks people should speak English to become citizens?" Anke asked, referring to a small anti-Catholic organization founded ten years previously a little north of Muscatine. "And that thing with the German Knights in Indiana?" with reference to English speakers' attempt to force German lodges of the Knights of Pythias to translate all their records into English. "Pfah!" she waved away the thought with one hand.

"Well, some of the English think we aren't patriotic to this country. And some think we're lazy!" Mary laughed as she pictured her own daily dawn to dusk labors.

Anke added, "I've even heard some think English is better suited to democracy than German."

Ada, waking up, let out a shrill yell. "That's telling them!" Mary said. "Heinrich believes *Gott Vater* will protect us. After all, our church has brought a lot of German souls to Him. It delights Heinrich no end to see these German congregations growing, and to know that he's playing a part in that."

"I hope you're right," Anke said.

"Where's Lydia? Do you see her?" Heinrich asked, having suddenly materialized.

"*Ach*, there they are!" Anke pointed toward a young couple strolling in their direction, then whispered, "I think we'll need to start planning a wedding soon. My nephew Heinrich Dietrich is truly smitten!"

*November, 2012*

Jessica rattled on as Cath picked her way through Saturday morning traffic. "So it looks like my German-American ancestors didn't think women should protest. Some of the men were politically active, but the attitude of the women seemed to be, stay home and let the men take care of it. I wonder why that was. Of course, I haven't been very political either, but, I mean, look how both Lydia and Mary had to uproot and move because of their husbands, even if they really didn't want to."

Keeping her eyes on the road, Cath replied distractedly, "I suppose that's how they grew up."

"Yeah, and they were so busy taking care of babies and husbands, they were probably too tired to do anything else. Some of the Anglo women, though, managed to get out and march for the vote and things like that."

Stopping at a red light, Cath looked over at Jessica. "You're really wound up this morning."

Jessica opened her mouth, then closed it. "I'm a little nervous, I guess." With one hand, she twisted the strap of her black leather bag around her fingers while rubbing her jeaned thigh with the other. Talking about the ancestors this morning distracted her from unbidden fantasies of Esteban kissing her, then running his hands up the inside of her shirt, then …

"Nervous about taking a public stand on Raza Studies? Or about seeing Esteban away from work?" Cath asked, as the light turned green. Passing through the intersection, she added, "Help me find a place to park. We're only a couple of blocks away."

Silence as both scanned the parked-up street. "There's one," Jessica pointed.

"Good eyes," Cath replied. As she pulled up to the space, she commented, "This will be a real test of my parallel parking skill. Get out and help me navigate."

Jessica hopped out of the car and stood on the sidewalk as Cath pulled into the narrow space with skill a driver's ed. instructor would envy. When she emerged from the car, Jessica marveled at Cath's ability to look interesting while appearing as though she hadn't tried. Her hair today, piled on her head, was held down with a couple of large black clips. Escaping tendrils framed Cath's handsome, unadorned face.

As they walked toward the rally, Jessica continued, "Sometimes I worry I might reenact patterns I've inherited, you know? Like, Willie could have helped address racism in Macon County after the lynching, but it looks like he just walked away. I could walk away too, but that wouldn't be right. Or I could stay home, like Mary, who probably didn't believe women should be out protesting. What I'm saying is, do we inherit these tendencies without realizing it?"

Cath stopped walking and turned to Jessica. "Jess, you're overanalyzing things. You make your own choices. I thought we're here today to support a school issue, not to rebel against your ancient ancestors."

Jessica blushed. "You're right, we're here to support Raza Studies. Maybe I get too immersed in the family history stuff."

They continued down the block, then turned toward the park where a crowd was forming.

Cath said, "I think what you're learning is great. You're inspiring me, although since I can get addicted to things pretty easily, I haven't tried looking up information about my own family like you're doing. But sometimes it seems you almost forget which century you're living in. Sure, we learn what's modeled and taught to us, but ..." her voice trailed off.

Jessica scanned the crowd for familiar faces. Adults, some with children in tow, were picking out posters from a pile on a table. She brightened and pointed. "There're some of our parents, over by that tree."

Cath squinted, then smiled. "Yeah, I see the Rodriguez family, and Mrs. Sanchez with a couple of her kids." A mischievous grin washed over her face. "Wait till you get little Hugo Sanchez in class, great artist, but can't hold one idea at a time in his head for more than two minutes. What a patience-tester!"

The two made a beeline for the Milford families. Jessica was greeting mothers of two of her students and wondering if another woman she glimpsed might be Marisela's mother, when she heard Esteban's enthusiastic voice behind her. "You made it!" He put his hand on her shoulder, then turned to Cath. "Cath, glad to see you. A stack of posters is over on that table, go grab one." Jessica's heart flipped, but she looked where he was pointing rather than at him, delicious warmth radiating through her body from her shoulder where his hand rested.

Participants of all ages, an excited buzz of confusion, sorted through posters, picking out just the right one to hold. A tall man wearing a poncho chose one showing a fist holding a pencil, while a couple of teenage girls, large hoop earrings glittering in the sunlight, picked out neon pink posters announcing: "What do we want? Raza Studies! When do we want it? Now!" A short older woman bundled in a heavy jacket as if snow were about to fall was studying a green poster on which someone had painted a picture of the book *Bless me, Ultima* and the announcement "BOOKS WE CAN RELATE TO." Joe, a teacher Jessica recognized from another school, grey hair and short grey beard setting off blue eyes and a lightly tanned face, was studying posters as if admiring artwork, his leashed Australian shepherd mix looking on curiously.

Jessica glanced at Esteban as he removed his hand from her shoulder. He was dressed more casually today than when he was teaching: a tan jacket partially covered a brown sweater, and boots peeked out from under his jeans. She wanted to touch his shiny black hair, ruffled in the morning breeze. She wanted to grab his hand and put it right back on her body.

Abruptly, he turned away to greet other new arrivals. Inwardly, Jessica sighed, then began to browse posters. Struck by their variety, she commented to Cath, "Wow, someone was really busy!"

"I had volunteers helping me after school," replied a stocky woman with short grey hair and purple-rimmed glasses. "I'm Dolores, I teach at Washington Middle."

189

"Oh, hi, I'm Jessica, and this is Cath. We're from Milford."

"Esteban's colleagues! Glad to have you here! Help yourself to whichever suits you," she said, sweeping a hand across the table. "Some of my helpers got pretty creative with their artwork." Jessica was studying a red poster featuring the United Farm Workers eagle juxtaposed with the fist and pencil, both in black paint.

"I think I'll take this one." She chose a white poster with dark blue graffiti lettering proclaiming "All Kids Deserve an Education they can Relate To." Cath selected a simple yellow one saying, "We Support Raza Studies."

As they turned away from the table, a short man wearing a cowboy-style hat and boots approached Jessica. He looked familiar, but she couldn't place him.

"Mrs. Westerfield," he said, "I'm happy you joined us. I'm Vicente Morales's father, I met you at Open House." Of course. Small and quiet, Vicente was easy to miss if you didn't intentionally pay attention to him, but after meeting his father at Open House, she had discovered that he was very smart.

Mr. Morales continued, "I appreciate all you are doing for Vicente. I think you're the only teacher he's had who helps him with his interest in *vaqueros*." Jessica immediately understood Mr. Morales's reference to the library book about Luis Ortega, master rawhide braider during the mid-twentieth century. Vicente had been fascinated to discover that Ortega had been his age when he learned braiding from an elderly Chumash Indian *vaquero*.

"I'm learning something from him," Jessica remarked. "Before I started working with Vicente, I had no idea how much cowboy culture drew from the Mexican *vaqueros*."

Just then, a tall, gangly man with a goatee approached, holding a megaphone. "Let's line up a couple of feet back from the sidewalk," he announced as he strode parallel to the street, motioning people to form a line.

As they moved into place, Jessica began to notice reactions of passing drivers. Many ignored them, but a few hollered things like, "Go back to Mexico if you don't like it here!" and "Quit complaining!" Others honked, thumbs up, as they passed.

Jessica had been jammed into a crowded line for a while, waving her poster, when two approaching cyclists slowed. Vic and Linda! "Hey there, Jessica! Cath! Good to see you two out here supporting this crowd," Vic greeted, stopping.

"Grab yourselves some posters and join us," Cath replied, smiling broadly.

"Just might do that," Vic remarked. He and Linda continued slowly down the sidewalk, stopping now and then to greet others. As she watched them, she noticed mothers of Marisela and Diana, who waved at her as they made eye contact. As she waved back, she remembered that she still hadn't followed up on their invitation to attend the *iglesia* with them.

A strikingly beautiful woman with black, wavy hair and tight jeans showcasing her slim figure grabbed Jessica's attention. One hand carried a poster, the other gripped Esteban's arm. As they stopped to talk with the man carrying the megaphone, Esteban slipped his arm around her, squeezing her closely. Definitely not a colleague-type of squeeze.

"… when we get to school on Monday?" she vaguely heard Cath ask. Then, "Jessica? Jess, what's wrong?"

Cath's eyes followed Jessica's gaze. "Oh, geez," she whispered, gripping Jessica's arm.

The blast of a passing car's horn unfroze Jessica, who turned to see two passengers waving angry fists at the crowd. She stared at the car as it receded down the street. Turning back toward Cath, she saw Esteban and the woman drifting in their direction.

"Want to go?" Cath asked quietly.

Too late. "Cath, Jessica," Esteban said, "I don't think you've met Brenda. Brenda, these two wonderful ladies are fellow teachers at Milford."

"Delighted to meet you," Brenda sparkled, both arms wrapped around one of Esteban's arms in a manner that suggested intimacy rather than possessiveness.

"You too," responded Cath for both of them. "You're a teacher, too?"

"Ah, no, I'm an immigration attorney. I don't think I have the patience to teach." Brenda's voice was warm and rich as honey.

Jessica felt as though she had turned into wood, unable to move. Esteban steered Brenda to another group of teachers.

"C'mon," Cath gently prodded Jessica's back, taking her poster and setting both down. Two high school girls next to Jessica looked curiously as Cath steered her away. Then a car passing noisily, this time with enthusiastic shouts of support, drew their attention.

Jessica could feel eyes of teachers and parents who had been near them, wondering why she was leaving. She hoped they would think she had suddenly become ill. She hoped they wouldn't connect her leaving with something Esteban said. Or think she had a change of heart about Raza Studies.

"He's sleeping with her," Jessica mumbled deadly when they got into Cath's car.

"C'mon, let me buy you a cup of coffee," Cath offered.

Jessica shook her head. "Just take me home. I feel like a fool. I had no right to expect anything from him, and probably if it weren't for my problems with Tim, I never would have."

"Don't beat yourself up," replied Cath. "Shit happens. How were you to know about her, anyway? He never talks about his personal life at school. The question is what you're going to do now."

"Go back to bed for the rest of the weekend, probably." Jessica fumbled in her bag for a tissue. "Maybe for the rest of my life. How am I going to face him when I see him at school? I must have been so obvious." She wiped her eyes.

Cath's silence was confirmation. Then Cath asked, "Have you talked with Tim lately?"

"Only a little."

They rode the rest of the way home in silence. When they reached Jessica's house, Cath asked, "Want to come to a Peace Action meeting with me tomorrow?"

"Not really," Jessica mumbled. "I'll be OK. I just need time to sort things out."

Cath reached over and gave her a hug. "OK, then, I'll see you Monday. Call me if you need me for anything."

*March, 1896*

"Mommy, when will we get there?" Six year-old Verne turned from the train window where he had been watching a wet, bleak winter landscape rush by.

"Pretty soon," Lydia replied.

"I miss Daddy," he complained, slapping his hands onto his lap.

"Shush." Lydia was amused at eleven-year-old Viola acting the adult whenever Verne began to whine. Curls peeking out from under her red knit winter bonnet, Viola explained, "Daddy's getting the house all nice and warm for us. He'll be waiting when we get to the station."

Seated across from Lydia and the two younger children, Orville and Ralston watched the passing landscape in silence, pointedly ignoring their siblings.

It had been only a month since Lydia and Orville had taken Willie from Boody to the Decatur train station. Lydia recalled bustling activity at the station that morning, despite cold wind tossing light snow. About sixty local residents, whole families as well as individuals like Willie, were bound for new homes in Storm Lake.

With Orville's help, Willie loaded trunks of personal items and farm equipment onto the train while Lydia paced. She smiled to herself now, remembering how jittery she had been. "Now, be sure to keep this basket of food with you in the passenger section, don't let it get packed with the trunks," she had advised Willie.

"Relax, Lydia, I'll be fine," Willie replied. Spying John and Tom, two neighbors who were also boarding, he added, "With them looking after me, what could happen?" He took Lydia in his arms, nuzzled hair escaping from her hat, and murmured, "By the time you and the kids join us next month, I'll have our little rental house all fixed up like home."

Lydia had laughed, knowing Willie's version of fixing up the house consisted of placing furniture haphazardly and making sure the wood stove worked.

"The train's slowing down!" Verne's loud announcement brought her back to the present. As it slowed, a blustery, cold rain gathered momentum. Lydia had to remind herself that they had planned to arrive toward the end of winter so they would have all spring to prepare the farm for planting.

A wooden sign proclaimed "Storm Lake" as the train slid to a stop, its sharp whistle knifing through frigid air. The excited throng scanning train windows for family members spilled out from under the narrow shelter covering the platform. "There's Daddy!" Verne suddenly hollered, pointing.

Spotting him, Orville and Ralston became animated. Smiles shattered their bored expressions as they stood to help their mother and siblings off the train. Willie, bundled in a heavy coat and a brown cap Lydia had knit years ago, folded them into his arms, the soggy, cold afternoon air momentarily forgotten.

Lydia's heart sank as soon as she saw the rental house that had been arranged for them. Rather than being located in the small town, it was perched by itself at the end of a bumpy road. Its single story contained claustrophobic rooms, no proper dining space, and a cramped kitchen.

As Lydia felt her face communicating disappointment, Willie hauled out sketches of the grand new house they would build once the weather improved. "It won't be in town, it'll be on the farm, but by then we'll have a good road."

Her eyes widened as she studied the handsome drawing of a large brick house set off by white wood trim. "My goodness!" she exclaimed, then added as she counted the rooms, "We'll have to get new furniture!"

Willie burst out laughing. Then he explained that he was still trying to ascertain what crops would actually flourish on his acreage, which appeared swampier than he had anticipated, although it would be difficult to know until May. The land agency's promised help draining water so far had not materialized.

Abruptly, his mood shifted. "There's some bad news." Lydia felt panic rise in her stomach as his voice took on a tone of someone about to announce disaster.

Willie ran a hand through his wavy hair. "John and the family just sold their land. They'll be moving to Council Bluffs, about 130 miles to the south."

"What?" Lydia had briefly imagined various potential disasters – loss of money, dead farm animals, diphtheria nearby. But she hadn't anticipated losing the nest of family. "Why?"

Willie shook his head. "It's a lot of things, Lydia. It's mostly that John's been upset about how this place has worked out for them. Or hasn't work out. He didn't tell me when I first got here, it came out a little bit at a time. His land is so swampy he's given up trying to do something with it. You know what a perfectionist John is."

Lydia screamed silently, What about our land? She stammered, "But – what a disaster this must be for him and Anna!"

"Yup. And, they have a baby due next month. They would have left last month but decided to wait until the baby arrives. John sold the land, thankfully, but he took a huge loss. And what doesn't help things, he still hasn't been paid for work he did for the land agency when he first arrived here. Lydia, the land agency is proving itself untrustworthy, which has me worried."

Lydia was still trying to grasp John's family's immanent departure. "Why Council Bluffs? Why don't they return to Boody?"

"Can you imagine how ashamed he feels? John was a big man in Boody. This move was to be a grand adventure, a better life for the family. A lot of our friends couldn't imagine why we left, but John was so sure. If he went back, it would be without a farm, without money ... I tried to get him to focus on his friends and family there, but he feels like such a failure. Anna persuaded him that Council Bluffs, you know, her father is *Pfarrer* there now, they might get a new start. Her family would welcome their son-in-law with open arms, no questions asked."

Lydia and Willie looked at each other in silence. Stunned, she wondered what John and Anna's experience would mean for their own new lives in Storm Lake.

*November, 2012*

Jessica felt like a fool for obsessing over Esteban. A fool for walking out of the rally way before it ended. Surely he noticed. Embarrassment washed over her whenever she thought of him.

To avoid running into him on Monday, she stayed in her classroom with the door shut, even during lunch. No one seemed to notice her absence from normal adult life except Cath, who texted her from the lounge: "Chicken! He isn't even in here."

Normally, Jessica stayed at school an hour or so after the children went home, but not today. At 3:10, shortly after they had cleared out, she prepared to follow suit. As she donned her jacket, she heard a tap on the doorframe. Whirling around, she saw Esteban standing there, arms folded and a quizzical look on his face.

"Have time for coffee?" he asked. When Jessica simply stared without responding, he added, "C'mon, I think we should talk."

"OK." She hesitated. "Not here though."

"I was thinking of Rolf's Coffee down the street," he suggested.

Rolf's predated Milford's teachers. Rolf himself was no longer around; his son Max ran the coffee shop. Newer customers, finding "Rolf's Coffee" hard to say, often asked why Max didn't rename the place. To long-timers, however, the name was part of the shop's identity. And as far as Max was concerned, the fact that anyone talked about its name was good for business. "Max's Coffee" would never be a name that prompted discussion, so he simply left it unchanged.

"OK," Jessica repeated, as though her vocabulary had suddenly shrunk. She picked up her book bag. "Let's take separate cars, I'll be going home directly from there."

"Meet you there in ten." Esteban nodded once, ducked out the door, and disappeared.

Jessica locked her classroom, then fled to the ladies' room, where she sat in a stall trying to collect herself. When she emerged, she threw back her shoulders as if she knew exactly what she was doing, and tried to look nonchalant strolling to the parking lot. As she climbed into her car, she noticed that Esteban's truck had already left.

She arrived at Rolf's to find him seated at a table in the back corner. Mutely, she slid into a seat opposite him.

He took a deep breath, then plunged in. "First, Jessica, I really want to thank you for your and Cath's participation in the rally on Saturday. I can't tell you how much difference it makes having white teachers support us. I personally value your commitment a lot." Maybe he hadn't noticed her early exit. Maybe, after shoving Brenda in her face, he hadn't noticed her at all.

Jessica was spared trying to figure out a response by a short, plump waitress wearing a white Rolf's Coffee polo shirt and jeans. "What wouldja like?" she asked, glancing toward the door as if the view there was better than the view in front of her.

"I'll take a small latte," Esteban replied.

"Me too," Jessica echoed.

"Be right up." The waitress turned on her heel and left.

Esteban's eyes briefly followed her, then turned back to Jessica. "Look, Jessica," he said. "Sometimes I'm pretty obtuse. Not observant. I didn't realize you and your husband had separated."

Jessica felt her face flush. Then she asked, "How did you find out?"

"Cath told me. I ran into her on the way in this morning. I asked why you two left early on Saturday."

So he had noticed.

"Cath practically bawled me out for not having figured it out for myself, and while she was at it, she mentioned that you and your husband had split. I guess when she said that, it put some things into perspective I should have seen earlier, but didn't."

"That's OK," Jessica said, staring at her hands on the table, thinking she shouldn't have chosen a phrase that implicitly let him off the hook.

"The thing is," Esteban continued, "I value you as a colleague and as a friend, and also as a potential ally. But you need to understand that – that I'm already taken."

The waitress picked that inconvenient time to plunk their lattes on the table and ask, "Will there be anything else?"

"No, thank you," Esteban answered for them both. The waitress retreated.

Jessica watched her hands curl around her latte for support. "I didn't mean to ..." She didn't mean to what? She wasn't sure how to finish the sentence. Didn't mean to fall for you? Follow you around? Imagine you had feelings for me?

"Jessica, I need to say something about my relationship with Brenda, but I also need you to realize how much I value your friendship. OK?" He sipped his latte, then said, "Brenda and I have been together on and off for years, since college. Well, we were off for a long time. But since she moved back here, we've been doing a dance trying to figure out whether we have a future together. And I think we do. She's like my second skin. She usually knows what I'm thinking before I do." He paused, then continued. "If she weren't in the world, and if you weren't married, who knows, you and I might get together. But that isn't how it is."

Staring at her untouched coffee, Jessica murmured, "I could see that. She's beautiful."

Esteban smiled. "She is, indeed. Inside even more than outside, once you get to know her. But what I want you to know is that I value you. Just not in the same way as Brenda. If I didn't value you, we wouldn't be sitting here stumbling through this conversation."

When a smile tugged at the corners of Jessica's lips, Esteban lowered his head to try to get into her field of vision. She finally raised her eyes to meet his.

He winked at her. "Of all the teachers at Milford, you're the one who gives me the most hope. You're willing to go the extra mile for our kids more than anyone else there. You're willing to make yourself vulnerable so you can learn, which is unusual. Cath too, but you even more."

"Well, I still have a lot to learn," Jessica managed to say.

"That's my point, you recognize that you do, and you dive right in. And the fact is, we need you. There aren't enough Mexican American teachers to carry the load with our kids, we really need teachers like you who understand that reaching everybody means paying attention to where everybody comes from." Having shifted the conversation onto familiar territory, Esteban talked more easily. "The Mexican American teachers and their allies are having regular meetings every couple of weeks. Will you join us? We need you."

Jessica took a deep breath, then exhaled. "I'll have to think about that. I care about my kids, and I'll keep learning more about the cultural stuff. But I'll have to think about whether I want to join your group." Her insides were screaming No, but she recognized that she should give herself time to process what he was saying. She craved being needed, but not needed this way, not by him, and not right now.

"A week from Thursday, November 29. Write it in your calendar." His eyes crinkled with a smile. "C'mon, open up your calendar and mark that date."

She did as he asked, although she doubted she would show up. To her, Raza Studies meant Esteban, and he was out of reach. Her kids weren't out of reach, though. She could continue to learn to teach them better, but would need to separate that from any feelings about him. Her heart had bound those things together far too closely.

He put out his hand, inviting her to shake it. "Friends?"

She took his hand and gave it a short shake. "Friends."

"I'll get it." He picked up the check as he stood, then added, noticing her full cup, "You didn't drink yours."

"I wasn't really thirsty. But thanks." Jessica rose, picked up her bag, and followed him to the cash register. He paid, and they left.

When she arrived home, Jessica ran straight upstairs and threw herself on the bed. At first, anger blazed through her – anger at Esteban for wanting to keep her on the Raza Studies teachers' side regardless of her feelings, anger at herself for imagining he cared. Then a cool voice chided her anger. He cares, Jessica, just not in the same way you do – or, did.

Like the tide of the ocean, anger receded, followed by tears and a deep sense of loss. Loss of what might have been but could never be with Esteban. Loss of Tim and their marriage. Loss of the hopes and dreams she and Tim had started out with, loss of their shared companionship, loss of someone who tickled her as she was waking up, someone who chowed down what she cooked with enthusiasm, even when she hadn't felt like cooking, someone who carted her off to a movie now and then, just because.

Loss of family. Her deceased parents had been an anchor in the world, an anchor she took for granted when they were alive. That anchor was no longer there.

Loss of sense of why she exists, whom she exists for, whom she exists with.

As sleep began to overtake her, thoughts of Thanksgiving in a few days intruded. Growing up, Thanksgiving was always a celebration of family. No gifts or hype like on Christmas. Just a day with nothing to do but hang out with extended family. Even if you didn't get along with all of them, they reminded you of who you are, who you are part of, where you come from.

How did she lose all that?

*May, 1898*

Lydia fussed as she peeled turnips and potatoes to cook with chicken for the mid-day meal. They never should have come to Storm Lake. Willie's land had proven considerably swampier than anticipated. What a disaster! Two years ago, having realized he couldn't drain it enough to plant anything, he rented another eighty arable acres. He was still planting crops on that land, still paying rent to use it, and still struggling to drain water from his own.

Thankfully, Lydia had persuaded him to agree to rent a larger house in town within easy walking distance of the school. They would delay building a new farmhouse until they figured out how to make the land usable. This house was at least much more comfortable than the tiny one they had occupied when first arriving in Storm Lake.

She sighed heavily as she watched yellow butterflies dance in bright sunlight through the kitchen window. Yes, they would have been better off staying in Boody! Maybe John would even still be alive.

She recalled that horrible day last December right before Christmas. She had been stitching up holes in one of Orville's old sweaters while Willie fed the pigs. Suddenly, an errand boy appeared at the door with a telegram from Anna. Lydia could still see it in her mind's eye:

JOHN DIED YESTERDAY OF TYPHOID FEVER – (STOP) – REST OF FAMILY IS WELL– (STOP) – FUNERAL WILL BE 23 DECEMBER IN BOODY, PLEASE COME – (STOP) – ANNA

They had immediately packed and caught the next day's train. At the funeral, Willie seemed lost, since John had always played an important part in his life, even after leaving Storm Lake. Lydia's heart wept for Anna. She couldn't imagine being suddenly widowed while living in a new place and caring for children, one of them still just a toddler.

John's death left a hole in their lives that Storm Lake's community, even its German church, was unable to fill. Although its German and German-American population was small and scattered, Storm Lake had a small German Methodist congregation that John, Anna, Willie and Lydia had joined. However, the congregation lacked a church building, so *Pfarrers* who rode a circuit led services in various locations. But frequent turnover of *Pfarrers* produced irregular attendance by all but the most devout (and elderly) members. As a result, the church never felt to Lydia like a community. The departure of John and Anna diminished it further, to the point that she and Willie participated only sporadically.

Lydia threw the vegetables into a pot with minced onions and chicken pieces. Orville and Willie, installing a new drainage system, would be back soon, hungry as usual.

A clatter on the front steps announced they were home early. She heard Orville saying, "Just lean on me, Pa, I've got you. There you go."

Lydia ran to the front door as Willie, supported by Orville, stumbled into the house, one hand clutching his belly.

"My God, what happened?" she cried.

"I must have eaten something this morning I shouldn't have," Willie muttered. "Help me upstairs to bed. I'm sure it'll pass."

Lydia couldn't imagine what he might have eaten that would affect him so. With Orville on one side and her on the other, Willie managed the stairs. As Orville removed his boots, Lydia fetched him some water.

"Ah, that's better," he sighed, then added, "Put the chamber pot right over there, so it's handy."

Orville retrieved it from under the bed, positioning it away from where Willie was likely to step.

Willie spent the rest of the day trying to sleep. By evening, the pain had not subsided and he felt too nauseous to eat. Lydia coaxed him to drink as much tea as possible, and gave him a mild laxative in hopes it would clear out his system. It did, but that didn't alleviate the pain.

With daybreak, the pain had worsened and Willie was feverish. Frightened, Lydia sent Orville to fetch Dr. Parkinson, Storm Lake's newest physician, just six years Orville's senior. What he lacked in experience Lydia hoped was compensated for by the recency of his training.

Dr. Parkinson arrived, boyish face looking freshly scrubbed, straw-colored hair combed, medical bag in hand. After looking Willie over – poking here, feeling there – he announced the onset of pneumonia. "Keep him warm and make him drink plenty of tea," the doctor advised.

Lydia did as instructed. She piled on blankets, forcing tea down Willie as often as she could. But the pain only seemed to worsen and the fever intensify.

The next day, absolutely distraught, Lydia went to the post office where the village's telephone was located to call her mother in Boody for advice. This was her first time using the newfangled contraption. The postmaster showed her how to place the call, which was answered by someone in Boody's post office. Then Lydia had to wait anxiously while her mother was fetched and instructed to place a call to Lydia, who waited by the phone in Storm Lake's post office.

By the time her mother came on the line, Lydia was crying inconsolably. "Get the doctor back to look at him again," her mother urged. "It sounds like you've tried everything I would know to do. You need to get him back with the doctor." Lydia gradually calmed. Before ringing off, her mother added, "By the way, your father took ill a few days ago, but I'm sure he'll be fine. Why don't we come for a visit when everyone is well again?"

Lydia replied that sounded like a good idea. Then she went to find Dr. Parkinson.

This time, the doctor found Willie delirious and his right side hot, acutely painful when touched. Concluding that his appendix must be infected, he sent Willie to the hospital. There, Willie underwent surgery to drain pus, standard procedure for an infected appendix.

The next afternoon, Willie died.

Grief cut through Lydia like a sword. During daytimes, she tried to shove her agony into a corner and cover it over with activity.

Indeed, there was a lot to do. She had to arrange for a burial plot and a funeral, she had to assure the younger children that life would go on, she had to help Orville and Ralston figure out what to do about swamp drainage and the rented farm.

During night times, she buried her face into the pillow and sobbed herself into fitful bouts of sleep, such a meager escape from her overpowering loss. She hated this place that had robbed her of her life! Gone was Willie who, forgetting his own father's premature death, had made no contingency plans for her. Gone were John and Anna, the only other family she and the children could count on day to day. And gone was the warm security and sense of belonging she had never questioned while living in Boody's community.

How did she lose all that?

*November, 2012*

Roast turkey with guacamole, buttered asparagus, fried rice, stuffed butternut squash, bean salad, and German chocolate cake. As Jessica filled her plate, she commented to no one in particular that this was the most eclectic Thanksgiving dinner she had ever seen.

"You should've been here last year," responded a middle-aged woman with a pale complexion, short reddish hair and long beaded earrings.

The man next to her looked up from squash he was heaping onto his plate. "Last year's curry was good. I wouldn't mind it again next year."

"Then are you going to make it?" asked the woman.

"Now, Grace." Jessica figured they must be married. She wondered what it was about marriage that chiseled jagged edges into what started out as romance.

Cath had invited Jessica to join a small group of her Peace Action friends for a potluck Thanksgiving dinner. Initially Jessica had begged off, but Cath had chided her: "You can't just sit around and feel sorry for yourself." Then she instructed, "Everyone brings whatever they want. Just make something you like." Relenting, Jessica decided to bake a couple of loaves of whole wheat bread. Still warm from the oven, they smelled rich and yeasty.

The small group was assembling around Sam and Frank's dining room table. Sam, who looked about forty, was tall and blond, a high bouffant hairdo (probably bleached) emphasizing his height. Frank, a little older with thinning dark hair, appeared to be of Italian, Mexican, or perhaps Portuguese descent.

The man who liked last year's curry sat down next to Sam. "Think the Court will take up Prop 8?" he asked, referring to California's proposition banning gay marriage. The U.S. Supreme Court had announced its intention to decide in early December whether to hear the case.

"I hope not. If it doesn't, you'll be getting a wedding announcement from us in January," Sam replied. Then he raised a bottle of white wine to the group, announcing, "This is our favorite Pinot Gris. It's heavenly! We stocked up last week at Trader Joe's, so don't be bashful."

"Hi, I'm Kimmie." Jessica, who had been following Sam's conversation, turned to find an Asian woman about her age sitting next to her. Kimmie's long black hair was pulled into a neat ponytail. "Did you bring the bread?"

"Yeah," replied Jessica.

"It's yummy! I just love homemade bread," Kimmie bubbled as she slathered a slice with butter.

"Did you bring the rice?" Jessica asked. "By the way, I'm Jessica."

"Hi, Jessica. Yeah, I always make it for occasions like this. It's easy and people seem to like it. I usually go home with an empty dish." Kimmie bit into the bread as though she had waited all week for this one pleasure.

"Are you with anyone else here?" Jessica asked, unsure how to figure out gracefully who was with whom.

"Not as in marriage or with a date. I'm friends with this group, so I sometimes do things with them. My family lives in Las Vegas. I go there for Christmas, but it's too much hassle for Thanksgiving."

Jessica laughed as she poured Pinot Gris into her glass. "I was supposed to join my brother and his family in Colorado. Not only too far, but who wants to spend Thanksgiving listening to criticism."

"I'm with you on that," said Kimmie, as she dove into the turkey. Then she asked, "I take it you're single?"

"Ah, no. Separated."

"Ouch. Sorry." Kimmie continued to eat as if she were ravenous.

Jessica had unexpectedly shared breakfast with Tim that morning. He called last night to ask what she was doing for Thanksgiving. He sounded genuinely concerned, then a bit relieved when Jessica told him she was going to a potluck dinner with Cath and her friends. Tim and Phil, Jessica learned, planned to hang out with a couple of single guys, watching football. One of them, apparently a decent cook, volunteered to prepare a turkey. Then he surprised Jessica by inviting her to meet for breakfast. "No agenda, I'd just like to see you. Especially this being a holiday and all." After trying to figure out what restaurant might be open, Jessica invited him to just come on over to the house.

Over breakfast, they exchanged updates about what they had been doing. Jessica talked mainly about teaching, and Tim, about happenings at Best Buy. While clearing the table, he said, "By the way, I'm thinking about doing a little bit of research on my own family."

"Really. Why?" Jessica had asked.

"I know I've poured cold water all over yours, and I still don't quite follow why it grabs you the way it does. But you got me wondering. I mean, a lot of my assumptions about things come from what my family went through and our parents told us. Growing up, you just take what they say at face value, you usually don't ask questions. So I got to thinking maybe I could find out more about what they actually did go through." Tim then looked away from her and began running water in the sink.

"That's interesting," Jessica said hesitantly. "Do you, uh, have thoughts about how you might start?"

Tim began washing the dishes. "No, I haven't had time to think much about it yet. You know how hectic work is this time of year. It's just an idea that's percolating."

Kimmie's voice abruptly brought her back to the present. "I almost got married last year, but then backed out. I'm trying to learn not to let a man run my life, if you know what I mean."

Jessica nodded affirmative, although having just met her, wasn't sure exactly what Kimmie meant. Kimmie went on, "I mean, here I am, a lawyer and a feisty one at that, but if a man I like says jump, I jump. Go figure. I'm learning to stand up for myself."

Cath, who had been plowing through the food on her plate with gusto she never displayed at school, chimed in, "Jessica, I've told this group a little bit about your family history research. Tell us what you're learning from it."

Jessica put down her fork. "Ah, what am I learning. Good question." She thought a moment. "One thing is that I'm part of something that extends back in time. I used to think of myself as this one isolated person, well, not isolated exactly. I have a brother I hardly see and a husband I'm separated from. Yeah, I guess that qualifies as isolated. But I'm discovering all these other people I'm connected to. Of course, they're all dead now."

She turned to Cath. "You know how I thought heart attacks ran in my family because so many of the men died off young? I just found out that Willie," she turned to the table at large to clarify, "on my dad's side, he was a great, great – well, he lived in the late 1800s. Anyway, he died of appendicitis. Back then, they didn't take it out of you, they only drained out the pus."

Grace put down her fork. "Eewww," she grimaced as though visualizing Willie's operation right in front of her.

"Sorry," Jessica apologized. "Anyway, I've been thinking a lot about my however-many-greats grandmother Lydia. Here she was, in an Iowa village she really didn't want to move to, with four kids, on a farm that was too swampy to work, and her husband dies on her. Then a week later, her father who she adored back home in Illinois, he died."

"Why did she let herself get talked into moving there in the first place?" asked Kimmie.

"I guess that's what women did in those days, although it seems like her husband's desires cost her a lot, and he never did realize that. Hmm." Jessica paused, realizing her own tendency to let men define her options. She continued, "Anyway, they were just starting to use the telephone, so news traveled pretty fast. Lydia's father was sixty-five, you kind of expect people might die when they get that old."

Jessica, into her story, missed raised eyebrows of an older woman sitting across from her. "So she went to the funeral, her second in a week! The two older kids looked after the two younger ones while she was gone, I imagine. Then as soon as she got back home, the general manager of the land agency that sold them the swampy farm tried to sue her, claiming Willie owed back rent on some other land he was renting from them."

"How on earth do you find this stuff out?" Sam asked as he set down his wine glass. "This all happened in the 1800s? Is your family famous or something?"

"This happened in 1898," Jessica replied. "Some of it was in old newspapers from Decatur, Illinois. I found out about the lawsuit by googling Willie's name. There was a description of it in an old book in Googlebooks about Iowa law cases back then."

Grace asked, voice sounding awed and earrings bobbing, "You googled your ancestor from over a century ago and found something? I can't even find out where my sister is living these days, and you're finding long-dead ancestors?"

"Just some. It's hit and miss," Jessica replied. "Anyway, imagine the stress of losing your husband and father, and then being dragged into court by this agent who it turns out was lying and just trying to milk her for money. She turned into such a basket case that her mother had to go to Iowa to look after her."

"Wait a minute," interrupted Cath. "If she hated Iowa, why didn't she just move back to Decatur?"

"Boody. It's a little village outside Decatur," Jessica explained to the group, then turned back to Cath. "Probably because the younger kids were still in school. But in the 1900 census, while the four kids were still in Iowa, Lydia was back in Illinois living with a recently widowed sister. They were probably helping each other deal with widowhood. Then Lydia took her mom with her back to Iowa, where they all stayed until the kids finished school."

"And then they all moved back to Boody?" Cath asked.

"Decatur, I think. I'm working on that."

"My word, what a story!" exclaimed Frank. "I wonder if I can find out what my Sicilian ancestors were up to back in the 1800s."

Jessica had been so engrossed that she hadn't noticed the older woman across from her rise and go to the kitchen.

"Estelle, let me help you with that." Sam pushed back his chair and stood, taking a carton of ice cream from Estelle, who went back to the kitchen, retrieved a cake, and brought it to the table.

Sam joked, "You know we only invited you because you bake the best German chocolate cake in California!"

Estelle smiled. "Speaking of grandmothers, this was my grandma's recipe."

As attention shifted from Jessica's story to Estelle's cake, Jessica's mind drifted back to why she seemed to feel she should apologize for who she was to men she cared about. She had spent much of her marriage trying not to appear too intellectually curious so as not to threaten Tim, and she had fantasized so intently about Esteban that she hadn't recognized his lack of real reciprocity. Now she had neither of them, but she still had herself. Maybe she was the best person to stand up for this self of hers. She wondered about Mary, back in the 1800s. Had Mary simply let Heinrich drag her from place to place? Or had she voluntarily signed on to the project of building the German church? In her own way, perhaps she had stood up for herself, alongside rather than behind, Heinrich.

*December, 2012*

Slowing the car, Jessica squinted at the address Álvaro had scrawled on a scrap of paper. He said they lived on Eighth Street near its intersection with Lincoln. There was Lincoln, so this must be the right block, but the addresses didn't match. Squinting, she realized she had read his smudgy "6" as an "8." Ahead lay a small blue house numbered 62. That must be it.

She pulled over and parked. A tiny, neat patch of garden in front and the door freshly painted white suggested care, while a torn window screen and chips in the exterior plaster suggested scarce resources. Gathering her bag, Jessica tried to figure out why she felt nervous. After all, Álvaro's mother *Señora* Pérez was expecting her. She had met both parents at Open House, it wasn't like she was dropping in on strangers. Maybe it was that they were more comfortable speaking Spanish than English. But since Jessica couldn't say much beyond "*¿Como está usted?*" *Señora* Pérez's English would have to suffice. Or maybe it was that she had never visited a Mexican home before. Ignorance she may not even be aware of will be on full display.

Initially Jessica's decision to embark on a series of home visits, concentrating on Mexican American families since she knew less about them, in general, than about white families, stemmed from guilt for eschewing further Raza Studies activities. Now on the group's email list, she deleted their weekly emails, unread. Yes, the point of Raza Studies was improving education for the students, but she still associated it with Esteban. Her misplaced crush on him still smarted. Becoming better acquainted with the kids' families, though, had nothing to do with him and everything to do with becoming a better teacher. When she broached the idea with a few students, they seemed so honored that a teacher might actually want to visit their homes that she realized home visits might be more valuable than she had initially thought.

Jessica's hand was poised to knock when the door burst open. "Come in, Mrs. Westerfield, *adelante*," greeted *Señora* Pérez with a broad smile. Clad in black slacks and a red sweater, and standing about four inches shorter than Jessica, *Señora* Pérez motioned her in.

Trying not to appear nosy as she entered, Jessica's eyes quickly took in two nondescript chairs flanking a couch draped with a bright multicolored woven blanket, a large print of *La Virgen de Guadalupe* above the couch, a small table of framed family photographs – a wedding photo and children's school pictures stood out – and an old TV. Further back in what appeared to be a tiny dining area, clear plastic covered a table displaying an embroidered white cloth, on which sat a large painted vase full of flowers. Grayish carpet typical of rental housing covered the floor. Jessica's nose detected delicious hints of stew and peppery spices.

As she sat on the couch and tried to decide whether to rest one arm on a crocheted doily, a door cracked open, allowing two dark-eyed young children to peek out. "*Vengan, vengan*," *Señora* Pérez called in their direction, motioning them in. A girl who looked about seven and a boy about four emerged. "These are my two youngest children, Teresa and Hernán. *Saluden, hijos*."

"Hello," greeted Jessica, making a mental note of how Teresa's mother pronounced her name. "Teresa, I think I've seen you at school. Who's your teacher?"

"Miss Peterson," Teresa replied as she twisted the bottom of her yellow T-shirt and studied her scuffed sneakers.

"Well, I'm happy to meet both of you." Jessica wasn't sure if she should try to shake hands with the children, something she would not think of doing at school. The children extended their hands, so she shook them gently.

"*Hola* Beatriz!" A greeting from the front door saved Jessica from deciding what to do next. Marisela's mother, wearing a black shirtwaist dress and pumps, bounded in, apparently not needing permission to enter. She said, "Mrs. Westerfield, I'm so happy to see you again. I hope you don't mind if I join you and Beatriz. Her English isn't as good as mine, so she asked me to come. By the way, please call me María Paz, since Mrs. Cruz, or *Señora* Cruz, sounds too formal."

"No, I don't mind at all." Jessica felt a small wave of relief, since the presence of Mrs. Cruz – María Paz – would make communication easier. "You can call me Jessica."

"Oh, no, I couldn't call a teacher by her given name," María Paz protested.

Jessica's brain raced to work out why she could address a parent by the first name, but it didn't go the other way. "I decided it would help me understand my students better if I learned more about their lives outside school and got to know their families a little bit. I know our school doesn't have a policy of home visits, but it just seemed like a good idea. When I mentioned it to some students, Álvaro was the first to volunteer." She looked around. "I wonder where he is."

As though he had been eavesdropping, Álvaro emerged from the kitchen with a plate of bright pink, sunny yellow, and light brown cookies. "Hello, Mrs. Westerfield," he said shyly, looking down as he set the plate on the worn coffee table in front of the couch. "*Hola, Doña* María Paz," he added.

*Señora* Pérez, who had vanished a minute earlier, followed him with a tray of coffee, cups, milk, and sugar. She set the tray down next to the plate of sweets, filled the cups, and handed one to Jessica. "Please," she said.

While María Paz heaped sugar into her cup, Jessica picked up a round yellow cookie. She thought it might be chewy, but biting into it, discovered a texture similar to baked meringue, but a sweeter flavor.

The children had been standing quietly, eyes glued to the cookies. *Señora* Perez gave them a firm smile and held up one finger. "*Una*," she said. They dove for the plate.

"No, I wanted the pink one," Hernán complained as he reached for Teresa's cookie.

"They all taste the same," she said, biting into it.

"*Es igual*," *Señora* Pérez handed Hernán a yellow cookie. "*Oigan, vayan a jugar afuera.*" She waved a hand in the direction of the back door. Watching the children scurry outside to play, Álvaro holding the door for the other two, then giving what sounded like directions, Jessica realized that, as eldest, he must be in charge. In the classroom, she thought of him as an imp who dodged responsibility, but was glimpsing a different side of him here.

"Thank you so much for your hospitality, *Señora* Pérez," Jessica said. "I'm interested in learning about your family." Jessica had earlier considered several opening questions, such as How long have you lived here? or What goals do you have for your children? But these sounded inquisitive. Asking where the family came from would sound too much like immigration enforcement. The phrasing she settled on seemed more like an invitation for the parent to define what to talk about.

*Señora* Pérez set down her cup, a smile lighting her round face. "Well, we came here from Guanajuato, just like the Cruz family," she said slowly, beaming at María Paz. "But my husband and I came before the children were born, many years ago."

"Have you ever been to Guanajuato? The city or the state? Or perhaps San Miguel de Allende, many Americans go there," María Paz asked Jessica.

Jessica shook her head. "The only places I've been in Mexico are Ensenada and Cancún." This hadn't seemed like limited exposure to Mexico until now. "What's Guanajuato like?"

"It's big," María Paz replied. "It's right in the middle of Mexico. It has everything from giant cities to small villages. It's full of mountains and valleys, very beautiful."

"Yes, very beautiful," repeated *Señora* Pérez as if to stress the idea. "You must visit. Wait here, I have pictures."

In the dining area she shuffled through a drawer in a low chest, returning with a photo album. Sitting next to Jessica, she opened it to the first page, where an older couple, seated in formal chairs, looked sternly outward. "My parents," she explained. "They are old now. We visit them when we can."

"We visit my parents as much as we can, too," added María Paz. "They are getting older, and I worry about them. When we were there a couple months ago, I tried to get them to come stay with us, but they said no."

"I try, too, but they say no. Their home is not here."

"Do other family members still live near your parents?" Jessica asked both women.

216

"*Sí, sí,* my brother and his family. They live in a town nearby," replied *Señora* Pérez.

"*¿Dónde viven exactamente?*" María Paz asked *Señora* Pérez. "Please pardon us for a minute," she added to Jessica.

The two women spoke in rapid Spanish, *Señora* Pérez emphasizing a point by patting her hand on her parents' photo. Then María Paz turned to Jessica.

"The problem is that their family farm was no longer able to support the entire family, so people left. Beatriz's brother went to work in León, which is a huge city in Guanajuato. He goes back to his parents' home as often as he can. Her sister, who lives near San Diego, sends her children to stay with their grandparents during summers. But they're alone most of the time, so Beatriz worries. Her husband, who's still at work, is from a different village and was the only one to leave, so his parents are cared for. In the case of my family, I was the only one to leave the country because my husband got a job here with a television station."

"What happened to their farm? Why can't it support the family anymore?" Jessica asked, unsure which piece of new information to follow up on.

Beatriz and María Paz looked at each other. María Paz explained, "A lot of Mexican farms used to sell crops for a fair price the farmers could live on. Now, with all this cheap American produce coming in, it's much more difficult. Her family depended on their farm. Mine didn't, you see, my family has a large ranch. One of my brothers runs it now that my parents are older. My other brother works as a financial advisor for a large company. But too much American produce creates problems for farmers."

Why didn't she know that, Jessica wondered, suddenly feeling as ignorant as she had when Vic began to tell her about Illinois history. So much was missing from her own education. And from a lot of news, at least the news she was used to paying attention to.

Beatriz began turning pages in the photo album, naming people as she went. "My uncle and his family," she pointed to a large family standing on a patio surrounded by vegetation. "My cousins Gloria and Sandra, with their children," standing in front of a large old church. With page after page, a very large extended family came into view against backdrops of living rooms, patios, distant mountains, and flower bushes.

"How many of these family members does Álvaro know?" Jessica finally asked.

"All of them. He forgets some names, but he sees all of them when we go visit," replied Beatriz.

"Might Álvaro, or your other children, go back and live there someday?" she asked both women.

Beatriz shrugged. "They were born here. They are U.S. citizens."

María Paz added, "It will depend on where they have the best opportunities. We want our children to feel comfortable in both worlds, the one here in the U.S. and the one where much of their family still lives. We want to keep as many options open for them as possible. If they get university degrees, then they'll be in the best position to decide where they want to live."

Jessica took another bite of her cookie, slowly chewing as she thought. She asked, "What do you think of the Raza Studies proposal? Will it help them?"

The two women quickly conferred in Spanish. Jessica heard the words "Raza Studies" and "Esteban" as they talked. Then María Paz turned to Jessica. "Sorry, but Beatriz wasn't sure what you were asking. I needed to explain it to her. The way we understand it, it will help our children connect to both worlds, Mexican and American. And the way Esteban explained it, it will prepare our children for the university. We think those things are very important. Right now when they go to school, our children learn mostly about American things. They need to learn all that, of course, but it would also be nice if they can learn some Mexican American things as well, things we might not be able to teach them at home, like some of the history of Mexicans in the U.S. and some of the writers."

Beatriz nodded affirmatively. "Our children are American, they should learn American things in school. But since America is part Mexican, they should learn all sides." Then she added emphatically, "And we want them to have a good education. We don't want them to have to do hard work like my husband and I, you know, cleaning and yard work, but maybe become teachers, like you."

Jessica tried to picture a grown-up Álvaro as a teacher. To her surprise, she realized she could conjure up an image in which he was a lot like Esteban. The hint of a smile crept across her face.

"This has been a wonderful visit, *Señora* Pérez and *Señora*, er, María Paz. You've given me much to think about."

"It is nothing, Mrs. Westerfield. We are honored you chose to visit our home," replied Beatriz Pérez modestly, as though Jessica were the President. "Please come again."

Jessica stood and began to collect her cup, saucer, and napkin, but Beatriz Pérez waved a hand indicating she would gather things up later. As the two women escorted her to the door, Jessica heard squeals of children playing in back of the house. She thanked the women again, then walked toward her car, still awed by a newly-formed image of Álvaro possibly following in Esteban's footsteps.

CHAPTER 31

*January, 2013*

"Do you have a few minutes?" Jessica poked her head into Cath's classroom as Cath stacked chairs on tables to facilitate the custodian's sweeping.

Cath motioned her to a chair that was still standing. "Sure, we're overdue for a catch-up. I've barely seen you at lunch."

"Well, you've barely been at lunch." Jessica entered, closed the door, and sank into a chair designed for a ten-year-old, knees approaching her chin. Usually an undignified position, but no matter today.

"Has it been only two days since we returned from winter break? It feels like a month already." Cath, locks of hair rebelliously escaping from their clips, slumped into a chair like a rag doll. "I was all rested up from my week-long yoga retreat, then come back to ..." she waved a hand vaguely "... this. Doesn't take long, does it." In an attempt to muster remaining energy, she straightened her back and met Jessica's eyes. "OK, so tell me how it went with Walt and what's-her-name."

Jessica rolled her eyes, then said, "Walt's actually trying, which was a pleasant surprise." She had decided to spend Christmas in cold, snowy Colorado Springs with Walt, Jan and their two noisy kids. María Paz, sensing Jessica's lack of holiday plans during a home visit, had invited her to spend Christmas Day with their family, but Jessica couldn't picture herself relaxing in the home of one of her fifth graders. Besides, she realized she wanted to give Walt another chance. He was, after all, the closest thing she had to living family. She couldn't continue to avoid her own brother while giving so much attention to ancestors who had passed on.

"Walt knew I was coming alone, but I didn't tell him why until I got there. As soon as I saw him in the airport, I told him Tim and I had separated, and he could either listen and support me, or criticize me, but if he chose the latter, I'd be on the next flight out."

Jessica pictured the surprised look on Walt's face. His mouth, opened as though to make an announcement, froze while his grey eyes widened, his brain probably racing to figure out this newly assertive sister. Jessica's subconscious, appreciating this rare moment, snapped a mental photo, even while her conscious mind was steeling itself for an argument.

Walt led her to his new Lexus in the airport parking lot as he made banal comments about the weather. As they left, he suggested stopping for a beer so they could talk before "having to deal with Jan and the kids," as he put it. So, in a cold depressing bar, Jessica had offered details of her separation from Tim. At first, Walt hadn't said much except "Okay," and "Go on."

When she finally stopped talking, he shocked her with, "You're braver than I thought, and braver than I am." It was Jessica's turn for a speechless jawdrop. "Jan's tough to live with in daily doses," he confessed. "Who knows, maybe she thinks I am, too. I fantasize leaving, but hate feeling like I failed, and I just won't walk away from the kids." The two kids, ages four and six, were spoiled brats in Jessica's estimation. She'd walk away from them in a heartbeat.

"I had no idea," Jessica said as her voice returned. "You never liked Tim, so I thought you'd blame me for picking the wrong guy." From a corner of the bar, loud laughter erupted, then gradually dissipated.

"I wouldn't have chosen him. But the one I did choose maybe isn't much better. Jan can be a know-it-all. That gets old after a while." Walt had stared at his beer, then looked up. "This is the first time my baby sister has stood up for herself. I like the new streak of iron down your back."

Cath laughed. "He said you have a streak of iron down your back?"

Jessica frowned. "Maybe it's just aluminum, but at least my back isn't a wet noodle anymore. Oh, and thanks for introducing me to your friends, you know, from Peace Action. Kimmie and I discovered we like the same movies, so we went to a couple while you were away doing yoga. Sam and Frank joined us for one of them and dinner afterward. Are they a hoot! Anyway, here's what I wanted to check in with you about in private. Has Ralph talked to you yet?"

Cath raised her eyebrows. "Ralph? Other than to ask how my holiday was on the way in yesterday, no. Why?"

Jessica exhaled. "You know how sweet Birthday Party Ralph always seems, like he loves everyone, and wants everyone to be happy."

"Birthday Party Boy is hitting on you?" Cath's eyes almost popped as her voice rose. "I didn't know he had it in him."

"Shhhh! No, that isn't it. Here's what happened. This morning I was getting my classroom ready before the kids arrive, you know, how we usually do in the morning. So in walked Ralph. I wondered what was up because he never just walks into my room in the morning like that, but I thought, whatever, maybe he's planning a surprise for someone. He was asking if I had a couple of minutes, when he picked up a Chicano history book on my desk." As Jessica unloaded her story, words tumbled out faster and faster, hands fluttering like mallard ducks. "You know the one Esteban loaned me? Actually, I gave it back to him last month, but since I wanted to read it, I got my own copy." Cath nodded while looking as though she wondered where the story was going.

"So Ralph picks up this book and then says, 'You know, Jessica, the Mexican teachers are trying to take over the high school curriculum.' And I went, 'Huh? What are you talking about?' And he went, 'Well, they have the school board considering a proposal for a Chicano Studies program to replace some of the classes students already take. This book here makes me wonder if you're in cahoots with them.' I was so stunned I asked Ralph if he lost his marbles. Then he went on to say it would be terrible for the kids, divisive, lower the academic quality, blah blah ... Cath, I couldn't believe what was coming out of his mouth! He said he was just trying to rally Milford teachers to stand up for academic standards, and he hadn't been sure where I stood."

"Birthday Party Ralph is sounding more like Lynch Party Ralph! That's a side of him I've never seen. Maybe I just wasn't paying attention." Cath narrowed her eyes, then asked, "When's it coming up at the board, do you know?"

Jessica shook her head. "I'm on the Raza group's email list, but I've been deleting their emails without reading them. I'll read the next one and let you know." She fumbled with the hem of her sweater, then added, "After the Esteban debacle, I figured I'd just stay out of it, you know. But now I'm not sure that's possible."

She stood as if to leave, then stopped and added, "I haven't even asked about your yoga retreat. How was it?"

Cath sprang up, spread her arms as if they were wings, and twirled, face glowing. "Fabulous! You don't do yoga, so you might not be able to imagine, but what a rejuvenator!" She let her arms drop. "I'm gonna try not to miss my session this afternoon, so I have to kick you out and finish cleaning up in here. But how about a bite after work tomorrow so we can catch up properly?"

"It's a date," Jessica agreed as she left.

Even though she hadn't finished preparing her classroom for tomorrow, Jessica's mind wasn't on it, so she decided to head home. She would come in early the next morning.

Sliding her car out of the parking lot, she reached for the radio to change from news to music, then hesitated as she heard a female voice mention immigration. As she pulled into early rush hour traffic, a reporter was describing discussions in Washington: "So the Republicans find themselves boxed into a corner. The beating they took in November sends a message that they can't ignore the growing Latino voting bloc asking for a pathway to citizenship for undocumented immigrants. But many of their white constituents oppose what they call amnesty for lawbreakers, and demand increased border security. We'll be following this issue closely. You have been listening to Latino USA on Public Radio, and this is ..."

Jessica punched the key for her favorite music station and relaxed as Green Day filled her car. "Sometimes I give myself the creeps, Sometimes my mind plays tricks on me," she sang along as she bounced to the beat. Unbidden, an image of Ralph materialized in her head. All smiles and curly hair like a big teddy bear, he was patrolling the U.S.-Mexico border, toting an AK 47. Was this Green Day's *21 Guns*?

How is it possible to be so kind and giving to some people, while simultaneously organizing against something other people really want?

As she pulled into the driveway, her thoughts shifted to dinner with Tim the night before she flew to Colorado Springs, and Tim and Phil drove to their parents' home in northern California. Tim had surprised her with a small package.

"I thought we said no gifts," she had said, as she took it hesitantly.

"We did, but when I saw this, I thought of you. Open it." Tim was smiling like a little boy anticipating an ice cream cone.

Jessica ripped open the package, finding a small silver bracelet in a translucent bag. She slid it from the bag and held it up, admiring a graceful bird in flight, silver chains attached to each wing. "Let me put it on you," said Tim, as he took one end of the bracelet. Jessica held out her arm so he could fasten it. Then she looked at him quizzically, wondering what the symbolism might mean.

"No particular message," he said, reading her thoughts. "It isn't about you flying away, just the fact that you're using your own wings. Which isn't a bad thing."

Later over dinner, Tim had shared ideas for his own family history research, which centered mainly on his parents' generation. His father's parents, born during the Great Depression, had been poor most of their lives, but Tim was under the impression they had wanted their son – his dad – to go to college and make something of himself.

Neither of his parents, however, did so. Tim's mother had no interest. His dad complained that he couldn't afford it, or couldn't get accepted because affirmative action, which he assumed, as did Tim, established special preferences for minorities.

"So what are you looking into, exactly?" Jessica asked.

"Well, while I'm at their house, I want to ask them more about their lives at that time." Tim picked at the chicken on his plate as he thought. "I really don't know what the story was. Was affirmative action really a problem for Dad, or is he using it as an excuse for something else?"

Surprised by this bit of introspection, Jessica watched Tim push carrots around the plate with his fork. She speared one and popped it into her mouth.

"Hey," he started to protest.

"You don't like carrots," she reminded him. "I was just helping out."

He jabbed a carrot, stuck it in his mouth, and grimaced. "You're right," he said. "Anyway, I guess it can't hurt to ask some questions while I'm there. How's your family history coming, by the way?"

"I kind of set it aside," Jessica confessed. "Not on purpose, I just got busy doing other things. I started doing home visits to get to know more about my kids." When Tim didn't respond, Jessica continued, "I think when I read about how my ancestor Willie died of appendicitis, and the terrible state of medical knowledge back then, I needed to give it a rest. One of his sons, my ancestor, became a doctor, who knows, maybe because of how his father died."

"Could be. Want dessert?"

"I'll split something with you."

Tim signaled the waiter for a dessert menu as Jessica continued, "The one who became a doctor married one of Heinrich and Mary's daughters. I assume they met in church, but the details I have on their lives so far put them in different states."

"Well, you've got two weeks of vacation," Tim had said as the waiter handed him a menu. He scanned it. "How does tiramisu sound?"

"Go for it," she had agreed.

Had that dinner been a turning point in their relationship? At least they had talked rather than bicker. But would she want to get back together with Tim? As she hung up her coat, the silver bracelet on her wrist caught a flash of afternoon sunlight. I wonder where that bird is going, she asked herself, looking at its graceful wingspan. Then she marched to the computer to piece together how Mamie and Ralston met.

CHAPTER 32

*July, 1906*

To Mary, nothing beat relaxing under the shade of a sprawling maple tree in the yard of a friend on a July afternoon. Of the places she had lived, Decatur turned out to be the most agreeable, a surprise, really. It was larger than the other towns, and she had always assumed large meant impersonal. But she found that community can flourish in a place of any size.

Decatur's German Methodist Church – Heinrich had been pastor there four years now – was elegant and spacious. Bright sunlight dancing through tall stained glass windows created brilliant patterns on walls, on the floor, even on the dullest grey of men's suits. More importantly, its congregation welcomed Heinrich's family, immediately regarding them as part of an extended family. And Mary realized that moving here didn't mean losing Muscatine's extended German family, but rather adding Decatur's.

"Please take another," offered Charlotte, the hostess and best baker of molasses jumbles Mary had ever tasted. Short and stocky, graying hair pulled into a bun, Charlotte bustled about in a long, nondescript brown and beige dress, reminding Mary of pocket gophers one saw everywhere. But Charlotte had a large heart and a larger oven she knew how to use. Three or four sweet, chewy bites, a molasses jumble (or two) was the perfect accompaniment for tea.

"Ah, there's Lydia." Mary followed Charlotte's gaze. A slender woman clad in a white shirtwaist blouse, its collar fastened with a simple brooch, was looking about as though lost. Charlotte motioned her over.

"Lydia, dear, have you met Mary yet? Mary, Lydia and her family moved here last month from Storm Lake, Iowa, although they're from Boody originally, so they really belong here." Busy with introductions, Charlotte missed the two women nodding in recognition.

"We met in church last week, although we haven't yet had the pleasure of a conversation," Mary explained.

Lydia seated herself in the wrought iron chair next to Mary. "I so enjoyed your husband's sermon. I must say, the church here is grander than any I've been used to. I grew up in the sweet little chapel in Boody, have you been there? The state of the German church in Storm Lake was, well ..." her voice drifted off as she waved a hand suggesting something insubstantial.

Charlotte disappeared, presumably to fetch more tea. Lydia asked Mary, "Have you lived here long?"

Mary laughed. "We haven't lived anywhere long! The life of a *Pfarrer* depends on where *Gott Vater* thinks he should be, which is never one place very long. We were sent here from Muscatine about four years ago. You're one of Bertha's sisters, aren't you?"

Lydia brightened. "Yes, both Bertha and Olivia are my sisters. You know them?"

"Of course, I see them at church as well as around town." Mary gazed at Lydia. "I can see the family resemblance."

Lydia blushed momentarily. "I thought Bertha was coming this afternoon, but she doesn't seem to be here. She's probably at my house seeing our mother, who's living with me and my two younger children. I tried to get Mother to join me, but she wasn't quite up to it."

Charlotte suddenly reappeared with a tray of tea and more molasses jumbles. Mary pointed. "Lydia, you must have one of these. Charlotte could give lessons to the rest of us who think we know how to bake." Mary's hand hovered, then dove for one more jumble while Charlotte beamed.

As Charlotte moved on to another small group, Lydia explained that after her husband died, she had stayed in Storm Lake until the two youngest finished secondary school. Shaking her head, she commented, "I wouldn't have survived without my older two boys. After Willie's death, they took over when I couldn't cope. They helped me sell our land, and did a little farming while we were figuring out what we would live on. But none of my children really wanted to become farmers!"

"They're still in Storm Lake?"

"Oh, no. Last year Orville married a lovely young woman. They moved to Cedar Rapids, where he's working in a jewelry store."

"Well, that's about as far from farming as you can get!"

"It is, isn't it? And Ralston is a student at the State University of Iowa. Since he's still in school, he isn't married yet, of course. He plans to study medicine. He always felt his father died needlessly because small towns like Storm Lake just don't provide adequate medical care. I think that awakened in him a passion to become a rural doctor. Then there's my daughter Viola, who sings and plans to continue studying voice at Millikin College. She's a schoolteacher, looking for a job here, but she was torn about leaving Storm Lake because of her beau there."

"Ah, I believe I heard her singing in church last Sunday. A beautiful girl with a magnificent voice," Mary commented. "You know, love can overcome distance. My eldest daughter – also named Lydia, quite a popular name. Anyway, she was living in Iowa when she met her husband. He lived in Illinois, but found work in Muscatine so they could court and then marry. That's where they live now. You know, the railroads these days make it so easy to visit."

"Yes, well, we may be seeing a lot of her young man. And then my youngest just finished secondary school. Being baby of the family, he hasn't figured out at all what he's doing next." Lydia sighed and rolled her eyes.

"Boys can be a challenge!" Mary agreed in a conspiratorial tone. "My eldest was very studious, I never worried much about him. But the other two, oh my! They were devoted to sports, especially basketball and track. It was always a chore to make them study. But after we came here, they involved themselves from time to time at the *Turnverein*, which started here maybe a dozen years ago."

"Oh, yes, that German gymnastics club. We never lived close to one, but I've heard they're marvelous for young people," agreed Lydia.

"They are indeed. My boys are all grown and gone now," she said wistfully.

A tall, graying blonde approached and introduced herself to Lydia. "My name is Alice. I overheard you say your son plans to become a rural doctor. How wonderful! I grew up in a village far from much of anything, and we could certainly have used a good doctor."

Mary gestured to a chair, inviting Alice to sit and join them, and commenting to Lydia that she was an active member of one of the English Methodist churches.

"You must visit us sometime, Lydia," Alice chirped. "We aren't German of course, but there's no need to choose one congregation or the other. We have some quite interesting activities."

Then to Mary, "Oh, I hope you don't mind me saying that, dear, because of course the German church also has wonderful activities."

Mary smiled. "Alice is right, our churches are more like comrades than competitors." Mary kept to herself her hunch that Alice had only a vague idea what went on in a German church, not attending one herself.

Alice continued, "The work of our Woman's Home Missionary Society is my particular passion. It helps women in the South, you know, Negro women who are trying to lift themselves up from slavery. We have a program every month where we read and discuss something that will broaden our knowledge about the problems of the downtrodden. We take on special projects from time to time to raise money for aid we send south. You must come. Our next meeting is ..." she paused to think, "let's see, it's three weeks from last Sunday."

As words tumbled from Alice's mouth like a waterfall, Mary sensed her forceful enthusiasm overpowering Lydia, so she returned to the topic of family.

"That's a wonderful idea, Alice. Thank you for mentioning it." Turning to Lydia, she continued, "You probably haven't met my daughters yet, but I believe your lovely Viola has. Our three daughters who still live with us are very actively involved in the church's music program."

"How nice that you still have three at home," Lydia replied.

"Yes, it is. Our eldest, Mamie, works as a stenographer. Our youngest is still in high school, and the middle one just finished school. I think she's aiming to become a teacher."

As the conversation shifted, Alice excused herself.

"Why don't you join us for supper after church on Sunday?" Mary invited. "And please bring your mother and the two children who still live with you. I'll see if your sister Bertha and her family can join us as well."

"My son Ralston might be here for the weekend," Lydia said hesitantly.

"Do bring him along. We'd love to meet him!"

As Lydia's face relaxed, Mary said to herself that hospitality was always the best medicine for someone who seemed lost.

\* \* \* \* \*

### September, 1906

Heinrich burst through the door, returning from one of his routine trips to St. Louis. Beaming, and without stopping to sit, he made announcement: "Mary, I have a new assignment. I was invited to become the new Secretary of the St. Louis German Conference. It's such an honor. The conference has been growing steadily, its membership is now up to nine thousand."

Mary just looked at him, thinking but not saying, Again?

Heinrich added quickly, "We don't have to move to St. Louis, we can stay right here in Decatur. The work I was given is here in Illinois.

Mary had ceased to find changes in his work assignment surprising, so she simply folded her hands and looked at him encouragingly, knowing she was about to get a full description of his new role anyway. Essentially, he explained he would be retiring from his work in the Decatur church. His first assignment as Secretary was to raise a $50,000 endowment for another Methodist church in the area. "I was so successful expanding the church in Muscatine, they want me to help churches here to grow."

Mary wrinkled her brow. "This is wonderful news, love. But you know, if you retire, we can't continue to stay on here in the parsonage."

"That's what I'm saying. We'll continue to live here in Decatur, but we'll need to buy a house. Our own house, for the first time. No more moving!"

Unbidden, tears sprang into Mary's eyes. Although she had become used to moving, until now when she finally had a chance to grow roots in one place, she didn't know how much that dream meant to her. Imagine! Their very own house!

CHAPTER 33

*January, 2013*

Jessica considered whether to buy the bag of tangerines she held. On the one hand, these sweet, juicy, seedless cuties were almost as sinful as chocolate and better for you. But on the other hand, she could scarcely finish a whole bag by herself before the last few began to resemble hard, shriveled walnuts fallen from her grandmother's tree.

She tossed the bag into her cart and continued. Shopping for one rather than two would feel depressing if she felt lonely. But in an odd kind of way, Jessica felt no lonelier now than she had when Tim was a regular part of her life.

Recently, in one of their sporadic conversations, he began to hint at reconciliation. "If we get back together," he had said more than once. But she steered the conversation in another direction. Although not ready for divorce, she also wasn't ready to fall back into the same old relationship. She realized she had relied on his presence to fill what was otherwise a void in her life, a void she now had to confront. Of course, there were other dimensions to their relationship based less on need and more on mutual enjoyment. But mutual regard had been the missing lead actor in their drama, all the more noticeable now that her life was beginning to be populated with friends who seemed to like her as she was.

Dinner, what will it be? A hamburger, perhaps? At the meat counter, Jessica picked up a pound of ground round. But a hamburger needs a bun, and the smallest bag contains eight. Maybe taco salad instead?

At the dairy cooler, Jessica pondered cheese. Cheddar – good on a hamburger, stronger than she liked on taco salad. Brie – good on crackers but not taco salad. Monterey Jack?

"Have you tried that farmers cheese?" A voice from behind startled her. Turning, Jessica almost bumped into María Paz, who reached into the cooler to retrieve a package. "I didn't mean to scare you!"

"Oh, hi," Jessica said, recovering. How did María Paz always manage to look stunning while raising three children? One would think she just came from a photo shoot, short black hair styled perfectly, eye shadow hinting the same shade of purple as her blouse, amethyst necklace and earrings matching effortlessly.

"No, I've never tried it. I'm contemplating what goes well on taco salad." She hoped María Paz wouldn't think she was asking for taco salad advice because she's Mexican. Jessica's brain went into overdrive. Is taco salad actually Mexican, or something Anglos cooked up and passed off as Mexican?

María Paz replied, "Most people use cheddar, but I prefer the Monterey Jack."

"Yeah, that's what I was thinking." Jessica picked up a package and added it to her cart. "Do you usually shop here?" She hadn't seen María Paz in this store before. She hoped her question didn't imply expecting her to shop someplace Mexican, like Mi Pueblo. She willed herself to try not to fixate on her own ignorance of Mexican adults.

"It depends on what I need. Tonight I am fixing spaghetti, the kids' favorite. My husband doesn't get home from work until later. By the way, Marisela loves what your class is doing in science."

Tension suddenly drained from Jessica's body like syrup running down the side of a bottle. "You mean the kitchen chemistry we're doing? I couldn't figure out a better way of getting at physical properties of common household items and chemical changes caused by heat and cold. The kids seem to be getting it."

María Paz laughed. "You should have seen her last night helping me make flan! She actually gave me a lesson about the relationship between sugar's melting point, the rate of heating it up, and resulting molecular change."

Jessica grinned. Planning the kitchen chemistry science unit had consumed the better part of two weekends. While intuitively it made sense to teach properties of matter through cooking, she hadn't been sure whether the cooking itself would eclipse attention to the science. This was good feedback.

The two strolled toward breads and desserts. "Can I ask you something?" Jessica ventured. When María Paz looked at her as though expecting her to continue, she did. "This might sound stupid, but how did your English get so good? I think you've lived here for a couple of years, but a lot of people who have lived here a long time don't speak it as well as you do." As soon as she closed her mouth, panic flitted through Jessica as she wondered briefly whether María Paz actually was a recent immigrant, or only presumed so because she was not Anglo.

"Thank you," María Paz replied. "My parents sent me to schools in Mexico where most of the curriculum was in English. I started to learn it when I was about seven."

"Oh, wow!" Jessica tried to picture herself learning science or history in another language. As she imagined feeling lost in such a classroom, she realized this was exactly what many Milford students experienced every day.

"Plus," María Paz continued, "the receptionist job I have involves using both languages everyday, depending on whom I'm talking to."

"Do you think you'll stay here in the States?" Jessica asked, pausing at a bin filled with a variety of fresh baked bread.

"Who knows? Right now my husband has a better job here than he would be able to find in Guanajuato. And the children are doing well. So we'll see. You'll be at the school board meeting next Tuesday?"

Jessica had avoided thinking about it. She knew the school board would be voting on the Raza Studies proposal, and its organizers wanted a good show of support. Maintaining distance from them, however, had gone hand in hand with distancing herself from Esteban. Until now, she hadn't considered the possibility that some of her students' parents would be there.

"I'm not sure yet. You're going?"

"Yes, of course. They've probably already made up their minds, and some of the board members seem stuck on the idea that school shouldn't teach what they think the parents can teach at home. But as I watch Marisela bring home from your classroom books by Mexican authors who I've never read – books by a whole range of authors, actually – I can see this proposal would give our kids something they otherwise don't seem to get. Except of course when teachers like you make such a welcome effort."

As Jessica gazed at María Paz, it hit her that this school board meeting wasn't about Esteban, nor was it about her embarrassment for having walked out of the rally. It wasn't about her at all. Here was the mother of one her students figuratively grabbing her hand, asking if she would join them, on behalf of the kids.

Silently she said, Thank you, I needed that. Jessica felt like hugging María Paz for giving her a kick. Aloud, she said, "Yes, of course, I'll be there."

A smile lit up María Paz's face. "Mrs. Westerfield, I truly appreciate what you're doing for my daughter. Well, I need to order a cake for Saturday, we're celebrating my youngest's birthday a couple of days early."

"I'm so glad I ran into you. You just made my day." Jessica smiled back at her.

"See you next Tuesday, then." María Paz turned toward the cake counter. Jessica stared after her, briefly wondering how she could walk so easily and gracefully in heels, especially after presumably tottering around in them all day. What an amazing person Marisela's mother was turning out to be!

A few minutes later, Jessica pulled out of the parking lot, glad the sky was finally staying light noticeably longer. Perhaps her darkest days were now past.

CHAPTER 34

*May, 1912*

What a relief! Viola's wedding was over. It had taken place in Lydia's living room earlier in the week. Although it was a simple affair, preparing had been exhausting. There was Viola's cream-colored lace dress to make, a four-course breakfast following the ceremony to plan and organize, the house – liberally decorated with roses from the garden – to prepare for guests, the German Methodist pastor to work with, and one of her own dresses to update.

Viola and her new husband – her beau from Storm Lake – left for their honeymoon, a trip that would take them to their new home in Sioux City, Iowa, where he owned a confectioner shop. He had waited to propose until he had a stable source of income to support a family, although Viola insisted she would continue to teach music. Lydia smiled as she pictured their planned stop in Rockford, Iowa, to visit Ralston, Mamie, and their new eight month-old boy.

A knock on the door startled her. Lydia pulled herself to her feet and opened it, finding on the doorstep her neighbor Heinrich and his two youngest daughters Flora and Ada. Flora, a 24 year-old German and French teacher, handed Lydia a basket of warm orange rolls. "My mother wanted you to have these. Viola's wedding was lovely. I'll miss her."

As Lydia welcomed the party inside, she marveled at the transformation of these two girls into pretty young women. Flora's auburn hair, piled on top of her head, complemented her fair, slender face, set off by the lace collar of her starched white blouse. Ada, a bit shorter and rounder than Flora, shared her sister's wavy auburn hair and vivid eyes.

"Your mother makes the best bread!" Lydia inhaled the yeasty aroma as she took the basket while motioning her visitors to sit. "Let me get some tea to go with them."

Heinrich shook his head. "*Danke*, but we don't want to cause you trouble, you're probably enjoying a chance to relax."

"On the contrary, I'm delighted to see you back in Decatur. And I crave conversation about something other than wedding preparations."

After completing his fund-raising assignment, Heinrich had served as substitute *Pfarrer* for a church in nearby Greenwood that had suddenly found itself without one. Mary and these two daughters had lived there with him temporarily, the older children remaining in the family's Decatur house.

"Tell me about your plans these days," Lydia prompted the two young women. Ada, just graduating from high school, replied that she was considering Millikin College.

"Viola liked it, and I can walk there from home," she added pragmatically.

Flora said, "I've decided to go back to Muscatine to teach. I've fallen in love with German literature, and there's more opportunity to teach it there than here."

Lydia raised her eyebrows. "German literature, how wonderful, although I confess to be fairly ignorant in that department."

Heinrich explained, "Flora's brother-in-law Heinrich Dietrich has been a marvelous instructor for Flora over the years when we've visited. He's not only read Goethe, he's actually studied Goethe's writing."

Lydia had heard of Goethe, but had read little of his work. She prompted Flora, "Tell me what you love about his work."

Ada sank back into her chair as if to say, Now we'll be here all day!

Flora brightened. "It's not just that Goethe used language brilliantly, and was a wonderful writer. He was also a strong intellectual, a Renaissance man in the truest sense of the word – poet, dramatist, scientist, philosopher. So his writing blends his intellect with his poetry and drama skills."

Ada stared intently at the ceiling while Flora went on, "The work I love most is *Faust*. Oh, if you haven't read it, you must. It's about a man who sells his soul to the devil for the love a beautiful woman. But the deeper question he asks is: what would you sell your soul for? What is your price, what do you want more than your own integrity and honor?"

Not having anticipated an academic lecture, Lydia vainly tried to think of a response, then commented to Heinrich, "That doesn't sound like a question the daughter of a servant of *Gott Vater* would be asking."

Heinrich replied, "But it is, if you take the notion of the devil as a metaphor for all that tempts us, and your soul as a metaphor for what you stand for."

Flora, hands waving like butterflies, agreed, "That's right. I've argued with some of the high school English teachers about the value of studying German literature."

Lydia tried to hide an amused smile as she pictured a schoolteacher trying to fend off the determinedly inquisitive Flora, who continued, "All the high schools teach Shakespeare. Why? Because Shakespeare used language brilliantly, and he wrote about human nature for a broad audience. But so did Goethe and other classic German writers. Then why is Goethe not taught? Because most English teachers have only read English authors. If they know Goethe at all, it's through translation. Goethe translated into English is good, but Goethe in German is exquisite," Flora rhapsodized in the tone one would use to describe one's beloved.

Lydia was perplexed as to why Flora would bubble so about long-dead German writers. Although she grew up speaking German at home and at church, her own schooling had been in English. So even though she had heard of a few German writers, she hadn't studied them, certainly not the way Flora was describing.

Bored listening to her sister's recitation, Ada reached for an orange roll.

"Honey, let me get you some lemonade to wash that down." Lydia jumped up and headed for the kitchen before Heinrich could stop her.

As Lydia returned with a tray of glasses of lemonade, Flora continued, "So that's why I'll return to Muscatine. There's more opportunity there than here to teach German, including German thinkers." Reaching for a glass, she added, "I'm also continuing to improve my French so I have that option as well."

While Lydia sought a response, Heinrich commented, "What she's saying has a ring of truth. It's not just German writers who aren't studied seriously in most schools here. German points of view are completely ignored, so when the English speakers discuss an issue, they have no idea we might have a slightly different perspective."

"You mean like what's in our newspapers, although I confess I don't read them very often," offered Lydia.

"Exactly. At least you're aware there's another point of view."

"I'm not so interested in politics, Father," Flora turned to Heinrich. "Although I suppose the viewpoints of philosophers and poets connect with those of politicians. Maybe."

"The point is that the German space these viewpoints come from has room for a lot of different ideas and viewpoints. The intellectual life of this country needs to be big enough to include that German intellectual space along with the English space." With that, Heinrich downed a glass of lemonade.

To try to draw Ada into the conversation, Lydia asked her, "When you go to Millikin, what will you study? Have you thought about taking German?"

"Yeah, I probably will because it's something I know. Not like Flora, I don't think I could be that passionate about it, but it's something I can do well. After all, we grew up with it."

"Are you thinking about being a teacher, too?" Lydia probed. Ada sighed, then said as though trying to sound more definite than she actually felt, "Of course, what else is there? At least until I get married."

Flora sent her a sharp glare, to which Ada stuck out her tongue.

"Marriage is fine, it just isn't our only option," Flora stated.

"Well, you're both very lovely and very smart, so I suppose you can do whatever it is you wish," Lydia replied, silently giving thanks that Viola had been less complicated to raise.

Henry stood. "We'll be on our way, Lydia. Thank you for the lemonade, I always enjoy seeing you."

"So what will you be doing now that you're back from Greenwood?" Lydia stood.

"Well, as Secretary of the German Conference, I'll be spending more time in St. Louis. I'm going there next week for a few days. I'm not sure what kind of work they'll give me next. Whatever it is, as long as I am continuing to grow our beloved German church, I am fulfilling the purpose *Gott Vater* gave me." Heinrich's voice rang of electric energy every time he talked about his work with the church. Lydia couldn't decide whether being around him was inspiring or tiring.

"Then we'll all see each other Sunday," she said warmly as she bade them goodbye.

*February, 2013*

Jessica quietly opened the door to the Board Room. The meeting had already begun and the room was packed. She slid on in, then along the back wall until she could stand comfortably. At the front, a tall white woman was reading from notes in her left hand.

"... and this would simply cause more segregation than we already have. My ninth-grade son enjoys hearing views of some of his Mexican classmates, but if they start taking different classes, he would have less exposure to them. As a mother, I don't think that would be good for his education, and as a citizen, I don't think it would be good for any of our children. So I hope the board votes no." She looked around nervously over reading glasses, then walked stiffly back to her seat near the back of the room.

Jessica recognized the procedure for school board meetings, having attended a couple before. They typically began with time for public comment. Those who wished to address the board signed a roster before the meeting began, then were allotted up to two minutes in the sign-in order. Although the board had invited discussion when the Raza Studies proposal was introduced in November, since they would be voting on it tonight and opinions were strongly divided, the roster was long.

Jessica scanned the crowd while a girl who appeared to be a Mexican-American high school student stood and walked confidently to the front of the room. She noticed three Milford teaching colleagues – Ralph, Rick, and Carolyn, huddled heads suggesting strategy planning. Behind them, standing against a side wall with arms folded across his chest, stood Joe, a teacher Jessica occasionally saw walking his dog. Near the front, she saw María Paz seated next to her husband, Diana's mother Graciela, and two more Mexican American Milford parents. Behind them, against the wall, was Esteban, who caught Jessica's eye. He smiled and winked. She blushed, then gave a small wave, noting Brenda at his side. To her relief, Brenda's presence bothered her only a little. Maybe her crush on Esteban was the signal she needed that her marriage was floundering, and the push she needed to understand and support Raza Studies.

"... and that's why we're counting on you to vote in favor of the proposal," the girl finished, silver earrings dancing playfully. Applause erupted from a group of high school students, about half of whom appeared Mexican American. "Go girl!" one yelled.

The gavel rapped sharply. "Only signed-in speakers have the floor, everyone else is to remain silent," board president Darin Armstrong reprimanded. Jessica thought he looked like Santa Claus minus the red suit, but the expression on his face was anything but jolly. "Mr. Walsh, you're next," he read from the speaker's roster.

A wiry man in his forties, thinning red hair, red mustache, and silver wire-rimmed glasses, approached the front of the room. Jessica recognized him as a sociology professor from a local university. As usual, he wore a plaid shirt, jeans, and boots.

"Thank you." His soft voice barely reached the back of the room. "Speak up, please!" someone shouted. "Shhh!" someone else admonished. The room fell quiet as the crowd struggled to hear.

"Thank you," he repeated with more volume. "I've heard objections that this proposal will segregate students by race. I want to point out two things wrong with this objection. One is that anyone can sign up for a Raza Studies class. Our university Mexican American history classes, for example, draw students from all ethnic groups, rather than segregating them. The other thing is that students are already segregated, but by housing. We all know which neighborhoods are predominantly white and which aren't. This proposal doesn't cause that segregation, although it might reflect it, since I don't think the proposal targets the white schools. But I just wanted you to stop and think about the fact that we already have segregation, and if we were concerned about eliminating it, we'd be talking about how to integrate housing."

Mr. Walsh walked back to his seat to a few light smatters of applause.

The next half hour continued in a similar vein. Jessica expected Ralph to take the stage, but he, Rick and Carolyn apparently had come just to watch.

The public comment period finally ended, and Mr. Armstrong moved to items on the agenda. Jessica's mind wandered while the chair of the Budget and Finance Committee droned through a short report in the language of number-speak. As she scanned the crowd, Ralph caught her eye and motioned her to join them. Not wanting to align herself with his politics, Jessica pretended not to see his nonverbal invitation.

The board went on to consider a proposal for a minor alteration to the district's suspension policy. Jessica glanced at her watch; it was almost 8:30 already, and her feet were complaining. Apparently other people's feet were doing the same; those standing along the wall were beginning to sway as they shifted from one foot to another.

"Let's move on to the next item, the proposal for Mexican American studies in several of our schools," Mr. Armstrong finally said. "We've had this proposal before us for about two months now. I think we've had ample time to consider it, and we've certainly had ample input into our thinking." He tipped his head toward the audience. "Are we ready for a vote?"

"I move adoption," said Monica Jones, an environmental activist whose long blond hair made her look like she was still in college, despite lines beginning to circle her mouth and eyes.

"Second," said Al Estrada, director of Clínica Salud and the only Latino on the board, certain to support the proposal. "We should do a roll call vote, to make sure the recorded count is accurate," he added.

"He just wants to make sure we all know who supported us and who didn't," a tall man with black hair standing next to Jessica loudly whispered to no one in particular.

Mr. Armstrong replied, "I think we can skip the roll call, but I will ask you to vote by raising your hand. We do need an accurate count. All in favor of the motion, please so signify."

Three hands shot up belonging to Jones, Estrada, and Lou Hammer. Hammer, the lone African American on the board and owner of a popular local restaurant, had occasionally requested looking into the high rate of African American student absenteeism, a request Armstrong said the board would "get to" at some unspecified future date.

"Those opposed, please signify."

Four hands went up. Jessica had figured Armstrong and two other white men would oppose it, all three being staunch advocates of sticking to the state standards and adopted textbooks, believing deviations would compromise quality education. Peter Nakamura, the fourth, had been a question mark in her mind. Although the young physical therapist tended to side with traditionalism, occasionally he surprised people, such as when he had opposed tying teacher evaluations to student test scores.

Mr. Armstrong rapped his gavel. "The motion fails." A few cheers went up and several people applauded.

Armstrong turned to the audience, many already packing up to leave, frustration and anger written on several faces. "I know many of you are sorely disappointed by this vote. Several of you in here have worked hard on this proposal, and some of you have creative ideas for the school curriculum. I personally opposed it because I think it makes changes that are too sweeping. I'm not sure we need a whole new set of courses, even if they are aligned to the state standards, as you have convinced me they would be. But I urge those of you who worked on this proposal to investigate ways you can infuse Mexican American content more strongly into the history and literature courses we already have. You don't need board authorization to do that."

Armstrong then moved the board on to the next agenda item. Jessica couldn't hear what it was, for the scooting of chairs and scuffling of feet as people headed toward the door. Being fairly close to it, she was one of the first out.

Standing in the cold, she realized she felt hollow. She hadn't expected the board to approve the proposal, although she had hoped they might. But neither had she expected to feel as though someone had sucked the air out of her. She stood to the side, watching people pass, as she sorted through her feelings. Several Latino families exited, dejected looks on their faces. Three teachers she had seen before but didn't know passed her, one of them saying. "We'll keep trying."

When her three Milford colleagues emerged, smug looks on their faces, anger shot through her body. How dare they advocate for something not in the best interests of the very students in their classes, she thought. Suddenly the anger brought tears to the corners of Jessica's eyes. She squeezed them shut in an effort to regain control.

"Are you alright?" Opening her eyes, she saw Esteban looking at her with concern. Next to him were Brenda, Dolores, and the tall, gangly teacher with a goatee who seemed to be the Raza Studies leader, but whose name escaped her.

"How can you stand to work with them?" she asked, nodding in the direction of Ralph, Rick, and Carolyn, now disappeared into the receding crowd.

"Practice," he replied. "You're just discovering their colors, but they've been obvious to me for a long time."

"I wish this would have passed. I guess I thought it had a chance," Jessica mumbled.

"We're disappointed, but not surprised," said Dolores. "We had a pretty good idea where everyone stood before going in. But at least it's all public now."

"What are you gonna do?" Jessica asked, assuming the work for Raza Studies was over.

"Keep at it," replied the goateed man. "I'm Donaldo, by the way."

"I'm Jessica, I teach at Milford."

"Esteban's colleague, right," he replied.

"Where's your sidekick?" asked Dolores. To Jessica's puzzled expression, she added, "The woman with long blond helicopter hair, I think she teaches with you?"

"Oh, Cath. She had planned to come, but a friend of hers got sick so she went to help out. I hope she doesn't bring germs to school tomorrow."

"Jessica." Donaldo pronounced her name as though committing it to memory. "You saw in there that we have a few white allies, but not enough. I was keeping track of the speakers." He pulled a rumpled page from a pocket. "Let's see, we had thirteen speakers in favor of the proposal and eleven of them were Latino.

There were fifteen speakers against, almost all white, one Latino and two, I couldn't tell."

"What would you want me to do?" Jessica asked. "I can't teach Mexican American studies, I don't have the background."

"Read the newspapers tomorrow," Donaldo said. "Then talk to Esteban."

No one replied to the puzzlement on Jessica's face. Instead, Dolores offered, "Walk you to your car?" Jessica walked silently with the group to the parking lot, wondering what Donaldo could be referring to.

* * * * *

Too wound up to sleep, Jessica decided to read articles she had downloaded from Newspaper Archive over the weekend, figuring they'd do the work of a sleeping pill. She bundled herself into pajamas, got in bed, balanced her computer on her lap, and dove in. She wanted to trace what happened to Decatur area German Americans after 1912. After ewar broke out between Austria and Serbia in summer of 1914, Germany declared war on Russia, France, and Belgium. She wondered how any of this might have affected her ancestors.

A quick scan of 1914 Decatur headlines showed newspapers, and probably the general public, lining up against Germany. While some headlines were simply descriptive – "Germans Capture 10,000 Prisoners" – others castigated Germany as dangerous and wrong. "Americans Scared," proclaimed one.

German Americans seemed caught in the middle, American yet also seeing Germany's point of view. A lengthy article written by a German-American attorney in the August 11 *Decatur Review* caught her attention: "A German-American citizen in expressing his view upon the very unfortunate war situation in Europe is liable to be misunderstood and have his loyalty to the government of the United States questioned. First, let me say, I believe every thoughtful honest German-American citizen cannot help resenting every insinuation, that because of his sympathy for the German people, that he is betraying disloyalty to the United States."

What he wrote makes sense, Jessica thought, then continued reading. The writer, after describing German Americans' active role in support of the Union during the Civil War, distinguished between the German Kaiser and ordinary German citizens who did not want war. He saw the conflict as resulting from European resentments toward Germany. England, in particular, "availed itself of this opportunity to reduce the world power of Germany, which had displaced the English marine in many parts of the world. ... This loss of trade not only made England jealous, but when the right time came to strike a fatal blow, she enrolled as an enemy against Germany." This was all news to Jessica, whose own forays into World War I history lessons hadn't mentioned England competing with Germany.

Another German American wrote: "The German people are looked upon as foreigners, the English as ancestors." That smacked Jessica in the gut. Even though she had little English ancestry herself, she realized she too took for granted English literature and philosophy as her heritage, England as her natural ally. The English were still viewed as the ancestors! Somehow not only non-English heritages vanished, but with them, memory of their very existence.

With a surge of energy, she continued reading. In August, the German Red Cross, raising money for relief of German soldiers on the battlefield, had drawn an enthusiastic Decatur crowd, which probably included her ancestors. "Staunch patriotism which neither years of exile nor American naturalization has weakened, flared brightly Thursday night when nearly 700 Decatur people, among them the representative German Americans of the city, assembled in St. Johannes' hall in the interests of the German Red Cross Society ... 'The Watch on the Rhine,' the national anthem swelling with a nation's pride and love of the country for which Germans are noted above all other people, rang through the hall again and again." Apparently a speaker told the crowd that the war "being waged in the Fatherland against nearly the whole of Europe was in reality one of defense of home territory." Self-defense, not aggression. Whether true or not in hindsight, Jessica couldn't say, but this speaker's viewpoint was the same as the lawyer's.

In an article printed later in 1914, she learned that a chapter of the National German-American Alliance, founded thirteen years previously to promote and preserve German language and culture in the U.S., was established in Decatur. Jessica could visualize Flora's active participation.

In 1915, Germany sank the Lusitania, believing it was carrying munitions. By 1917, as Germany increased its submarine attacks against non-German ships, German Americans, now downplaying their German roots, redoubled their efforts to affirm loyalty to the U.S. Jessica learned that in early February, a convention of the National German-American Alliance passed resolutions "endorsing the action of President Wilson in severing diplomatic relations with Germany and pledging its loyalty to the United States," and giving German Red Cross funds to Americans rather than continuing to send them to Germany. The Alliance also encouraged German Americans to enlist.

Its members, however, lamented growing backlash against them. In early April, President Wilson requested a declaration of war from Congress. The article, laced with anti-German rhetoric, characterized Wisconsin Senator La Follette's anti-war speech as "pro-German, pro-Goth, pro-vandal" and "anti-president, anti-congress, and anti-American." Former President Teddy Roosevelt announced that "some senators, congressmen, and newspaper editors" were "standing where the copperheads stood in the civil war" – traitors, in other words. He demanded "suppression of the German language press" and "deportation of 'fifty-fifty Americans.'" My god, thought Jessica, that would certainly include German-born Heinrich!

She learned that the Post Office Department considered "exclusion from the mails of certain influential German language newspapers ... as a part of the government's determination to prevent circulation of anti-war propaganda." Citizens of Harbine, Nebraska drove to a nearby town and "placarded the place with notices demanding that the use of the German language be stopped." German ministers in various places were told "to preach in English and that the songs be sung in English." Oddly, even use of the German language in German opera was banned in New York. Jessica wondered how German opera could possibly be sung that way. German Americans, particularly those born in Germany, were targeted as spies, violence toward them escalating. Jessica read that German civilians were detained in military camps, and that some German Americans – now widely referred to by the epithet "Huns" – were actually lynched.

In Decatur, the teaching of high school German was suspended. When the superintendent was asked in 1919 whether it might be restored after the war, he replied, "I suppose it will be put back sometime. But there will not be any hurry about it so far as I am concerned. The more I learn of the German conduct of this war the less I am in sympathy with things German." How did Flora, a German teacher, fare? She must have been outraged!

Even Methodist church publications concurred with banning German. Writing in *The Christian Advocate*, a weekly newspaper of the Methodist Church, Bishop Cooke proclaimed that, "nothing separates humanity like diversity of tongues ... let our preachers and people use only the English language ... we should preserve the unity of the nation and foreign language is not the language of the young people of America." With English-speaking congregations turning against their fellow German Methodists – or at least against that which made them German – how did German Americans manage to survive?

Jessica filed the newspaper articles, closed her laptop, and set it on the floor next to the bed. This bedtime reading, rather than making her drowsy, stirred her thoughts even more. To try to empty out her brain, she concentrated on slow, deep breathing: in ... out ... in ... out ...

\* \* \* \* \*

*"I urge you to please vote for this proposal," Jessica implored the school board. "Everyone should be able to enroll in a class on German-American history and literature. It isn't just for Germans, it's for everyone." Her voice became desperate. "We need it because the regular curriculum doesn't include German authors at all, not even Goethe. Nothing about our history is in the curriculum, nothing at all. It's as if we didn't exist."*

*The board members glared coldly back at her. Then, as one, they stood and began to chant: "Seditious, lock her up. Seditious, lock her up. Seditious, lock her up." As they approached her, Jessica grabbed her pillow and tried to bury herself under it. "No, I'm American," she pleaded. "I'm not a Hun, I'm a loyal American!" She felt something wrapping tightly around her as she twisted.*

Jessica had to go to the bathroom. She stopped twisting, trying to figure out where she was. She opened her eyes. An echo of a streetlight filtered through closed blinds of her bedroom window. The school board had vanished.

She looked at the clock on her bedside table. The alarm wouldn't sound for another half hour, but Jessica was suddenly wide awake, so she got up, practically stumbling over the laptop on the floor.

A half hour later, showered and dressed, she opened the front door to see if the newspaper had arrived yet. She usually read news online, but had subscribed to a local paper after Tim left, a substitute for breakfast conversation.

She tossed the paper onto the kitchen table while she made coffee and rummaged through the refrigerator for fruit and milk to put on her daily dose of Wheat Chex. Then, breakfast in hand, she opened the paper. There at the top of the front page was a picture of the tall mother of a ninth grader reading her statement to the school board, objecting to the Raza Studies proposal because she believed resulting segregation would compromise her son's education. The headline read: "School Board Rejects Curriculum Segregation."

Jessica almost dropped her coffee mug. Curriculum segregation? That wasn't what the proposal was about. She set the mug down and read through the article, trying to remember if she had noticed reporters with cameras in the room. Obviously at least one had been there.

The article quoted various statements made during the public comment period. After reporting the tall mother's arguments, it quoted another person Jessica barely remembered, who had claimed there is nothing wrong with learning about Mexico later on, but what students really need is more knowledge of basic American culture, American institutions, American history, and American heroes.

Recalling Donaldo's tally, Jessica frowned as she read the article's assertion that a clear majority of public comments had opposed the Raza Studies proposal. Technically the article was correct, but only by two speakers. It went on to report detailed comments of someone who spoke against the proposal, then briefly mentioned two who spoke in favor, including the high school student. But in her case, the article described how poised and energetic she was, barely mentioning what she had actually said.

Jessica flipped to the last page of Section A to finish the article. As she read, her eyes caught the adjacent editorial page. In the center, the newspaper's opinion about the school board's decision on the Raza Studies proposal was featured prominently. Jessica wondered how they could have prepared something to publish so quickly, considering a vote wasn't taken until after 8:30 pm. They must have had it already to go, just waiting for the vote.

The editorial commended the school board for its "wise decision" to reject a "heart-felt and well-meaning but misguided proposal." Well-meaning? How patronizing!

It went on to argue that a strength of American schools is that they treat everyone as individuals rather than as members of ethnic groups, and they promote free inquiry rather than brainwashing young people to accept a certain political viewpoint. The editorial praised the nation's roots in the Enlightenment, democracy, and English legal institutions, and the importance of upholding a tradition of turning immigrants from foreign countries into true Americans.

In other words, Jessica thought, Mexican people are foreigners, the English are the ancestors.

This prominent editorial was flanked by two letters to the editor that must have been written earlier and saved for today. A short letter simply condemned what the writer believed was a program designed to overthrow the U.S. government, and teachers whose loyalty to the U.S. was questionable. The other, assuming the Raza Studies curriculum would be taught in Spanish, argued that "foreign" students need to learn to speak English, which the writer felt is impossible when some of their classes are taught in Spanish. There wasn't a letter in support.

So this was what Donaldo anticipated when he told her to read today's newspaper. She shoved it aside and finished breakfast.

Arriving at school a bit earlier than usual, Jessica went straight to her classroom and organized materials for the day. Then she marched down the hall to Cath's classroom, where she found Cath arranging strips of paper in different colors and sizes on a large table in the center of the room.

"What are you doing?" Jessica pointed at the colored paper.

Cath looked up. "Getting ready to try out a new arithmetic activity. A lot of my kids still get mixed up on place value when numbers are over 100, so I'm trying something. We can talk while I work, but I've gotta get this stuff organized before they start showing up."

"Did you read the paper this morning?" Jessica asked.

"Do I ever read a newspaper in the morning? No. If it's about the school board meeting, I hear things didn't go well." Cath carefully stacked some large blue squares, then looked up at Jessica. "You look terrible, what happened?"

"I didn't sleep well last night," Jessica said. "I made the mistake of reading old newspapers about persecution of Germans in the U.S. during World War I. Cath, the same thing is happening now."

Cath put down a stack of long green paper strips. "What are you talking about?"

"Now I know why I didn't know anything about my German-American ancestors, about how they lived, about their German churches, their German community. Everything German got squashed during World War I. Non-Germans were afraid of them. Even when they just tried to offer a different point of view, people accused them of sedition. This morning, when I opened up the newspaper, I saw the same arguments being leveled against the Mexican Americans. And Cath, some of these very same people are probably German descendants, who don't even know their own history." Jessica exhaled loudly. "I don't know what to do with that."

A bell sounded, signaling that students could now enter the building. Cath hesitated, then said, "Hold that thought until lunch."

"OK, but in my room. I can't talk about this stuff in the lounge, not around Ralph and Carolyn and Rick. They were there last night, and they're probably gloating."

A lively cacophony of clatter punctuated by squeals of children's voices rolled down the hall like a wave. Jessica ducked out of Cath's room, returning to her own just seconds ahead of her first students.

When Cath arrived for lunch, Jessica showed her the morning's newspaper. Cath sat down, opened her lunch bag, and read it while eating. Jessica silently munched on a ham sandwich.

"Whew, looks like they already had their guns lined up," Cath commented.

"What bothers me is that the article about the board meeting is skewed, but technically accurate. Alongside those letters the paper must have saved up, it makes the board look open-minded for even considering the proposal, but reasonable for voting it down. I should write a letter to the editor, myself."

"Saying?"

Jessica studied the remains of her sandwich. "Well, maybe just saying, from a teacher's point of view, I can see how my kids respond when I integrate Mexican-American literature into my classroom. What gets me is that we're doing pretty much the same things to immigrants now as what was done to our ancestors a century ago. But we don't know what happened then, so we don't stop to think."

"So you're suggesting there should be a German studies program, too?"

"No, that wouldn't be relevant here and now, although I might sign up for German classes if they were available here. But, it was relevant in the Midwest a hundred years ago. The thing is, it's like there's this big funnel," Jessica's hands outlined its shape, "and this country takes all these different people, puts them through the funnel, and out comes people like you and me." Her hands grabbed at imaginary people, tossing them into the imaginary funnel. "People who think the English are our real ancestors, but couldn't tell you who they are beyond something like, 'Oh, I'm a sports fan. White bread, Wonder Bread no less.'"

"So you're going to write about Wonder Bread?"

"Something like that. I'm not sure."

The two sat silently with their thoughts, then Jessica announced, "That's what I'll do, I'll write a letter to the editor about, something about this funnel, or whatever, that erased my history, erased a lot of other people's histories. And here we are at it again, no memory. What do you think?"

Cath nodded slowly. "I like the general idea. The details will need work. Can I read it before you send it?"

"Hell, yes, I'll need your help. I'll probably need Esteban's help, too, to get this right. Oh, by the way, he was there last night with Brenda. I was only a little bit bothered. I think I'm moving on."

"Good girl, I'm glad to hear it."

The door swung open abruptly. "Can we come back in?" asked Joey, out of breath from running.

"Sure, we're done." Jessica and Cath stood. "C'mon in," Jessica gently laid a hand on Joey's shoulder, motioning him into the room.

"My signal to get back to my classroom." Cath scooted out the door. "Catch you later!"

CHAPTER 36

*May, 1918*

"Well, that's it." Ralston slapped the newspaper onto the worn kitchen table. "German's gone from Iowa. The deed's been done."

He pointed at the chicken Mamie was deboning. "That's baked chicken, or whatever you do to it. You're not fixing *Hähnchenschnitzel* anymore."

Mamie replied as she continued working on the chicken, "For all intents and purposes, German's been gone from here for a while, at least outside people's homes. The German Methodist Church over in Flood Creek stopped using it some months ago."

Ralston, eight years a physician in Rockford, slumped down wearily. "I know, a couple of my patients told me. At least Pastor Feuer here in Rockford can retire. He certainly has aged a lot. Gretchen and her family still make the trip all the way over to Flood Creek, although I suspect they'll stop."

"I spoke with Gretchen on the telephone not ten minutes ago. She's distraught. They've banned the very language that connects her with the world."

Shortly after arriving in Rockford and establishing an office, Ralston married Mamie. A former stenographer, she lent her skills to the business end of his work. After their first child Bobby arrived, they remodeled the back of their house to serve as Rockford's only hospital. Ralston and another novice physician now used it as their surgery. Mamie kept the books, and a hired matron kept the hospital rooms scrubbed.

"Unless it's absolutely necessary to use German to communicate with a patient, we need to use English all the time. Otherwise people start to think we're pro-German spies," he said.

Mamie sighed, "I keep thinking about Dad and how he's put his whole life into building the German community's church. Now his life's work is being eradicated right before his eyes. I think it's slowly killing him."

Ralston stood and looked out the kitchen window at auburn-haired Bobby digging a hole with a stick, dirt flying in what would soon become the vegetable garden. Clouds scudded across a robin's egg blue sky, shiny green buds burst from a sprawling oak. Their two-year-old, napping in the other room, occasionally grunted.

"We can't tell the children about all this," Ralston remarked. "It's best if they grow up not knowing what happened. They're just plain white bread. I guess now we are too, for that matter."

"White bread." She gazed at a golden loaf she had pulled from the oven a few minutes ago, filling the kitchen with its rich yeasty aroma. "I guess that will have to do."

"It's still hard for me to believe people think Germany's actually trying to colonize the U.S. by planting spies over here to work for the Kaiser. Poor elderly Mrs. Luecht, can you imagine anyone actually thinking she's a spy? She can barely walk across a room!"

Mamie said, "It's just as well Flora went back to Decatur to teach French and help Ada care for Mom and Dad. Her career teaching German literature at that high school in Muscatine was certainly short-lived, what with German texts being banned. English isn't actually the official language of the U.S., is it? I thought there wasn't one, but the Governor seems to think differently."

"It might as well be. We can't be angry with him, though," Ralston said as he sat down again and thumbed through the newspaper. "He's just reflecting what the general population feels."

"The general non-German population," Mamie corrected. "Almost half the people in this town have German ancestry. No one I know supports the Kaiser."

"Even so, the English-speakers would happily jail anyone they suspect of being pro-German. The Governor says he's just trying to prevent violence by banning the language." Ralston stood and put his arms around Mamie's waist. "We'll get through it."

"We will, yes. I'm not so sure about the older people like Gretchen, and Mom and Dad, who can't simply hide their German-ness."

Looking at Bobby tossing dirt, Mamie asked, "Do you think they'll want to know? You know, one day when they're older."

"Can't think why they would." He looked at her, resignation in his eyes giving way to something less defined as he gazed off over her shoulder. "We'll just tell them one of their grandpas was a farmer in Iowa – or Illinois, actually, he didn't get much farming done in Iowa before he died. And their other grandpa was a preacher. That's all they need to know. We have a few pictures we can show them. Kids usually don't want to know much more than that, anyway."

As they gazed out the window, he continued, "The future belongs to our kids. They have American-sounding names, they'll grow up in English, they'll blend right in. They won't even know what we lost." He visualized an opera he had seen years ago. The stage was filled with eye-catching props, set against a brightly painted backdrop. But when it ended, the abruptly pulled curtain blocked everything from view except the lead actors, who suddenly appeared suspended in mid-air without the scenery, the trees, the fence post, the sofas, and the tables they had waltzed among just seconds earlier. "We'll have to invent normal. Maybe we'll even move out West. I hear it doesn't snow much out there."

From outside the kitchen window, Bobby's sudden laughter rose up, even as deepening clouds gathered over the afternoon sun.

\* \* \* \* \*

## August, 1928

Mary collapsed into the wooden chair in front of the desk and dropped her face into her hands. It had been three months since Heinrich had succumbed to a stroke, but she couldn't get used to his absence. Just this morning as she was waking, she had rolled over to put her hand on his chest as she often did, before remembering he was gone. He would tell her she shouldn't grieve because he was now in the arms of *Gott Vater*, but she grieved anyway.

Raising her head, she surveyed the empty cubbyholes in the old wooden desk. All their married life, this desk had been a cacophony of bits of paper, newspaper articles, letters, books propped open to this or that quotation to use in a sermon, and notebooks filled with Heinrich's longhand scrawl. Last month Flora and Ada finally cleared it out, since Mary didn't have the heart to do so. It stood here now in a corner of the living room, an empty monument to his work. One of the girls should just take it.

Mary was convinced that what killed him was having to spend three years watching his life's work unravel like a sweater when a cat runs away with a loose end of yarn. But really, things had started to disintegrate much earlier, with the mounting pressure during the war for churches to dispense with German. Even before the war, there had always been that element that felt threatened by things German. Mary hadn't thought they held much sway, but then look what happened once fear took hold in more English-speakers.

The German churches had complied with wartime demands. Heinrich, occasionally invited to deliver guest sermons, had done them all in English. She, too, had complied when hosting meetings of the German Methodist Woman's Missionary Society entirely in English. Somehow that compliance seemed only to confuse things, however. English-speaking congregations began to wonder why German churches were still needed, if they could do just as well in English. Why not make everything English, unite the Methodists once and for all.

At the time, the German churches replied that their continued growth was evidence of why they were needed. Indeed, the Decatur church boasted a healthy congregation, at least until the middle of the war. But the English remained suspicious that rather than bringing souls to *Gott*, *Pfarrers* like Heinrich were actually bringing them to the *Kaiser*. Nonsense, really, but when people are afraid, they believe all sorts of things they might question in other circumstances.

Then the newspapers he read were stopped. After all, the argument went, it was through German newspapers that the Kaiser delivered orders as part of his grand design to conquer the U.S. Of course Heinrich could read the English newspapers just as well, but he preferred the German papers simply because they covered more events of interest to him.

Then German churches began to close, in some cases through pressure from English neighbors who were offended by anything hinting of Germany in their midst, in other cases because of loss of members who feared that continuing to attend a German church, even if services were all conducted in English, would brand them as pro-German and anti-American. While Lydia never actually said that was why she shifted affiliation – she preferred to say she liked the English church's Women's Auxiliary activities better – Mary suspected that being viewed as German wore on her, and attending the English church sealed her American loyalty in the eyes of neighbors.

After the war was over, Lydia had gone to Sioux City to live out the rest of her days with Viola and her family. Viola had sent the sweetest note letting her know Lydia died. Consumption or something of that nature. Lydia and Willie, whom Mary had never met, were reunited at last.

The biggest blow came three years ago, when the St. Louis Conference of the German Methodist church was simply folded into neighboring English-speaking conferences, and the German churches were shuttered forever. German *Pfarrers* could either retire or accept assignment to English congregations. Those Mary knew chose retirement. That was when Heinrich's health began to fail, never to recover. His heart had broken.

Wood creaked as the house sighed. Mary was not used to being alone, and suspected she would never stop listening for family noises. She wasn't actually entirely alone – Flora and Ada, both teachers, still lived with her and would be home later. But having spent her entire life surrounded by family and friends, she was finding the hours to drag very slowly indeed, like a lame old man moving haltingly down the sidewalk.

Her eyes fell on two framed photos from their golden wedding anniversary ten years ago. In one photo, Heinrich and herself, both white haired, bespeckled, and unsmiling, stared back. The other, a larger photo taken by the newspaper photographer, captured her and Heinrich surrounded by family. There were all the children – now adults – except poor Carl who had died two years earlier, God rest his soul. A son-in-law and a daughter-in-law – one living on the east coast and the other on the west coast, both with young children – had been unable to come. But the rest were there. Even a nephew and two nieces made the trek from Iowa. Tears welled as she felt the love her family had showered on them.

Most had returned for Heinrich's funeral, a distinctly more somber affair. But afterward, they flew back off to their scattered lives. And here she was now, marking time, watching the hours trudge by.

Since Heinrich's death, Mary's thoughts increasingly returned to the family of her childhood, particularly her younger sister Annie, who still lived in Burlington. Scrounging through drawers, She found a bit of stationary Flora had missed. Picking up a pen, she began to write:

*Dearest Annie,*

*It has been three months now since the funeral of my dear husband Heinrich ...*

*February, 2013*

Jessica jumped out of bed and dashed to the front door. Flinging it open, she scanned the dark porch and walkway. No newspaper yet, not surprising considering it wasn't yet six a.m.

As jittery as she had been on her wedding day, she dove into the shower, then dressed. She was hooking an earring into her ear when she heard it. Thump! The earring still in one hand, she ran downstairs and threw open the front door. She scooped up the newspaper, wondering if today would be the day.

Yesterday she had awakened early, anticipating publication of her letter to the editor. But it hadn't appeared. Not terribly surprising, since she had emailed it to the editorial office just the day before. Today was more likely.

Jessica kicked the door shut while she opened the paper to the editorial page. Bouncing into the kitchen, she scanned the page. There it was!

---

German-American Descendant Supports
Mexican-American Studies

I write as a teacher whose Mexican-American students, like anyone else, love reading literature they can relate to. When I started using Mexican-American books in class, the uptick in their learning was obvious to me.

I also write as a descendant partially of German Americans, only recently having recovered their story in the Midwest over a century ago. It took a lot of effort to reconstruct what I could; most of the stories are gone forever. What I learned is that my ancestors had to bury their stories, language, and literature so as not to be seen as anti-American.

Fast forward to today, and many of us who are German-American descendants are pushing hard to do to other groups, such as Mexican Americans, what was done to our ancestors. When I place what has been said in objection to Mexican-American Studies

---

alongside what was said in objection to anything German American during World War I, the parallels are striking. I think the objections are rooted in fear, but the result is loss, rather than gain, for all of us.

Those of us who are white may have lost our stories, but we don't have to make others today lose theirs. I, for one, urge us to rethink our stance toward Mexican-American Studies, giving it our full support.

Jessica Westerfield
Fifth grade teacher

Jessica was so excited she couldn't sit. She danced around the kitchen as she prepared coffee, spilling water in the process. She ran back to the bedroom to finish putting in her earrings, her shaking hands struggling to find their target. She expected the phone to start ringing as friends and acquaintances began their day with the newspaper.

But nothing happened. No bells, no phone calls or texts, no emails. With the silence, her burst of hyper-energy gradually dissipated.

Jessica was backing the car down the driveway when her cell phone rang. Rooting through her bag, she found it just before it went over into voicemail.

"Jessica, it's Kimmie," a voice bubbled from the phone's speaker.

"Kimmie! What's up?"

"Hey, I just read your letter in the paper. Wow, girl, you rock!"

"Thanks! I really appreciate hearing that, you're the first person I know who's read it." A rush of elation shot through Jessica's body like a hot geyser.

"I gotta get to work, but maybe a movie this weekend? Let's talk later." With that, the call abruptly ended.

A Cheshire cat grin plastered on her face, Jessica drove to school. As she was parking, her cell phone rang again. Tim this time. "That's a really good letter you wrote," he said. "I just want you to know I'm proud of you."

Speechless, Jessica replied stupidly with the first thing that popped into her head, "You read the paper in the morning?"

"No, Linda and Vic read the paper. Linda called me, read it to me, then told me I'd be the biggest airhead in the world if didn't at least congratulate you for taking a courageous stand. I'll have to say, I'm not surprised. I'm truly proud."

Tears welled in Jessica's eyes. "Thank you, Tim. Just ... Thank you, it means a lot to me for you to say that."

"You must be at school," he said. "Go teach those kids, we'll talk later."

Jessica gathered herself together, stepped out of the car, and headed into school. On the way to her classroom she passed Ralph, who looked at her without smiling, tipped his head to acknowledge her existence, and kept walking. "Well, same to you," she muttered as she unlocked her classroom door.

Jessica was arranging furniture and props for book talks six students would do this morning, impersonating authors of books they had just read, when Sarah walked in, high heels clicking purposefully. Uh oh, Jessica said under her breath, trouble ahead. "Morning, Sarah," she said as cheerfully as she could muster.

"I won't take up your time, I know mornings are important for getting ready for the day. I just wanted to say," and she brandished the morning newspaper.

Jessica wondered if her letter had violated some rule. Maybe she shouldn't have said she is a teacher.

"I'm so glad you did this. I'm mostly Swedish and Norwegian on my father's side, and Russian on my mother's side. I think the Russians might have been Jewish, but I don't know, all that's been lost. Maybe sometime you can show me how you dug up your own family's history, I'd like to try doing that with mine."

"Uh, sure. I'd be glad to." Jessica hadn't expected Sarah's reaction.

"Well, I wasn't sure what to think about the Mexican-American Studies proposal, and I'm still not sure, but you've given me a fresh angle. Now I'll let you get back to your work." With that, Sarah spun a quick 180 degrees and marched out.

Jessica stared after her, taken aback. Then she returned to arranging chairs and setting out materials on a table for the book talks. She was writing a math puzzler on the board when Esteban stuck his head in her room, giving her a thumbs up. "You're now a full-fledged member of the Raza Studies *familia*."

"Thanks," she said as his head disappeared.

She realized her arm had frozen hovered over the math puzzler as warmth surged through her body. Not warmth for Esteban this time. No, it was more than that. Somehow Jessica had crossed over from standing on the outside looking in, to becoming part of something greater than herself.

The rest of the morning followed normal routines, with the normal wear and tear a room full of children incurs. Nothing out the ordinary happened, but Jessica felt different. Confident, perhaps. More securely herself than she had felt even yesterday.

Jessica was locking her classroom before going to the lounge for lunch when Andrea, a new second grade teacher, suddenly appeared at her elbow. Jessica barely knew her. Small in stature with mousy brown hair, Andrea was extremely quiet in faculty meetings. She was someone you didn't notice, and didn't notice not noticing.

"Do you have a minute?" Andrea asked tentatively.

"Sure, what is it?" Jessica tried to steer Andrea into walking down the hall with her, but Andrea's feet were firmly planted right where they were.

"I saw your letter in the newspaper this morning. I didn't know you were part German, but I guess a lot of us are. I'm German on my father's side. They were from the St. Louis area, and I think they went through the same thing as your family during the World Wars. Do you know if any of yours were from St. Louis?"

"No, I don't think so," said Jessica, wondering where this was going.

"I did some family history research a couple of years ago, and tracked down a lot of them. They all spoke German until the war. Most of them were German Evangelicals. Did you know Germans in St. Louis organized to oppose slavery? I wasn't able to find out if any of my ancestors were involved, but I think that is so interesting. I'd like to share notes about our families sometime."

"Okay," said Jessica, thinking this would never happen, having just experienced an all-talk, no-listen side of Andrea she hadn't known existed.

"Well, I won't take up any more of your time now. I just want you to know I'm proud to be in the same school as you." Andrea smiled shyly, then like a mouse turned and scuttled around the corner.

Jessica reached the door to the lounge just as Cath arrived. "Do you know Andrea very well?"

"Yeah, we're both in the primary grades team. Why?"

"I just had the strangest conversation with her." Jessica opened the door and stepped into the lounge.

"You had a conversation, that's good. Most of us only get three-word sentences out of her. The kids seem to like her, though. I figure she relates to seven-year-olds better than twenty-seven-year-olds."

They took their usual seats, Jessica's radar on high alert for more reactions from colleagues. Carolyn stared at her without smiling, then turned back to a conversation with Rick and another teacher.

"So did they print it yet?" Cath asked quietly as she sat down.

Jessica handed her the newspaper, folded open to the page. While Cath read, Jessica opened her lunch bag with one hand and checked for text messages with the other, having heard a couple of pings earlier. From María Paz, "¡*Felicidades y gracias*!" From Sam, "U finally came out, good on U!"

"I came out?" she wondered out loud.

Cath looked up, puzzled. "A text from Sam," Jessica clarified, showing her the message.

A smile washed over Cath's face. "Yeah, Jess, you came out, as a firm advocate. On the right side of things."

"Not everyone thinks so." Jessica rolled her eyes in the direction of Carolyn and Rick.

"Maybe if they did the work you've been doing on your own roots, they'd see things differently. Of course, depending on how they look at what they find, they could end up with stories that bolster how they already think."

As the two dug into their lunches, Cath surprised Jessica by touching her hand lightly. "I'm proud of you. You have more courage than I do, but maybe it will rub off."

Jessica, who regarded Cath as admirably self-contained and grounded, was taken aback. She opened her mouth, hoping an appropriate reply would find its way out, when Cath stopped her.

"You don't need to say anything. Just letting you know I appreciate you for who you are." Cath turned her attention back to her salad, so Jessica followed suit.

"By the way," Jessica said, "this morning I tried out that Authors Chair activity you told me about. Great idea, the kids got into it!" She proceeded to fill in details.

That afternoon after the kids left, Jessica checked her email. Funny, she never thought to check email at work, but today was certainly different. An email from teacher Joe read: "Nice going, the parallel you drew in the newspaper works. Keep it up." Another from Donaldo: "You have good instincts. We'll see you at the next Raza Studies meeting, I hope."

As she straightened the chairs and picked up a few scraps of paper from the floor, Jessica started humming John Legend's rendition of "Wake up Everybody, No More Sleeping in Bed." A knock on the doorframe startled her.

"Raza Studies, next Thursday at four," Esteban said, smiling broadly. "You'll be there?"

"Be there or be square," she replied, then thought how stupid that cliché sounded. "Yes, I'll be there," she corrected herself.

"I said it earlier and I mean it, you're part of us now."

As she was gathering her things to go home, her cell phone pinged. A text from Tim: "Dinner this weekend?"

Jessica frowned. She would need to think about that.

Driving home, a warmth toward the world enveloped her that she hadn't experienced for a long time. Somehow, suddenly, she was part of a community of sorts. Not exactly the kind her ancestors had over one hundred years ago, but community nonetheless. Some of the people who touched her today she had known for quite a while, others were new acquaintances. But they embraced her, and one reason was that she stood for something. More than that, she stood with others for something.

She pulled into her driveway. Ping! Another text, this time from Vic: "Go girl! ☺"

\* \* \* \* \*

Phil popped open a can of beer, spread out the sports page, and helped himself to a piece of KFC chicken. Tim had been getting on his case about learning to cook so his meals would be healthier, but by the time he got off work everyday, the idea of grocery shopping and then trying to cook just didn't work. He peered into the box. At least coleslaw counts as a vegetable.

Phil didn't always buy a newspaper on the way home, but since the box outside KFC still had a couple of today's papers, he decided to catch up on sports gossip while eating. He scanned the page for stories about local teams, while in the background a TV news commentator filled in the world about the latest details of Oscar Pistorius's pending arrest for killing his girlfriend. As his ear caught Pistorius's name, Phil put down the newspaper and listened. When a commercial came on, he switched back to the newspaper.

Finished with the sports section, he folded it and set it aside, then picked up the front section to see if he could learn more about Pistorius. Nothing until he got to the editorial page, where he saw a letter to the editor entitled "Pistorius Throws it All Away." Phil read it, written by someone who presumed he was guilty, about the stupidity of committing murder after winning a world championship on prosthetic legs.

Phil was about to add this section to the discard pile for the recycling bin when he noticed the name of the previous letter-writer: Jessica Westerfield. He read, then re-read her letter.

So that's what all this has been about, he said to himself. She's been reconstituting the stories she didn't grow up with.

Phil had been puzzled, when visiting the parents over Christmas, why Tim had started asking what life was like for them during the 1970s, what the economy had been like, what their grandparents' lives had been like. Was whatever Jessica had catching or something?

The first evening, Tim's questions had prompted music and sports stories from the '70s. Mom even hauled out some old vinyl records she still had that were pretty scratched up from wear, although they didn't have a stereo to play them on anymore.

"Why are you still keeping those?" Dad asked her, baffled, apparently not having seen them for decades.

"These songs bring back memories," she replied. Then holding up the album *America: A Horse with No Name*, she asked him wistfully, "Like, remember dancing to this one? Remember how you used to hold me?"

At that point, Phil went to the kitchen for a beer. He preferred thinking of his parents as just plain parents, not as kids dancing and holding onto each other.

When Tim moved on to questions about how the economy affected them, they continued with stories that, as far as Phil could see, didn't really address whatever it was Tim wanted to know. They talked about how they passed time while sitting in the car for hours on end one spring during a gas shortage, waiting for a turn at the pump. Mom, a former secretary, described making copies of letters using carbon paper and corrections using whiteout ("My boss even expected me to correct the carbon copies!"). Dad relayed stories about Chip, the other guy he used to bag groceries with.

But as soon as Tim would touch on the topic of college and why they decided against it, their mother went silent and their dad went into a rant about affirmative action.

Tim and Phil hadn't yet processed in much detail this attempted foray into their parents' past. Maybe now was the time. Phil hunted around for his cell phone. It wasn't on the kitchen counter or the dining table. Checking the pockets of the jacket he had worn home, he found it. He opened the favorites menu and called Tim.

After preliminaries, Phil said, "Hey, did you see that letter in the newspaper Jessica wrote?"

"How do you happen to be reading letters to the editor?"

"I read the newspaper. Sometimes," replied Phil defensively. "Anyway, it gave me kind of a better idea of what she's been doing."

He flopped down on the couch and turned down the volume on the TV.

"Yeah, I read it. Y'know, I wasn't fair to her when she started. I didn't realize how much it meant to her to have the stories about her people's lives. I also have to say I never thought about the historical parallel she's come up with."

"Well, speaking of, what did you make of your digging around about Mom and Dad's lives?" Phil asked. "I couldn't quite figure out where your questions were going, but it didn't sound like you got there."

"Well, yeah, I did and I didn't. You know how Dad always managed to close off some of my questions about his life by saying he got screwed because he's white. I had always thought of affirmative action as this liberal get-back-at-white-people thing that set up a quota system. So after we returned from Christmas, I did a little reading, and learned that's not exactly right. Affirmative action tries to correct for ongoing racial discrimination, which apparently still exists, but it isn't this thing to keep white people out. Maybe I should pay more attention to it. Anyway, when our folks were thinking about college – if they even thought about it, and truthfully, I'm not sure they did –"

"Our folks might not have thought about college?" Phil interjected, sitting up. "That isn't what Dad always said."

"Well, whenever we press them on it, they never really say what they did to try to get in somewhere. Like, how many places did they apply to?" Phil was silent. "See? You don't know. We always hear about how they didn't get into Berkeley, but there's a shitload of other places they could've gone."

When Phil was still silent, Tim continued. "I don't think affirmative action had anything to do with it. They just weren't all that interested, as nearly as I can figure. But Dad's folks badly wanted him to go, so he needed an excuse. You notice Dad is the only one who always goes off about Blacks and affirmative action, Mom usually doesn't say anything, she just goes to the kitchen or something. I think Dad's just ashamed he didn't make more of himself. He was his folks' only son, they expected more out of him than he delivered."

271

Phil finally said, "Shit, I've gotta think about that. I can sort of see what you're getting at, but it puts a different spin on things."

"And that's why we never got much encouragement about school," Tim continued. "Or stories about our own family's past, for that matter. Back to Jessica, I've been kind of an ass about her being smart because I bought into Dad's idea that school isn't that important, that it's for prissy kids. Sure, some of my classes were boring, but I ducked out rather than dealing with them."

"This is heavy," Phil said.

"It is. I'm seeing Dad reflected in me in ways I don't like. Like getting too defensive about what kind of house we can afford to live in right now, but bitching about her salary being higher than mine. Putting her down because she's curious because it's easier than dealing with my own stuff. I'm sort of used to Mom going along with Dad's put-downs. But Jessica isn't like Mom."

"No, she's not," Phil agreed, remembering the first time Tim brought Jessica to meet their parents. Jessica had been nervous, so she chattered on and on about some English class she was taking. Their mother just smiled and nodded, and when Jessica ran out of steam, Mom disappeared into the kitchen to get dinner ready. When Tim had announced he and Jessica were getting married, their parents had taken a collective deep breath and wished them luck. Phil now realized Jessica was like the child their dad's parents had wanted.

And Phil had regarded Jessica as the sister he never had since the first time he met her. She might be smarter than he was, but she teased him like a kid sister would, and seemed to enjoy being teased in return.

"She might not want me back," Tim was saying.

"Want you back? You're trying to get back with her?" Two weeks ago Phil and Tim had double dated, and Phil had been under the impression Tim liked his date. "What happened with Judie?" Tim's date Judie, tall and shapely with long blond hair, had been all over Tim.

"Judie?" Tim asked as if he couldn't remember who she was. "Oh, she's history. Not my type."

"Send her on over here." Phil could just picture running his own hands up and down her body.

"I've gotta go, guy. Jessica was going to get back to me about whether we're having dinner this weekend."

"Oh, man, you sound hooked!"

"Knock it off. If we have dinner, great, if we don't, we don't."

After they hung up, Phil pondered what had just happened. Tim had rearranged some of the pieces in Phil's image of their parents, as well as his own understanding of Tim.

Then it then occurred to him that Tim was right – Jessica might not want him back.

*February, 2013*

Jessica stared at the phone. She had just agreed to have dinner with Tim on Friday. That would be the day after Valentine's Day, although neither had mentioned that fact.

She wasn't sure what she was feeling, and maybe it was best to leave it that way for now. They had talked almost an hour, something they hadn't done since – well, she couldn't remember the last time they had talked like that. The conversation had not started with what Tim wanted, which was how they usually started. Even questions that might be about Jessica ("Jess, what are you doing?") were usually based, however obliquely, in Tim's wishes ("When are you gonna start dinner?").

But not this time. He really wanted to know more about the historical parallels she found from her family history research, and, perhaps more importantly, how she felt about what she found. He listened, asked questions, seemed genuinely interested. That was the first pleasant surprise.

The second was his confession that he realized he resembled his father in ways he didn't like. Not that he didn't like his father. He said he loved his parents, although he wasn't entirely sure what that meant, but there were things about his father not worth emulating. The greatest was that over time, he had started to belittle Jessica, just like his father belittled his mother. And a little digging into his own family history helped him see why.

So the idea of dinner with Tim on Friday sounded good.

The idea of Tim moving back in was a different matter, however, one Jessica was not ready to entertain. As far as she was concerned, the possibility of divorce was not off the table, although perhaps Tim had begun to nudge it further away. But the future of their relationship would depend on the depth of friendship and mutual respect that took root. She no longer felt she needed to grab at someone to fill a void in her life. The void itself was dissipating, pushed away by friends and a sense of purpose.

Jessica retrieved the letter Mary had written to Annie over eighty years ago, and smoothed the creases. "Thank you, multiple-greats grandma Mary," she told the letter. "You helped me find part of my own story, my own community, my own past. By doing that, you helped me hear the stories of my students and understand how they're anchored to their own communities. Maybe it's time now to lay you to rest."

Opening her laptop, Jessica searched Newspaper Archives for Mary's and Heinrich's obituaries, which turned out to be more complicated than she had anticipated. Heinrich's was fairly easy to locate once she added "Rev." to the search terms. His obituary confirmed information she already had regarding his birth in Volkerode, Hesse-Kassel, Germany, his service as a pastor, and his date of death "following a stroke of apoplexy," a term that at the time simply meant loss of consciousness before death.

Locating Mary's obituary was more challenging. Initially, Jessica forgot that back then women's given names disappeared when they married. Entering "Mrs. Heinrich" surfaced several articles, mostly about their golden wedding anniversary in 1927, complete with photos and descriptions of who attended and how far they had traveled to get there.

Finally, she found it. Mary had died in June of 1930 of a cerebral hemorrhage. The blurry copy was hard to read, but Jessica learned that a severe illness five years prior to her death had partially incapacitated Mary. You wouldn't have known that by her subsequent activities, however, which centered largely around what became the First Methodist Church.

Jessica filed the obituaries, closed her computer, and sat back, looking outward at nothing in particular, but inward at everything that had happened in the last six months. These obituaries placed the period at the end of a long and complex sentence. They wrote "The End" at the conclusion of a story, not just a story of Mary, Heinrich, Lydia, and Willie, but a larger story of the German-American communities that had been a prominent feature of the American Midwest.

And yet, she realized, the obituaries did not mark the end. Rather, she was a continuation of that story. The story itself, like a winding river, may have shifted directions, but like the river it continued to flow, and she was now one of its authors. How she could choose to make sense of the small story of her life and the larger, ongoing story of her family could become the next chapter.

Jessica retrieved the last two emails about Raza Studies meetings, filed but unread. Opening them, she learned that the group was considering a petition campaign. A bullet point in the most recent email caught her eye: "to strategize how to get white support for a Raza Studies program." Donaldo had sent the email. His phone number was beneath his name.

Jessica punched his number into her cell phone. When Donaldo answered, she identified herself, then said, "I want to help with the petition, and I want to target white support. I think I know how to reach a lot of people I could bring on board."

As Donaldo responded enthusiastically, she watched a shaft of late afternoon sunlight brush the wall mirror, painting the room brilliant gold.

# AUTHOR'S NOTE

The historical sections of this book are based on extensive research into my own family's history. After gathering as much detailed information as I could about the families, individuals within the families, and the contexts in which they lived, I let my imagination loose. In some cases, I crafted stories that embellish on newspaper accounts; in other cases, I had only scraps of information to start with.

I made good use of the census and other well-known genealogy tools. In 2008, I traveled to Decatur, where I had an opportunity to meet a knowledgable cousin, and to visit the church in Boody that Wilhelm founded. While there, I was able to talk with church members who generously shared stories and artifacts, including the church's earliest records, kept in German, and the *Pistorius Family Memory Book*.

Central Illinois maintained a thriving newspaper business that has been digitized. I was able to glean many details and stories about the lives of people between 1879 and 1928, background information about local contexts, and details about the lynching that occurred from the *Decatur Morning Review*, the *Decatur Daily Republican*, the *Saturday Herald*, the *Decatur Daily Review, The Evening Bulletin*, the *Decatur Evening Herald*, the *Decatur Herald*, the *Weekly Herald-Dispatch*, and (in Iowa), the *Burlington Hawkeye*.

For background historical information about towns mentioned in this book, I drew on *Appleton's Annual Cyclopaedia and Register of Important Events of the Year 1893*, Volume 18, Appleton & Co., 1894; A. M. Antrobus's *History of Des Moines County, IA*, S. J. Clarke Publishing Company, 1915; I. B. Richman's *History of Muscatine County, Iowa*, S. J. Clarke Publishing Company, 1911; and N. M. Baker, "The pioneers of Macon County," *Journal of the Illinois State Historical Society*, Vol. 16, 1923, pp. 92-106. For background information about some specific people, I consulted W. H. Perrin's *Biographical Review of Cass, Schuyler, and Brown Counties, Illinois*, O. L. Baskin & Co. Historical Publishers, 1882; and *Portrait and Biographical Album of Des Moines County*, Iowa, Acme Publishing Company, 1888.

I first learned of the extent of German language use in the Midwest through Amanda Kibler's "Speaking like a 'good American': National identity and the legacy of German language education, *Teachers College Record*, Vol. 110, 2008, pp. 1241-1268. I drew extensively on D. H. Tolzmann's *The German-American Experience*, Humanity Books, 2000, for background about German American history. For background about German immigration, I used R. W. Frizzell's *Independent Immigrants: A Settlement of Hanoverian Germans in Western Missouri*, University of Missouri Press, 2007; and J. C. Theibault's *German Villages in Crisis: Rural Life in Hesse-Kassel and the Thirty-years War*, Humanities Press, 1995.

For information about the German Methodist Episcopal Church and some of its congregations, I consulted many sources. They include digitized Central Wesleyan College Archives in Pickler Memorial Library at Truman State University (http://library.truman.edu/manuscripts/C3-CWC%20Archives.asp); Rev. G. Davies, editor, *Journal and Year Book of the Illinois Annual Conference of the Methodist Episcopal Church*, Wagoner Printing Co., 1929; M. L. Davis, *The Methodist Unification: Christianity and the Politics of Race in the Jim Crow Era*, New York University Press, 2008; *History of the German Methodist Episcopal Church, Storm Lake, Buena Vista County, Iowa* (http://tinyurl.com/ko9mhkm); O. E. Kriege's "German," page 367 in Samuel McCauley Jackson's edited *The New Schaff-Herzog Encyclopedia of Religious Knowledge*, Vol VII., Kessinger Publishing, 2006; L. McCleary's *German Methodist Episcopal Church, Muscatine, Muscatine County, Iowa* (http://iagenweb.org/muscatine/churches/GMEintro.htm); M. M. Schmid, compiler and translator, *Records of German Methodist– Jackson Street Methodist Church, Belleville, Illinois, 1840–1998*, St. Clair, IL Genealogical Society, 1999 (www.stclair-ilgs.org/bvmethch.htm), and Joshua Hollingshead's *Prejudice and Purging: World War I and the Demise of the German American Church in America* (http://faculty.mckendree.edu/scholars/summer2006/ hollingsead.htm).

Information about the Northwest Land Agency as well as the suit it brought against Lydia comes from C. A. Helgeson's *The*

*Promotion of Agricultural Settlement in Northern Wisconsin 1880-1925*, Unpublished PhD dissertation, University of Wisconsin, 1951; H. F. Peterson's "Some colonization projects of the Northern Pacific Railroad," a paper presented at the St. Paul Minnesota Historical Society in June, 1929; and N. B. Raymond, B. I. Salinger, U.G. Whitney, W. W. Cornwall, R. Reichman, F. F. Faville, C. H. Scholz, & W. C. Barlow's *Reports of Cases at Law and in Equity Determined by the Supreme Court of the State of Iowa, Vol. 143*, Geo. H. Ragsdale, Publisher, 1910.

For background about African Americans in Decatur and Muscatine, I drew from Sundiata K. Cha-Jua's "'A warlike demonstration:' Legalism, armed resistance, and Black political mobilization in Decatur, Illinois, 1894-1898," *The Journal of Negro History*, Vol. 83, 1998, pp. 52-72; I. L. Thomas's *Methodism and the Negro*, Eaton & Mains, 1910; R. R. Dykstra's *Bright Radical Star: Black Freedom and White Supremacy on the Hawkeye Frontier*, Harvard University Press, 1993; and K. L. Anderson's "German Americans, African Americans, and the Republican Party in St. Louis, 1865-1872," *Journal of American Ethnic History 28*, 2008, pp. 34-51.

Finally, for a description of diagnosis and treatment of appendicitis during the late 1890s, I turned to P. I. Nixon's "Can we diagnose appendicitis?" pages 469-471 in G. F. Shrady and T. L. Stedman's *Medical Record Vol 89*, William Wood & Co, 1916.

# ABOUT THE AUTHOR

Christine Sleeter is Professor Emerita in the College of Professional Studies at California State University Monterey Bay, where she was a founding faculty member. Sleeter is an internationally recognized leader in social justice multicultural education and teacher education. She is author of several non-fiction books, including *Power, Teaching and Teacher Education* (Peter Lang, 2013), *The Academic and Social Value of Ethnic Studies* (National Education Association, 2011), *Un-Standardizing Curriculum* (Teachers College Press, 2005), *Culture, Difference & Power* (Teachers College Press, 2001), and *Multicultural Education as Social Activism* (State University of New York Press, 1996). Her best-known co-authored works include *Doing Multicultural Education for Achievement and Equity* (with C. A. Grant, Routledge, 2011) and *Making Choices for Multicultural Education* (with C. A. Grant, Wiley, 2009). *White Bread* is her first work of fiction. Sleeter's work has been translated into several languages. In 2009, the American Educational Research Association honored Sleeter with its prestigious Social Justice in Education Award. She currently resides in Monterey, California. For more information, please visit www.christinesleeter.org.

CPSIA information can be obtained
at www.ICGtesting.com
Printed in the USA
LVOW13s0142120818
586724LV00006BA/51/P

9 789463 000659